# The Dynamics of Policy Implementation in Nigeria:

The Case of Sokoto State

# The Dynamics of Policy Implementation in Nigeria:

## The Case of Sokoto State

MOHAMMAD AHMAD WALI

iUniverse, Inc.
New York   Bloomington

The Dynamics of Policy Implementation in Nigeria:
The Case of Sokoto State

iUniverse books may be ordered through booksellers or by contacting:

iUniverse
1663 Liberty Drive
Bloomington, IN 47403
www.iuniverse.com
1-800-Authors (1-800-288-4677)

Because of the dynamic nature of the Internet, any Web addresses or links contained in this book may have changed since publication and may no longer be valid. The views expressed in this work are solely those of the author and do not necessarily reflect the views of the publisher, and the publisher hereby disclaims any responsibility for them.

ISBN: 978-1-4502-1795-8 (sc)
ISBN: 978-1-4502-1796-5 (ebook)
ISBN: 978-1-4502-1797-2 (dj)

Printed in the United States of America

iUniverse rev. date: 7/30/2010

# Contents

# Figures

# Tables

# DEDICATION

For our mother, Hajiya Amina, and in memory of our father, Dangaladima Wali Sanyinna

# ACKNOWLEDGMENTS

I would like first and foremost to register my sincere indebtedness to my brothers, sisters, and friends for their enormous support and encouragement in the course of updating and revising this thesis for publication. I should mention Dr. Usman M. Wali, Ambassador (Senator) Abdallah Wali and Alhaji Umar Wali, Professor M. J. Balogun, Professor T. M. Bande, Professor Rizkuwa A. Shehu, Professor Lawal Bilbis, Dr. S. S. Muhammad, and Dr. Ibrahim M. B. Zagga. In particular, Professor Shehu's encouragement has been very inspiring, and Professor T. M. Bande's reading of the entire manuscript and suggestions have improved the quality of this book. Moreover, Professor M. J. Balogun has remarkably made the initial edits of the manuscript by providing absolutely valuable comments and criticisms that undoubtedly enhanced the standard and quality of this book. I am indeed grateful to all of them.

Gratitude is due to my supervisor (the chairman of my supervisory board), Mr. Antony Barker, who, apart from his critical comments and helpful suggestions, has encouraged me enormously in this work. He has introduced me to useful literature on Nigeria, and his attention to precision and detail has been inspiring and insightful. I am also appreciative of the comments and suggestions made by other members of my supervisory board, particularly by Professor Ian Budge and Dr. Christian Anglad. Professor Budge drew my attention to a number of secondary material on policy implementation that I found most helpful. His initial supervision of my work was encouraging. Dr. Gerry Stoker, who took over the final supervision of my work, also made useful observations and suggestions. I am indeed grateful to him.

Professor R. A. W. Rhodes and Dr. Dave Marsh have shown interest in my work. Professor Rhodes has made useful comments on some of the draft chapters of this study. I am indebted to him and to Dr. Marsh.

I am very grateful to the late Dr. Onujabe Ademoh Onido of University of Sokoto for his encouragement and useful suggestions at the initial stage of the doctoral research.

My coming to the UK for the study has been made possible by the Commonwealth Office in London. I am highly indebted to the office as well as to the federal government of Nigeria, which nominated me for the award, and to the Sokoto State government, which granted me study leave. Dr. Hassan Abdul Raheem Al-Tayyib of Urdoman University, Khartoum, deserves special mention, if for no other reason than the encouragement he gave me when I was planning to come over to the University of Essex.

I am appreciative of the interest shown by my friends and colleagues in my personal and academic life at the University of Essex. Specifically, I would like to mention Dr. A. Al-Hameed, Dr. O. Al-Omery, Dr. Y. Khalifa, Dr. M. Tufail, and Ahmad Abul. Others are Dr. A. Fadl, Dr. H. Al-Ghamdi, Dr. M. Khudairi, Abdulkadeer Maazouz, Dr. Faisal Malik, Dr. Mubaidin Okleh, Dr. Mukhtar Yusuf, Dr. Kashifa Mahmood and Dr. Muneerah Al-Muhannadi.

My stay in the UK has been facilitated by the efficient way in which my program officers (Paul Harvey, Simon Schofield, and Nerissa Johnson) executed my award and the understanding shown by the secretariat of the Commonwealth Scholarship Commission in the UK.

In Colchester, in particular, I would like to acknowledge the friendship of Dr. Nisar Ahmad and his wife, Dr. Tayyiba Ahmad, and Mr. M. Luqueman.

I am highly indebted to my relations and long-life friends for their interest in my scholarly endeavors and for supporting me at various points. Among these are Muhammad H. Sanyinna, Sani Abdullahi, Abubakar J. Suru, the late Umaru Zagga, Muhammed Siddiq, Malami Ahmed, Muhammad Hassan, Altine Abubakar, Alhaji Mode H. Gyara, the late Abdulqadir A. Bashir, Yaqub D. Yusuf, and Shehu Bagudu. They are a tower of strength and an inspiration.

Last, but by no means the least, I am greatly indebted to my wife, Fadima, and our children, Islam, Nusrah, Saleem, Muslimah, Salsabilah, and Ismael, for not only their understanding, but also for creating a peaceful and conducive atmosphere for both my academic work and social affairs. I am equally indebted to my brothers and sisters for their remarkable understanding, prayers, forbearance, discipline, and commitment, and for looking after our parents (Dangaladima Wali and Hajiya Amina) during my long absence from home up to the passing away of our father. To them all (including Hajiya A'i, Hauwa, Imamatu, Maria, Fatima, and Asmau) this book is dedicated.

Finally, I thank my publisher, iUniverse, for showing interest in the work and for taking me through the nitty-gritty of the publishing process. Their editorial support has been absolutely wonderful.

On the whole, I am grateful to God for His mercy upon us.

# FOREWORD

This book came about from research undertaken for a PhD degree at the University of Essex, UK, titiled *The Implementation of Public Policy in the Sokoto State Bureaucracy.* It examines the state of policy implementation in Nigeria and sheds light on what policy makers, academics, students, and the public can do to improve the current system. My experience and involvement in the Nigerian bureaucracy and, in particular, Sokoto State bureaucracy as an insider, and not a participant observer, has been another empirical source of this work. I have been in the service of the Sokoto State government for over two decades. As a generalist administrative officer, I worked in different departments, but mostly in the military governor's office, the nerve center of the state administration. Of particular significance is the fact that I worked in the secretariat of the state executive council as one of its secretaries. I worked in the Policy Implementation Unit as its sectional head. I also served in the Administration and Political Affairs Department as principal assistant secretary, and then I served in the Office of the Secretary to the Military Government and Head of Service (where overall implementation of government policies are coordinated) as principal secretary. I also participated in different government board meetings and government committees where policies were initiated and made. I visited all the eighty-four districts of the state officially and acquainted myself with most of the government projects, including schools, hospitals, and water and housing projects.

Mohammad Ahmad Wali

# PREFACE

Taking the top-down as opposed to the bottom-up approach, this book examines the implementation of public policy in Nigeria, the Sokoto State of Nigeria (1976–1991). Specifically, it investigates the implementation of an education policy designated "Operation Move Ahead" and shows that while the policy has achieved some successes, it has failed to achieve its overall objectives. The failure of the policy, it is argued, was due neither to the structure of the bureaucracy nor the character of the bureaucrats, nor even to the contents and directions of the policy (as is generally believed), but to governmental instability, governmental overload, socioeconomic problems, and infrastructural inadequacies confronting the implementers of the policy. These four variables, interacting at the same time, constitute the main obstacles to implementation in the Sokoto State bureaucracy. This is most probably the case in most of Nigeria's bureaucracies.

Mohammad Ahmad Wali

# Chapter One
# Statement of the Problem

## Introduction

Successive administrations in Sokoto State of Nigeria have formulated and implemented a number of policies in pursuit of the socioeconomic progress of the state. However, many of the policies have failed to achieve their overall objectives. Among such policies are:

1. the 1976 transport policy, which established the Rima Transport (Bus) Service and SUDA Bus Service. The aim of the policy was to provide transport services in the state at an affordable cost. Although both services were initially acclaimed by the people, by 1980, they had been grounded.
2. the 1980 health policy, which provided for the establishment of first aid centers in all the villages of the state. The aim of the scheme was to ensure accessibility to health facilities by the rural populace. However, no sooner had the scheme taken off than it collapsed.
3. the 1982 Marriage Law, whose purpose was to minimize the high cost of marriage. Signs of the policy's failure were visible by 1983.
4. the 1984 Environmental Sanitation Edict (a law first promulgated by the federal military government at the national level as a decree and then by state governments

at state level as an edict), which was meant to ensure the total cleanliness of the environment. The edict was received with mixed feelings. Whereas some saw it as a way of creating a healthy environment, others considered it as a draconian law imposed to regulate their behavior. The law makes it compulsory for everybody, except those on special duties (particularly officers associated with the movement of ambulances, telephone services, electricity, etc.), to stay at home every Saturday from 7:00 AM to 10:00 AM, to clean their houses and surroundings. Later, the weekly cleaning was found to be too demanding and hence changed to once every month (the last Saturday of every month). However, by 1986 it was clear that the policy had been abandoned.

5. the 1986 education policy: "Operation Move Ahead." The policy, which is examined in detail in Chapter Seven, was meant to improve the falling standard of education particularly at the primary-school level. The government gave important emphasis to the program. The implementation of the policy started in late 1985, and it was formally launched in January 1986. However, by the end of 1987 it was apparent that the implementation process had lost its steam.

Why did the aforementioned policies prove so difficult to implement in Sokoto State? Is it the fault of the bureaucracy and "bureaucrats," as some scholars have argued? This question becomes salient when it is noted that virtually all public policies are implemented by bureaucrats. A related question is whether the failure lies within the policies themselves and the context in which they were formulated, as others have concluded. If the fault lies neither with the bureaucracy nor with the policies, where does the problem lie? This book makes an an attempt to answer these questions from the implementation perspective. It proceeds by examining the explanations so far provided for implementation success (or failure), and by asking whether the explanations prove adequate in light of the experience of Sokoto State. If the explanations fall short, the book looks for alternatives. After all, the crucial role of implementation analysis is to identify the factors that affect the achievement of policy objectives (Mazmanian and Sabatier 1981, 541). In doing so, the concept of implementation will be reviewed and the theoretical focus will be provided.

# Background of and Rationale
# for Choice of Topic

This study examines the process and problems of policy implementation in Sokoto State, a subject that has received little or no attention up to now.

The subject has been of interest for some time. However, it was further stimulated by an event that took place on Sunday, January 4, 1987. On that date, the National Television Authority (NTA) Sokoto carried the following news analysis: "Why Nothing Works in Sokoto." The news analysis traced, among other things, the origin of the 1976 transport policy that established SUDA Bus and the Rima Transport Services. Both services were introduced in 1976, but by 1981, the policy had virtually failed. The NTA news analysis thus drew attention to the problems encountered in the implementation of otherwise laudable policies.

Implementation of public policy is a major issue in the policy process. Thus, in order to succeed or consolidate themselves, governments have to implement various policies. One of the factors in the popularity of any government is its ability to meet basic needs of, and provide social services required by, its people. This cannot be achieved unless the policies for providing those services are implemented. In other words, no matter how good government programs may look on paper, unless they are implemented they will amount to nothing. Governments are changed, through either democratic or violent means, when presumably they fail to provide satisfactory services to their people. In Nigeria, with the exception of the second military coup d'état of July 29, 1966, all the other coups' leaders have condemned their predecessors for failing to provide the basic needs of the people—notably, education, health services, water, and roads. In other words, every effort of the government at providing social services is dependent on the success of policy and program implementation.

At any rate, the relevance of a policy cannot be tested unless and until it is implemented. Revolutions are carried out, government reforms are contemplated, and military coups d'état are staged— all in the expectation that the world would change for the better. The hope for a better society is given expression in various policy areas: political, social, economic, and technological. However, until the policies are implemented, they remain just that (i.e., "policies," ideas, or intentions). Evaluation of policy cannot be effectively carried out unless the policy is implemented, even if it is partial implementation.

Much has been said and is being said (by government and public service leaders, civic groups, and academics) about the problems of policy implementation in Nigeria. In this connection, President Ibrahim Babangida (1985–1993) had this to say in his address to federal ministers and permanent secretaries on January 21, 1986:

> As I reminded you in my Budget Speech, Government recognizes that … policies, no matter how soundly formulated, become empty words, unless they are vigorously implemented. We cannot therefore afford to allow the machinery of policy implementation to jog along its leisurely pace.… We are aware of the problems of policy implementation and we shall begin to tackle the problems with the machinery of government itself; we shall instill the spirit of the times by promoting fresh commitment to the values of efficient performance and dedicated service and by installing a proper mechanism for close monitoring and control (1986, 1–3).

The significance of the president's address is that the problem of policy implementation is anticipated by, and therefore put firmly on the agenda of, the government. Yet, in spite of the centrality of implementation in the policy process and despite the extensive discussion about implementation problems in Sokoto State and in Nigeria as a whole, very little has been done to study the problem.

It is true that in 1976, Ahmadu Bello University, Zaria, organized a national conference on research and public policy, the purpose of which was "to draw the nation's attention to the need to adopt new approaches to inform the dynamics of policy making within existing policy making structures in the country" (Kumo and Aliyu 1977, ix).

The conference stressed the need to conduct research in the field of public policy, the aim being the development of policies that would be instrumental to the achievement of the needs of a rapidly developing society (Kumo and Aliyu 1977, ix).

In all, thirty-one papers were presented by both academics and practitioners in the field of public policy. Although most of the papers mentioned implementation, none actually discussed it in any meaningful way. This neglect is due partly to the implicit assumption in many studies that

> implementation process is ... a series of mundane decisions and interactions unworthy of the attention of scholars seeking the heady stuff of politics. Implementation is deceptively simple; it does not appear to involve any great issues. Most of the crucial policy issues are often seen to have been resolved in the prior decisions of executives, legislators and judges (Van Meter and Van Horn 1975, 450).

As a matter of fact, there is no single published comprehensive study of implementation on Nigeria as a whole and Sokoto State in particular. Although there are a few unpublished works whose titles remotely suggest interest in implementation, they are not actually implementation studies. Examples include *The Extent to Which Corruption Has Hindered the Effective Implementation of Economic Development in Africa: A Case of Nigeria from 1979 to 1983*, by Uzobeyi Anigboh. However, except for the unpublished doctoral thesis of Haruna Dlakwa—*Implementing Federal Government Development Project at the State Level in Nigeria: The Case of Federal Low-Cost Housing Scheme 1980–83*—and the unpublished doctoral thesis of Thomas Odunlami (1986)—*The Effectiveness of Land Use Policies: A Case of Nigeria*—which attempt to examine some implementation literature, even unpublished works on implementation are very scanty. While Dlakwa (1984) has reviewed some implementation literature, his subsequent treatment of the subject shows that his thesis is about project planning and management in the field of development administration (1984, 20). His study, like others, is concerned with factors that hinder overall socioeconomic development from the perspective of development administration, which is concerned with the management and direction of social and economic development by governments in the Third World. In particular, it focuses on the structure and organization of bureaucracy, bureaucratic attitudes and behavior, politico-administrative leadership, and the question of political legitimacy. Thus, bureaucratic reform is seen as crucial in order to cope with development challenges (Tukur 1971), to solve the leadership tussle between policy makers and higher civil servants (Adedeji 1969), or to ensure the legitimacy of political leadership (Nwosu 1977).

All these studies focus either on agency or individual behavior but ignore the importance of policy variables in explaining much of the bureaucratic behavior (Mazmanian and Sabatier 1981, 25). This is not to deny the importance of those issues. However, it is necessary to change the perspective from which the issues are perceived and "the language and context in which they are discussed." This could be done only by examining the implementation process and dynamics. Implementation analysis, unlike the classical public administration and organization theory, is essentially about how to achieve planned or desired change (Mazmanian and Sabatier 1981, 11).

The current study therefore is an attempt to, on the one hand, fill the gap in the implementation study in Sokoto State and, on the other hand, to contribute to the development of implementation literature as a whole.

The choice of Sokoto State (instead of Nigeria as a whole) will permit in-depth analysis of factors helping or militating against the implementation of public policy. Besides, with a population of over 8 million, covering 102,500 square kilometers, Sokoto State is large and populous enough to warrant this research. It is bigger than the Republic of Benin, the Gambia, Jordan, Kuwait, Fiji, the Republic of Niger, and Senegal in terms of population. Furthermore, apart from the few unpublished local case studies, most of the literature on Nigerian politics and administration tend to focus on Nigeria as a whole, paying little attention to its constituent parts (i.e., the states that form the federation). Secondly, the focus on Sokoto State confers the advantage of access to data—data that an outsider may find hard to obtain, not because they are secret documents but because of the cumbersome process involved in collecting data. This is borne out by Augustine Agu's experience while collecting data on the implementation of universal primary education in Kaduna State of Nigeria. As she recalls,

> In Kaduna State, entry was not easy. It was and probably still is the state policy that for one to get any research done in the schools or any educational agency, one needs to get clearance from the Permanent Secretary of the Ministry of Education. It took a week of hard negotiation for me to be cleared (Agu 1986, 75).

Similarly, Odunlami had this to say in his study of land use policy in Nigeria:

> [A]lthough difficulties in obtaining factual information had been anticipated, the extent of difficulty involved during the empirical studies far exceeded that envisaged. Records were seldom available for consultation either because they did not exist or because they were regarded as confidential (Odunlami 1986, 151).

# The Education Policy

I have chosen an education policy formulated by the Sokoto State government to illustrate the problems of implementation. The intention is to establish, among other things, a pattern in the implementation of Sokoto State's education policy.

Effective implementation of education policy is capable of transforming the socioeconomic condition of the state. For instance, the federal government of Nigeria adopted education "as an instrument par excellence for effecting national development" (National Policy on Education 1981, 5). Education, as James S. Coleman observed, "is the master determinant of all aspects of change" (Coleman 1965, 3). As the World Bank sees it, education is a basic need; it is a means of meeting basic needs; and it is an activity that sustains and accelerates overall development (Bunza 1984, 163). Thus the management of education is very important in facilitating the overall progress of the nation, specifically in providing the needed manpower for the states and the federation, as well as for the public and private sectors of the economy. It enhances economic growth as it facilitates the deployment of the productive capacity of labor and machines, as well as the efficient use of land, labor, and capital (Maipose 1984, 169). An educated population provides opportunities for rapid socioeconomic development.

The choice of education policy is predicated on the understanding that previous studies of education in the state have been concerned with: the growth and development of grade II teachers colleges (Gulma 1983), the development and expansion of higher education (Bunza 1982), the working of the College of Education in Sokoto, and the quality of training it gives to prospective secondary school teachers (Boorer 1985) and nomadic education (Junaidu 1987). In all this, there has never been any attempt to examine the implementation of any education policy in the state. The intention, therefore, is to fill the vacuum. That apart, an educationist observed:

> The history of education in Nigeria right from pre-independence period to the current time is replete with vacillations and failures by both federal and state governments when it comes to translating policies into action.

This raises the question: what factors account for the persistent failure to "translate policies into action"—that is, to implement policies once formulated? This is the question that this book sets out to answer.

# Methodology

The research is problem-oriented: the implementation problem is identified from the outset, and relevant literature is examined in order to frame the research question. The methods of investigation adopted are content analysis of secondary and primary materials and interviews. The purpose here is not to try to justify one data gathering method as opposed to another—for each has its own virtue—but to rely on unstructured personal interviews where that methodology provides enormous chances for finding out not only about respondents' attitudes to a research question, but also their convictions as manifested in their body language. A face-to-face interview, like any method of data collection, has its weaknesses. However, some of the weaknesses are ameliorated in this research by recourse to reliable secondary sources, particularly authoritative documents and records. Thus, the study relies on both primary and secondary sources of data.

## Secondary Sources

The study proceeds by undertaking content analysis of books, journals, magazines, and newspapers focusing on theoretical and empirical policy implementation issues. The information from these sources are particularly used for literature review, for highlighting and substantiating some points, and for comparative analysis.

## Statistical Data

Statistical data are used to show the growth and development of Western education in Nigeria as a whole and in Sokoto State in particular. However, statistical data alone are insufficient and not always reliable. To this extent, statistics are employed to complement arguments and to provide background information.

# Primary Sources

A number of respondents comprising commissioners, permanent secretaries, chief executives of government parastatals, and professional officers in the Sokoto State bureaucracy were both randomly and deliberately selected and interviewed on the problems of policy implementation and on the role of the bureaucracy as a whole: its development and the implementation of the policy area chosen for examination.

A total of fifty people were interviewed. Among these were: three commissioners, three retired permanent secretaries, seven existing permanent secretaries, two ministerial secretaries, two principal assistant secretaries, three senior assistant secretaries, two executive officers, four directors of education, two chief inspectors of education, four education officers, two zonal education officers, two principals of post primary institutions, two post-primary school teachers, three primary school head teachers, three primary school teachers, two inspectors of local government, two local government secretaries, and two university students.

The interviews were conducted in the offices or homes of the interviewees. The first part of the interviews was conducted between June and September 1987. The second part was conducted between May and June 1989.

Two broader sets of unstructured questions were asked: those related to the bureaucracy and general problems of implementation, and those related to the conception, formulation, and implementation of the education policy, "Operation Move Ahead."

Aside from the interviews, ministry files, records, and documents were consulted to verify and corroborate the substance of the interviews. These records have been of immense advantage where interviewees could not provide specific data on the implementation of "Operation Move Ahead." These documents have further helped to minimize biases the interviewee or the interviewer might have.

That apart, my active involvement in the Sokoto State bureaucracy as an insider, and not a participant observer, has been another empirical source of this work. This experience, apart from exposing myself to the practical issues of policies and implementation, have been influential in the decision to focus on implementation problems in the state. As I pointed out earlier, there has not been any study of this kind in Sokoto State and, hence, the problem of implementation has not been documented. Thus this work, apart from anything else, is an attempt to bring implementation problems into focus, and I hope that it will sensitize both the policy makers and implementers in Sokoto State in particular and Nigeria as a whole to the implementation problem and how to cope with it.

# Arrangement of Chapters

Chapter Two reviews selectively the implementation literature and shows the dominance of two approaches in the field: the top-down and bottom-up perspectives. The bottom-up school has questioned the assumptions of its top-down counterparts. However, the criticisms on both sides are found to be inadequate. Although, methodologically, the two approaches could be distinguished in their focus: the substantive analytic concepts of the implementation process put forward by the bottom-uppers are neither new nor adequate to challenge the position of the top-downers. Thus, the distinction between the two approaches is challenged. The top-down perspective is found to be more appropriate for analyzing implementation process and for identifying implementation problems.

In Chapters Three and Four the environment of the Nigerian bureaucracy as a whole and Sokoto State in particular are presented, arguing that the Nigerian bureaucracy is development-oriented, contrary to the conventional view.

Chapter Five focuses on the policy process and implementation constraints in the Sokoto civil service and advances explanations for policy success or failure.

Chapter Six discusses the development of Western education and shows its unequal development between Northern and Southern Nigeria. It argues, contrary to the popular view, that the backwardness of Northern Nigeria regarding Western education was not due to its conservatism or Islam, but rather largely to a century-long difference, deliberate colonial education policy, and the Christianization of education. It thus sets the context for the formulation of the education policy designated "Operation Move Ahead," whose implementation is appraised in the following chapters.

Chapter Seven, applying the top-down perspective, examines the implementation of the education policy, "Operation Move Ahead." It shows that although the policy achieved some remarkable successes, it failed to achieve its overall objectives. The failure, it is argued, is due neither to the structure of the Sokoto State bureaucracy, to the character of the bureaucrats, nor to the nature of the policy and its context, as the conventional explanations would lead us to believe. The failure has been due essentially to a combination of factors, notably, governmental instability, governmental overload, socioeconomic constraints, and infrastructural inadequacies. These are the alternative explanations presented.

Chapter Eight concludes the thesis by drawing together the main arguments and showing the main contribution of the book: identifying the main problems of implementation in the Sokoto State bureaucracy as well as in other Nigerian states and the federal civil services.

# Chapter Two
# Policy Implementation: Meaning, Significance, and Intervening Variables

The purpose of this chapter is to interrogate the meaning, significance, as well as the factors helping or hindering the implementation of public policy. In pursuance of this objective, the chapter reviews the literature, focuses on contemporary approaches to the study of implementation, and outlines a framework for the analysis of the policy implementation process in Sokoto State.

## Domain of Implementation

Implementation studies came to prominence as the first flush of enthusiasm in policy analysis subsided. It started in the early 1970s in the United States of America (USA) partly as a result of a growing concern about the failures of Great Society programs. It became apparent that mere rationalization of development programs and effective utilization of financial resources were not sufficient for the realization of policy objectives. Policy analysts began to refocus their attention "on the implementation process itself in a search for the factor that 'interferes' with effective implementation" (Hanf 1982, 159). Their hope is that "systematic investigation of implementation … can provide more direct, more useful, and more readily generalized advice to policy makers" (Berman 1978, 158).

The pioneers were Jeffery Pressman and Aaron Wildavsky (1973). Although not the first to observe the problems of implementation, and whereas, even before their seminal work, implementation had been variously called policy execution, policy application, policy activation, sanction and control, and carrying-out of policy (Bunker 1972, 71–2), Pressman and Wildavsky deserve credit for generating enormous interest in the subject and giving it an analytical cutting edge. It was not until in the late 1970s that such studies gained root in Europe, pioneered by Hood (1976) and filling what Dunsire calls the "implementation gap" (Dunsire 1978, 18) or what Hargrove (1975) calls the "missing link" between the concern with policy-making and the evaluation of policy outcome (Ham and Hill 1984, 94).

In the Third World, the concern with implementation problems arose as a result of the growing recognition that the development plans promulgated did not often lead to the desired objectives (Love and Sederberg 1987, 155). The first major work on implementation in the Third World was undertaken by M. S. Grindle (1980). There has been, since the late 1970s, much literature on implementation: many case studies of implementation failure and success in various policy areas have been produced, attempts at producing a body of implementation theory have been made, all designed to enhance understanding of the dynamics of the implementation process.

The study of implementation, as argued by Van Meter and Van Horn, is about examining those factors that facilitate the realization or nonrealization of policy goals (Van Meter and Van Horn 1975, 448). In line with this, Berman submits:

> Implementation is not about whether a policy's goals are fit and proper, which is a matter of values; nor does it concern itself with how they were chosen, which is a study of policy-making. Rather it … presumes that P does not invariably lead to O. Implementation analysis is, in short, the study of why authoritative decisions [policies, plans, laws, and the like] do not lead to expected results. To speak in more positive terms, it is the study of the conditions under which authoritative decisions do lead to desired outcome (Berman 1978, 160).

Or, more technically, as Goggin asserts:

> Implementation is a problem-solving activity that involves behaviors that have both administrative and political content. The manner, or style, of implementation is a result of certain implementing decisions that are made and action taken between the time that a plan is adopted by the authorities and the time when it is more or less successfully put in place. These implementation behaviors are shaped by the decision making environment, the type of policy at stake, and the characteristics of both the implementing organizations and the people who manage the program (Goggin 1986, 330).

In short, implementation study is an attempt to sensitize policy makers to variables that can be manipulated to improve the provision of goods and services to the people (Van Meter and Van Horn 1975, 484) and regulation of their behavior (Sabatier and Mazmanian, 1979, 540).

This is notwithstanding the fact that students of implementation are not in agreement about what constitutes their subject of inquiry (O'Toole, Jr. 1986, 183). Their common ground, however, is:

> a belief that the carrying out of policy, the installation of technology, the realization of a plan, or the enforcement of a law is neither automatic nor assured. On the contrary, both casual observation and systematic investigation suggest that the outcomes of social policies and innovative plans generally have been unpredictable and unfortunate, at least in the eyes of their designers (Berman 1978, 160).

# Perspectives in the Study of Policy Implementation

From the late 1970s, a distinction began to be made in the implementation literature between a "top-down" and a "bottom-up" perspective. The first to make this distinction was Richard F. Elmore (1979–80), arguing that "there are at least two clearly distinguishable approaches to implementation analysis: forward mapping and backward mapping," which represent top-down and bottom-up perspectives respectively. Since then analysis of implementation process tends to center around the two approaches. This distinction is artificial. This section, therefore, reviews not only the literature but also this distinction.

## Top-Down Perspective

The "top-downers," to use Sabatier's term (1986), include Pressman and Wildavsky (1973), Van Meter and Van Horn (1975), Hood (1976), O'Toole Jr. and Montjoy (1979, 1984, 1986), and Sabatier and Mazmanian (1979, 1980, 1983, 1986). They draw an analytical distinction between policy formulation and policy implementation, but their aim was to integrate them so that implementation would be taken into account when policy is being formulated. As Pressman and Wildavsky pointed out:

> The separation of policy design from implementation is fatal. It is no better than mindless implementation without a sense of direction. Though we can isolate policy and implementation for separate discussion, the purpose of our analysis is to bring them into closer correspondence with one another (Pressman and Wildavsky 1973, xvii).

Policy can be seen as "a hypothesis containing initial conditions and predicted consequences. If X is done at t1, then Y will result at t2" (Pressman and Wildavsky 1973, xiv). Policy thus contains both its goals and the means for realizing them. However, for the initial condition to exist, a program has to be initiated:

> A program consists of governmental action initiated in order to secure objectives whose attainment is problematical. A program exists when the initial conditions—the "if" stage of the policy hypothesis—have been met. The word "program" signifies the conversion of a hypothesis into governmental action. The initial premises of the hypothesis have been

authorized. The degree to which the predicted consequences [the "then" stage] take place we will call implementation (Pressman and Wildavsky 1973, xiv–v).

To this extent, successful implementation is defined by policy goals since "implementation cannot succeed or fail without a goal against which to judge it" (Pressman and Wildavsky 1973, xiv).

It is within this framework that Pressman and Wildavsky define implementation as "a process of interaction between the setting of goals and actions geared to achieving them" (1973, xv).

Similarly, in their attempt to identify the key findings of previous implementation studies, Van Meter and Van Horn (1975, 447) see implementation as

> those actions by public or private individuals [or groups] that are directed at the achievement of objectives set forth in prior policy decisions. This includes both one-time efforts to transform decisions into operational terms, as well as continuing efforts to achieve the large and small changes mandated by policy decisions.

More elaborately, Mazmanian and Sabatier define implementation as:

> the carrying out of a basic policy decision, usually made in a statute [although also possible through important executive orders or court decisions]. Ideally, that decision identifies the problem[s] to be addressed, stipulates the objective[s] to be pursued and, in a variety of ways, structure the implementation process.... [T]he implementation process normally runs through a number of stages beginning with passage of the basic statute, followed by the policy output [decisions] of the implementing agencies, the compliance of target groups with those decisions, the actual impacts—both intended and unintended—of those output, the perceived impacts of agency decisions, and, finally, important revisions

[or attempted revisions] in the basic statute (Mazmanian and Sabatier 1980, 540–1).

Implementation, in this sense, is seen as the process between the enactment of policy and its ultimate impact on the society (Sabatier and Mazmanian 1983, 6).

The last two definitions only elaborate on the earlier one. All have emphasized the centrality of stated policy goals in any implementation study. As Pressman and Wildavsky argued:

There must be something out there prior to implementation; otherwise there would be nothing to move toward in the process of implementation. A verb like implement must have an object like policy (Pressman and Wildavsky 1973, xiii).

Pressman and Wildavsky further contend that:

Policies imply theories. Whether stated explicitly or not, policies point to a chain of causation between initial conditions and future consequences. If X, then Y. Policies become programs when, by authoritative action, the initial conditions are created. X now exists. Programs make the theories operational by forging the first link in causal chain connecting actions to objectives. Given X, we act to obtain Y. Implementation, then, is the ability to forge subsequent links in the causal chain so as to obtain the desired results (Pressman and Wildavsky 1973, xv).

The focus on the stated objectives enables scholars to analyze and distinguish the objectives contained in legal documents from both those arising from the political rhetoric on the policy, on the one hand, and those arising from mistaken perception of the objectives of the policy, on the other (Sabatier 1986, 28).

All assume that policies are made by the politicians—whether in civilian gown or military uniform—who are accountable to the people, and that the policies are implemented by the bureaucratic officials who exercise some discretion in the implementation process, for it is inevitable and necessary (Majone and Wildavsky 1978, 113), and that separation of policy from implementation makes it possible to evaluate policy (Sabatier 1986, 31).

This policy-centered perspective takes policy as the starting point for implementation. It sees the whole policy process in terms of what Nakamura called "sequential, differentiated by function, and cumulative." It is sequential in the sense that one stage leads to the next. It is differentiated functionally in the sense that each stage represents a distinctive activity required by a system to move to the next stage. And it is cumulative in the sense that each round of activities produces results that are fed back into the process (1987, 142). Within this framework, it focuses on what is done and examines whether what is done, over time, was in conformity with the stated policy objectives and the factors responsible for that (Sabatier 1986, 22). Policy comes from the top (central authority or politicians) and is passed down (to local authority or bureaucrats) through organizational hierarchies for implementation, and in doing so to ensure the realization of the policy objective. In short, taking policy as the central focus, the approach asks the following questions:

1. To what extent were the actions of implementing officials and target groups consistent with (the objectives and procedures outlined in) that policy decision?
2. To what extent were the objectives attained over time (i.e., to what extent were the impacts consistent with the objectives)?
3. What were the principal factors affecting policy outputs and impacts, both those relevant to the official policy as well as other politically significant ones?
4. How was the policy reformulated over time on the basis of experience (Sabatier 1986, 22)?

## Bottom-Up Perspective

The "bottom-uppers" include Elmore (1978, 1979-89), Barrett and Fudge (1981), Barrett and Hill (1984), and Hjern and Hull (1982). They make no distinction between policy and implementation, as they argue that policy and implementation are not separable. According to them, it is difficult to show where policy stops and implementation starts. Besides, what is implementation to one group of actors may be policy to another group (Barrett and Fudge 1981, 11). The adherents of the bottom-up school, therefore, criticize the top-down approach. Barrett & Fudge and Barrett & Hill (whose work may be considered quite representative of the works of bottom-uppers and who have been more concerned about conceptualization of implementation process) define implementation as

> a policy-action continuum in which an interactive and negotiative process is taking place over time, between those seeking to put policy into effect and those upon whom action depends (Barrett and Fudge 1981, 25).

This is graphically represented in Figure 2.1.

## Figure 2.1
## The Policy-Action Relationship

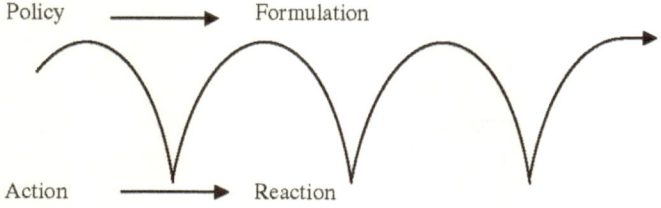

Source: Barrett, Susan and Fudge, Colin (eds). 1981. *Policy and Action: Essays on the Implementation of Public Policy*. London: Methuen. 25.

The bottom-up definition of implementation is derived from the following assumptions (which also encapsulate their criticisms of the top-down perspective):

1.  Policy-action is not just a mere transmission process, but rather a complex network of actions involving the aggregating of different interests and priorities. Thus, the political process involved in the policy formulation does

not stop with the enactment or promulgation of policy, but continues during implementation to influence the behavior of those implementing policy and those affected by it.

2.  The policy-action relationship is not a linear, step-by-step progression by which policy is translated into desired objectives but is "interactive and recursive" and, in that sense, individuals' and organizations' actions and reactions determine policy and are determined by it.

3.  Policy is not constant. It is mediated by actors who may have different assumptions and perceptions of the world from those who formulate it. To this extent, it undergoes some changes arising from interpretation and modification, as a result of what is happening in both the environment of implementation and outside it. "Thus it becomes difficult to identify a distinct and sequential `implementation process' which starts with the formulation of policy and ends with action" (Barret and Fudge 1981, 25).

4.  Policy does not necessarily have to come from the top: "policy may be a response to pressures and problems experienced on the ground. Equally, policy may be developed from specific innovations, that is action precedes policy. Not all action relates to a specific or explicit policy" (Barret and Fudge 1981, 12).

5.  The relationship between policy makers and implementers is not hierarchical. Implementers are not agents of the policy makers. Implementation agencies are either autonomous or semi-autonomous and have their own interests and priorities to pursue and their own policy-making role. In other words, "the implementation of much of public policy is dependent on action by groups that are relatively autonomous and not subject to the direct authority of those making policy" (Barrett and Hill 1984, 227). In brief, they see implementation in terms of a power relation.

This implementer-centered perspective, unlike the policy-centered, takes individual implementers as the central focus of analysis

(Lewis and Flynn 1979, 141). The implementers operate not under any hierarchical organization structure but within "implementation structure." The structure comprises both official and private actors who interact within a policy field. Instead of focusing on the factors affecting the implementation of a policy, it looks at the problem-solving activities of the actors involved in the policy at operational level (Sabatier and Hanf 1985, 306–7). It "starts by identifying the network of actors involved in service delivery in one or more local areas and asks them about their goals, strategies, activities, and contacts. It then uses the contacts as a vehicle for developing a network of planning, financing, and execution of the relevant and non-governmental programs" (Sabatier 1986, 32). This provides an outline for studying implementation from bureaucrats (the bottom) up to policy makers (the top).

Although there are other criticisms levied by the bottom-uppers against the top-downers, the enumerated ones are dominant. Yet, what is interesting is that most of the criticisms (notably, policy cannot be separated from implementation; policy-action is not just a mere transmission process; policy-action relationship is not a linear step-by-step progression; policy is not constant) are not serious challenges to the position of the top-downers and have even made the distinction between the two approaches artificial.

## A Critical Review of the Two Perspectives

The bottom-up approach is inadequate in that it limits implementation to the actions of those explicitly charged with the handling of a policy. Hence it excludes some actors who are not officially designated, even if they are politically and technically essential in the process of translating policy into action. And it ignores the issue of whether or not the prescribed actions are likely to lead to the desired objective (O'Toole Jr. 1986, 183). Although the bottom-uppers are concerned with actions and the interaction of the actors (which are essential variables in any implementation study), they are not basically concerned with policy implementation per se (Sabatier 1986, 36), for they ignore the relevance of policy and policy objective in guiding the action and the behavior of the actors in organizations. Even at the level of action it is impossible to understand the behavior of the actors in isolation from the context within which they operate. An understanding of the context will invariably lead one to an understanding of policy objectives and policy goals. However, the goals may not be precise or clear, and they may even change over time. But without a goal, implementation will have no determinate focus, and without a goal, there will be nothing to implement (Linder and Peters 1987, 465). In other words, there is no implementation without policy (Pressman and Wildavsky 1973, xiii), but there may be policies waiting for implementation.

Still, the bottom-uppers' criticism of the separation of implementation from policy is not defensible, since it is really possible to distinguish between policy and implementation. Policy provides the guideline, establishes the parameters, and sets the agenda for implementation. Whereas policy is concerned with setting the initial condition, implementation is concerned with taking further the initial condition to the intended goal. A policy may be formulated in a given time, but its implementation (its coming into effect) may be much later. Similarly, a policy document is one thing; its coming into being is another. In a phrase, "a yet-to-be implemented policy and an implemented one do not belong to the same logical category" (Majone and Wildavsky 1978, 107). In his analysis of land use policy, Odunlami observes that "the way planning authorities and planning responsibilities are often structured ... in Nigeria partly confirms the ... distinction between policy making and implementation" (Odunlami 1986, 59). Many policy case studies in education, employment, and industry have confirmed that there is even a difference between the language of policy and the language of implementation, which Lewis termed the "language of politics and language of administration" (1984, 203–11).

However, the top-downers are quick to point out that circumstance may change in the course of implementation of a policy, which may change the earlier policy goal and invariably affect the initial condition. To that extent, Mazmanian and Sabatier conceptualize a "formulation-implementation-reformulation cycle" (Sabatier 1986, 28) in order to explain the nature of policy shift in the implementation process. This conceptualization is within the general conceptualization of policy cycle. "Policy cycle ... does not refer to some predetermined, definitive number of steps through which all policies must inevitably go, but refers instead to how, in thinking about the policy process, one's attention is drawn to beginnings, middles, and endings that may lead to new beginning" (May and Wildavsky 1978, 12–13).

It is impossible in the formulation of any policy to anticipate every likely constraint on, or consequence for, implementation, even at the level of developing a program for the implementation of the policy. This is because of both cognitive limitations and the dynamic nature of the environment, as some of these constraints usually remain hidden in the formulation stage and emerge only in the implementation process (Majone and Wildavsky 1978, 106 –8).

These shifts in the policy goals are aptly identified by Love and Sederberg in their study of the implementation of refugee policy in Somalia (1987). They pointed out that the initial policy goal was to provide for a temporary relief support to refugees who fled from neighboring Ethiopia. However, as the circumstance changed, so also the policy goal: from relief to self-reliance and finally to self-sufficiency. They summarized the situation as follows:

> We have identified three broad stages in Somali refugee policy: relief, self-reliance, and self-sufficiency.... [E]ach was undertaken in response to the unfolding situation.... The original influx of refugees demanded emergency relief provisions for refugee care and feeding. The longer the refugees remained in their camps, the more routinized their care feeding became; the emergency faded. But then a second problem arose: The absence of any firm prospects for prompt repatriation created the danger of long-term refugee populations idling their time away in the camps. Consequently, the articulation of the self-reliance policy was intended to serve as a medium-term solution, providing refugees with activities to enhance both their skills and their contribution to their own support. Finally, the government had to admit that many of the refugees were never going to return to their original homes, and provisions had to be made for their self-sufficiency (Love and Sederberg 1987, 163).

To this extent, the argument that policies are changed in accordance with the desires of implementers (Palumbo and Harder 1981, x) is only one side of the story. More importantly, policies are reformulated in the implementation process to accommodate changing circumstances.

Similarly, the assertion that actions determine policy and are determined by it is incorrect. Although the implementation of the Somali refugee policy has revealed different stages in the policy shift, it does not show that implementation has shaped the policy. Rather, as Love and Sederberg pointed out, when the circumstance changed, so also the direction of the policy, which invariably affected the character of the implementation. Love and Sederberg indicated that all the different stages of the policy goals required different responses from the implementing agencies: relief requires immediate, short-term response; self-reliance, on the other hand, requires medium-term planning; while self-sufficiency demands not only long-term planning, but also more of the implementing agencies (1987, 163). It is not the implementation that shaped the policy but the other way around. In this regard, Majone and Wildavsky contend:

> Some of the ways in which policy affects implementation are fairly obvious. Policy content shapes implementation by defining the arena in which the process takes place, the identity and role of the principal actors, the range of permissible tools for action, and of course by supplying resources. The underlying theory provides not only the data, information and hypotheses on which subsequent debate and action will rely, but also, and most importantly, a conceptualization of the policy problem (Majone and Wildavsky 1978, 112).

Of course, in the process of implementing a policy other issues may arise, new ideas are learned, mistakes of previous policies are noted, and, as a result of all these, the policy being implemented may be reformulated or new policies are formulated to solve other problems. In other words, policies are reformulated because of what are happening both outside and inside implementation process (Hill 197, 8). Government actions are continuous; it does not wait for implementation of a particular policy to end before it formulates and implements other policies. Policies intended to cope with certain problems are themselves the causes of new problems for which new policy solution has to be formulated (May and Wildavsky 1978, 13). As implementation of policies may generate ideas for policy reformulation and formulation of other policies, so also policies are reformulated and formulated without any ideas arising from the implementation of particular policies.

However, the point that it is hard to say where policy stops and implementation starts does not in any way invalidate the distinction between policy and implementation. Besides, there is a difference between formulation of a policy and reformulation of a policy. Whereas the former refers to a new policy, the latter refers to an existing policy with some modification.

Equally, the argument that one person's implementation is another person's policy does not help the matter either. To emphasize that point is to ignore the nature of the bureaucratic communication process and the routinization of policy into the bureaucratic process. Bureaucracy has various procedures—at both horizontal and vertical levels—for implementing policy. It is clear that what one group of actors may see as implementation others may see as a policy. "That is, the policy passes through and is implemented sequentially by various organizations, so that the output of one implementing organization becomes the input for other organizations. The final implemented programme, and hence the policy's outcome, depends on these passages" (Berman 1978, 166). That is how policy is implemented, although the process is neither smooth nor does it follow a step-by-step progression. Bureaucrats are not restricted to the implementation of a single policy at a time, but many of them to the extent that some actors may not even know or remember which policy they are implementing. Implementation of policies becomes routinized. This seems to be partially noted by some of the bottom-uppers when they contend "there may be an important distinction—at least in degree—between processes of 'getting things done' whereby the 'policies' have become routinized into the day to day procedural frameworks for action, and the implementation of new policy" (Barrett and Hill

1984, 222). However, this distinction is crude since even new policies have to become routinized into the day-to-day procedural action.

The distinction between policy and implementation is central to the understanding of the concepts of policy failure and policy success. Without this distinction, there will be no basis for analyzing policy failure or policy success. This is the underlying logic behind the bottom-uppers' neglect of analysis of policy failure or success. They contend that it is difficult to show whether a policy has achieved its goal or not, for policy goals keep changing. Besides, what is policy success to some actors may be failure to others (Hill 1979, 7). Illustrating this argument, Ingram and Mann (1980, 13), using the American minimum-wage policy as an example, ask:

> What are we to think of the existing policy on the minimum wage? For organized labour, the minimum wage policy is a necessity, a protection for the skilled and organized workers, but also an insult grudgingly afforded by a government that responds too willingly to business interests. To others, business and particularly some economists, it is an irrational policy that prevents a large segment of our employable population—mostly teen-agers and relatively unproductive workers—from reaching agreement with employers on mutually beneficial terms. Is minimum wage policy a success or a failure? For organized labour it is a qualified success. To business generally and most economists, it is a failure. Is there an objective measure of success acceptable to all conflicting value positions?

The preceding quotation suggests that bottom-uppers are not dealing with specific policy goals, let alone deliberating on whether the policy goals have been achieved or not; rather they are primarily concerned with the rationality of the policy, which is a matter of value judgment. Of course, what a group of people may consider as good policy others may not. For instance, a policy for nationalizing private companies or privatizing public companies is largely dependent on the value judgment of the policy makers. Similarly, the definition of policy goals is the responsibility of the policy makers and is not shared with other actors in the implementation process. However, the measurement of the policy goals may be undertaken by other actors as well. What is basic in all this is that there has to be a policy goal against which to judge implementation. A policy may have many goals. Some of the goals may be realized while others may not be. Some of the goals may be more fundamental than others. Thus, to say whether a policy has succeeded or not would, to a large extent, depend on one's position in the policy process (either as a policy maker, implementer, policy analyst, or as a target group) and the categories one uses in the measurement of success in the implementation process.

However, if a policy goal is not achieved, it does not necessarily mean that implementation has failed (Bowen 1982, 12). In order to understand whether or not implementation has succeeded or failed, policy goal should not be seen as the only source of reference, but also the program designed to accomplish the objective. It is the program that operationalizes the policy. When a policy goal is not realized, one of the following three factors, or all the factors, might have been responsible: First, the policy is not well executed by the implementers. Second, the policy is not based on a sound theory about the causes of the policy problems and the effects the policy will have upon its implementation (Pressman and Wildavsky 1973, xvii). In this respect, conceptualization of policy problems and solutions has to be linked with adequate conceptualization of the implementation process (Weimer 1983, 168).

In view of this, no matter how well the policy is implemented it may not achieve its goal; the policy may not have impact on those it is intended for or the impact may be different from those envisaged (Hill 1979, 47). In this regard, Bardach contends that if a "theory is fundamentally incorrect, the policy will probably fail no matter how well it is implemented" (Bardach 1977, 251–2). All this arises because of inadequate knowledge of the environment (Hill 1979, 47). Hence, implementation may be a necessary, but insufficient condition for the realization of policy goal (Van Meter and Van Horn 1975, 449). Third, the policy may be abandoned midway. This may happen not just because of inadequate theoretical understanding of the policy problem, but also because of success in other policy or other external exigencies.

One argument that cannot be substantiated empirically is that the relationship between policy makers and implementers is not hierarchical; implementers are not agents of policy makers. In this connection, Wildavsky (1989, 77) asserts,

> [W]hile one hears talk of building bureaucracies without hierarchy, I was not aware that the great day had come. The idea of what might be called 'bureaucracy without authority' would require considerable discussion.

Giving policy makers and implementers equal status is to imply that they perform the same function; performing the same functions undoubtedly removes any difference between the two. The difference, if any, is only in the division of labor between the two groups. This position is reinforced by the assumption that policy and implementation are not separable. However, as policy is distinguished from implementation so also policy makers are distinguishable from implementers.

Of course, there is an important area of overlap between policy and implementation, and there are more substantial areas of relatively independent functioning that are analyzable and observable in practice (Hogwood and Gunn 1984, 207). Policies are generally made by politicians in either civilian or military uniform, whether at legislative or executive level, while their implementation is performed by bureaucrats. This fits in with what even the most forceful advocate of bottom-up approach termed "those seeking to put policy into effect" and "those upon whom action depends" (Barrett and Fudge 1981, 25). In terms of recruitment, while civilian politicians are in most cases elected by the people (to make policies and ensure their implementation), and hence responsible to them, bureaucrats are in most cases appointed on the basis of qualification (to implement government policies) and are responsible to the government of the day. Furthermore, their method of operation differs remarkably: what legislators do in the legislature is not what bureaucrats do in the bureaucracy. Whereas the legislative method of operation tends to be open, bureaucratic method is characterized by secrecy and anonymity.

Associated with the argument affirming policy makers' and the implementers' equal status is the assumption that implementers have their own interests and priorities to pursue, which may be in direct conflict with the priorities of policy makers. In addition, the implementers have their own policy-making role. Hence, implementation is a process of negotiation, bargaining, and conflict between policy makers and implementers (Barrett and Fudge 1981, 21). Barrett and Hill maintained that their

> focus on policy implementation highlights a particular range of interactions in which one set of actors is actively trying to influence or change the behaviour of others to get policy implemented; and other actors are responding according to whether the desired action fits in with or furthers their own interests (Barret and Hill 1984, 230).

There is no doubt that implementers have a great deal to do with either the success or failure of public policies. However, as argued by Linder and Peters (1987, 465),

> [T]o place goal definition in the hands of that element of the public sector [empirically, analytically, or managerially] is to admit defeat and the inability of the policy making hierarchies in government to function effectively to produce governance.

In line with this argument, Majone and Wildavsky (1978, 107) note:

> [W]e disagree with the idea that the function of the implementation process is to satisfy the psychological and social needs of the participants, regardless of the actual policy results. This view is strangely reminiscent of old syndicalist doctrines summarized in once-popular slogans like "The Railroads to the Railroadmen," and "The Mines

to the Miners" ... We feel the emphasis on consensus, bargaining, and political maneuvering can easily lead [and has, in fact, led] to the conception that implementation is its own reward.

It is certainly true that implementers may have different views or interests from those of the policy makers on a given policy area. However, it is equally true that implementers themselves, whether within organization or between organizations, may have different interests on certain policy issues. The 1988 Civil Service Reform in Nigeria clearly highlights these different interests among implementers. The reform, among other things, abolishes the distinction between the professional and administrative officers. Whereas professional officers supported the reform, administrative officers were cool toward it. The reform, however, is being implemented effectively. These differences of interests, furthermore, are not only limited to the implementers alone, but also to the policy makers. This is the norm in all government organizations. Yet, in all this, when policy is sanctioned, its implementation is not dependent on the consensus of the implementers, as formulation of policy itself is not always dependent on the consensus of the policy makers. There may be policies that are in direct conflict with the interests of even the influential members among the implementers, but such policies eventually get implemented without any bargaining and negotiation.

In Britain, for example, King observed that the senior civil servants were unhappy about many of Margaret Thatcher's economic policies but in the end they accepted the situation, for "it is their job to do what their political masters tell them to do. Thatcher and her colleagues told them what to do. They did it" (King 1984, 485). In Sokoto State, a policy on government rentals of private residential houses for its officials was enacted in 1984. The policy document indicates that the government would no longer rent any private residential houses for its staff except, in special circumstance, for expatriate officers (where government could not provide its own houses). In this connection, all the existing government-rented accommodations were to be released. This policy not only affected some of the policy makers (commissioners), but also many of the influential implementers, notably, permanent secretaries, secretaries, professional sectional heads, and other senior officers who owned a large number of the rented accommodation. Despite this, the policy was, to some extent, implemented. Most of the private property rented by government were released and the government saved about one million naira (N1,000,000.00). This is to show that although there are incentives to motivate implementers, there are also sanctions to keep their behavior within bounds. Compliance based on legal rational authority has not yet been replaced by negotiation and bargaining.

In the same vein, to consider central government officials as the policy makers who interact through negotiation, bargaining, and conflict—with the local officials as implementers—is too simplistic. In the first place, implementation is neither the monopoly of the central nor of the local government. Central government formulates and implements policy at its own level; so also does local government. In other words, there are policy makers and implementers at the central and local government levels. Yet, whenever a policy comes from the center to be implemented by local government, both the policy makers and implementers at the local level become implementers of the policy. In the second place, implementation is not all about bargaining, compromise, and conflict between policy makers and implementers. In line with this position, Hogwood and Gunn (1984, 208) contend:

> If parliament decided to move from left-hand to right-hand drive on our roads, would we be happy to leave to 'negotiation' between road-users, local authorities, and the central government such questions as when, how, and whether the change-over should take effect?.

Linder and Peters (1987, 464) agree that "[g]overnance is not about negotiation, it is about the use of legitimate authority."

Thus, implementation is essentially about the mechanisms the government uses for executing policies. Among the mechanisms are issuance of directives, communication, coordination, control, and monitoring of actors' performance.

In short, and as the relationship between the policy makers and implementers in Sokoto shows, bargaining and negotiation have limited relevance where one group has control over another. On the other hand, where all groups are mutually dependent, and no one group is dominant, agreement may be reached by negotiation and bargaining (Barrett and Hill 1984, 228). The concepts of bargaining, conflict, and compromise are most useful if they are analyzed in relation to two or more groups with more or less equal power—such as among implementers, legislators, and policy makers on the one hand and the target group on the other (Pressman and Wildavsky 1973, 134; Barrett and Fudge 1981, 21). Where this condition does not exist, the whole framework of bargaining and negotiation as the dominant factors in the implementation process is called into question. Anyway, it seems that the problem with the bottom-uppers in their analysis of bargaining and compromise is their failure to recognize that much of the negotiation and compromise takes place between the central policy makers or their representatives and local policy makers or their representatives, and not just between policy makers at the center and implementers at the locality. However, in this kind of relationship the position of the local policy makers becomes that of implementers. But, based on this, it will be incorrect to assume that implementation is bargaining and compromise between policy makers and implementers without qualification. This notwithstanding, much of the bargaining, negotiation, and compromise can take place during the policy formulation stage (Majone and Wildavsky 1978, 113; Hogwood and Gunn 1984, 208).

Apart from that, the argument focusing on the implementation structure to the exclusion of policy is inadequate as a unit of analysis. Relying on the perceptions of the actors in the implementation structure to arrive at a conclusion—in isolation from the direct and indirect organizational, socioeconomic, and policy influences on their behavior—is fallacious. There is no doubt that informal implementation structure may exist and may serve as a unit of analysis but cannot be seen as independent of the formal organizational arrangement. Yet, that is the very assumption underlying the concept of implementation structure. An implementation structure can hardly develop without a policy. It is the policy that determines not only the development of implementation structure but also its character. It determines the kinds of organizations, both formal and informal, to be part of the implementation structure and the kinds of actors to be involved. For example, health, education, communication, and agricultural policies will each have its unique set of policy network or policy community (stakeholders, interests, and structure of interactions). Each formal actor in the implementation process represents his organization, and his loyalty to the implementation structure is derived from his loyalty to his organization. The power relation of the actors in the network is dependent on first their position in their respective organizations and second their relative roles in the implementation process. Actors whose support is crucial in the implementation process may tend to be more powerful in the implementation structure.

At this point it could be said that both perspectives have been motivated by different concerns and, as a result, developed somewhat different strategies for studying implementation. Some of the implementation scholars from both perspectives have attempted in different ways to explain these concerns.

# Concerns of the Top-Downers and Bottom-Uppers

Lewis and Flynn see the different concerns of the two approaches in terms of their varying definitions of implementation. As they indicate, "The term implementation tends to be used in two rather different ways; either as an analytical category or as a description of actual behaviour" (Lewis and Flynn 1979, 124).

This distinction corresponds to the top-down and bottom-up perspectives, respectively. Top-downers treat implementation as something separate from policy and merely as a stage in the policy process. Within the implementation process itself, they identify three analytical phases: First, there is an interpretation phase in which the policy is translated into guidelines and regulations by the implementing agency or agencies. Second, there is an organization phase when departmental units assume responsibility for putting the policy into operation. And third, there is an application phase in which service delivery becomes routinized by the implementing agencies (Larson 1980, 4). Thus the strategy and problems of policy implementation are more or less different from those of policy formulation. And since implementation is a stage within the policy process, it is taken into account during the formulation stage. In this connection, implementation:

> is an action-oriented phenomenon that, within the context of public bureaucracies, unfolds over time. As such, it has a beginning, a middle, and an end, with each stage of the process characterized by its own goals, strategies, and agents (Goggin 1986, 335).

In contrast, bottom-uppers do not see any distinction between policy and implementation, and hence their definition of implementation is not analytical; rather, it is a description of certain aspects of the implementation process. In other words, bottom-uppers do not say what implementation is but what it involves: interaction, bargaining, and negotiation. The top-downers regard all this as a description of what actually happens in real life (Hogwood and Gunn 1984, 207) or, to put it differently, as a politics of implementation that is just part of the implementation process. The problem here is that bottom-uppers seem to confuse the characteristics of the implementation process with the product of what happens during implementation. This important distinction, Goggin (1986, 330) contends, has been unfortunately blurred in many of the conceptual frameworks and empirical studies of implementation.

## Policy Objective versus Actors' Strategy

Unlike Lewis and Flynn, Sabatier asserts that the top-downers have been concerned with: (1) the effectiveness of specific governmental programs and (2) the ability of elected officials to guide and constrain the behavior of civil servants and target groups.

Addressing such concerns requires a careful analysis of the formally approved objectives of elected officials, an examination of relevant performance indicators, and an analysis of the factors affecting such performance. Bottom-uppers, on the other hand, are far less preoccupied with the extent to which a formally enacted policy decision is carried out and much more concerned with accurately mapping the strategies of actors concerned with a policy problem. They are not primarily concerned with the implementation (carrying out) of a policy per se, but rather with understanding patterns of actor interaction in a specific policy sector (1986, 35–6).

In short, Sabatier points out that whereas top-downers are concerned with policy objectives, bottom-uppers are concerned with actors' strategies in the implementation process.

## Programmed versus Adaptive Strategy

As for Hyder, the focus should be on the different concerns of the two perspectives in relation to their differing strategies to implementation. Whereas the top-downers adopt what Berman (1980) termed "programmed" strategy, bottom-uppers adopt "adaptive" strategy. Rewording the terms and comparing their methods, Hyder points out:

> In broad terms, a programmed strategy seeks to prepare carefully, in terms of defining goals, assigning responsibilities, and laying down clear and detailed programmes of the activities necessary to achieve the goals, so that implementation can proceed without any great need for subsequent changes or adjustments. An adaptive strategy on the other hand deliberately leaves the content of the policy flexible, and gives the implementers scope to adapt the policy to varying circumstances, and perhaps in so doing to clarify its goals (1984:5).

## Accountability versus Trust

In contrast to Hyder, Lane argues that implementation is about two issues: the relationship between objectives and outcome, which he terms the responsibility side, and the process of putting policy into effect, which he terms the trust side (Lane 1987, 542). These sides correspond to the concerns of the top-downers and bottom-uppers respectively. On the responsibility side, Lane contends that political as well as administrative accountability is impossible without the notion of implementation of public policy.

If it is not possible to evaluate the extent to which objectives and outcomes match, then public accountability is meaning-less. The fact that objectives sometimes do not find their outcomes or that outcomes sometimes cannot find their objectives does not imply that accountability is impossible (1987, 542).

On the trust side, furthermore, Lane argues that implementation in a democratic system of government is predicated upon the public power entrusted to politicians and public officials who are supposed to deliver on policies. Nonetheless, how implementation is carried out is a duty of the implementers for which they are held accountable where relative autonomy exists.Without some leverage for independent action, it will be impossible for the implementers to make judgment about appropriate means for achieving policy ends, taking into account environmental exigencies and the need for flexibility.

However, Lane (1987, 542–543) is quick to point out:

[C]omplete autonomy on the part of the implementors would mean a total absence of restrictions on the behaviour of the implementors so negating the fundamental accountability nature of the interaction between citizens and implementors. On the other hand, too many restrictions following a distrust in the implementors would jeopardize the possibility of successful implementation as it is impossible to outline once and for all a detailed plan as to how objectives are to be accomplished. Trust is basic to the implementation process, but this does not do away with the responsibility side of the implementation.

The problem, however, is that top-down models place too much emphasis on the responsibility side, ensuring as far as possible that the inherent uncertainties of implementation processes are minimized with the aid of a firm plan or an outlined structure of control. Bottom-up models, on the other hand, underline the trust side too high in an attempt to safeguard as many degrees of freedom as possible to the implementors as a tool for handling the uncertainties by flexibility and learning. If responsibility is stressed unduly, then there will be too many restrictions on the implementors in the choice of alternative technologies for the accomplishment of objectives. On the other hand, if trust is the sole basis of the activities of the implementors, then there will be too few restrictions on the implementors, allowing even the replacement of the original objectives by new goals (Lane 1987, 543).

Although both perspectives have been motivated by different concerns in their focus and method of inquiry, and although the controversy between the two approaches has stimulated further interest in the implementation research, the essential question is whether or not they are completely different. The answer, however, is that they are not. They both "spring from the same basic root and share a common focus on governmental organizations as endogenous political actors" (Linder and Peters 1987, 467). In this respect Lane argues:

> An implementation process is a combination of responsibility and trust both in the relation between citizens and the public sector in general and in the relation between politicians and officials. Without the notion of implementation as policy accomplishment there is no basis for evaluating policies and holding politicians, administrators, and professionals accountable. On the other hand, implementation ... rests upon trust or a certain amount of degrees of freedom for politicians and implementors to make choices about alternative means for the accomplishment of goals (1987, 543).

Each perspective emphasizes certain aspects of implementation. Even in each of the perspectives there are variations in the emphasis on crucial variables in the implementation process. Expressing this concern, Lester et al. assert:

After almost twenty years of implementation research, there is still no overarching implementation perspective that adequately explains and predicts how and why the joint efforts of the federal government and states and localities to put public laws into effect in the American states turn out the way they do (Lester et al. 1987, 208).

So far all implementation studies have identified only those variables they consider important in the implementation process without specifying a fully developed framework of implementation (O'Toole Jr. 1986, 184). However, "the available literature does attempt to specify the common causes and cures for policy failures."

# Toward a Framework for the Analysis of Policy Implementation

The first elaborate, analytical framework for examining the policy implementation process was advanced by Van Meter and Van Horn in their article "The Policy Implementation Process: A Conceptual Framework" (1975). It is, of course, one thing to present a framework in a textual form, and it is another thing to reproduce it in a meaningful graphic form. Van Meter and Van Horn's have met this requirement as shown in Table 2.2. They first identify six independent variables that shape the linkages between policy and performance. Second, they depict the relationship among the variables. The variables are: policy standards and objectives; policy resources; interorganizational communication and enforcement; the characteristics of the implementing agencies; economic, social, and political conditions; and the disposition of implementers. On the linkages between the six independent variables, on one hand, and the dependent variable, on the other, Van Meter and Van Horn show that policy standards and objectives, and policy resources, apart from elaborating on the overall policy goals and the means for achieving them, provide objective standards for measuring performance.

Finally, all the components of the framework (the independent variables) discussed must be fitted through the perception of the implementers (disposition of the implementers). Three elements of the implementers' response may affect their ability and willingness to implement policy: their understanding of the policy; their acceptance of, neutrality toward, or rejection of, the policy; and the intensity of that response (Van Meter and Van Horn 1975, 462–474).

As regards the relationship among the independent variables on how they affect implementation, Van Meter and Van Horn contend that policy standards and objectives have indirect effect on performance. At the same time, the policy standards' influence on the dependent variable is mediated by other independent variables. Clearly, Van Meter and Van Horn (1975, 474) argue, "[T]he delivery of public services will be influenced by the manner in which standards and objectives are communicated to implementors and the extent to which standards and objectives facilitate oversight and enforcement."

Van Meter and Van Horn further point out that standards and objectives have indirect impact on the implementers' disposition through interorganizational communication activities, as their response to the policy will be influenced partly by their perception and interpretation of its objectives as well as the way in which they are communicated. Standards and objectives, moreover, have an indirect impact on the implementers' disposition through enforcement activities; they define the relationship between policy makers and implementers and their powers and discretion respectively.

Second, policy resources affect communication and enforcement activities in that services can only be given if provided in the policy, and enforcement can only be achieved if there are sufficient resources to support such activity. Availability of resources directly influences the disposition of implementers when they perceive the prospect of receiving a share of these resources.

**Figure 2.2**
**A Model of the Policy Implementation Process**

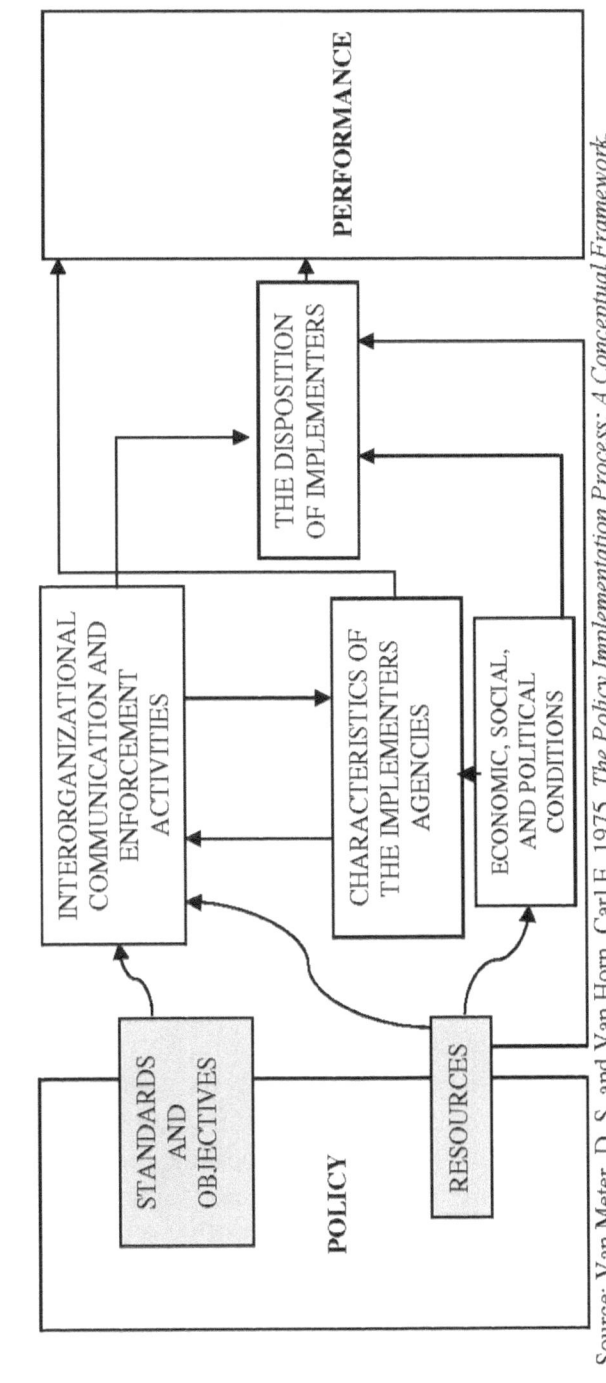

Source: Van Meter, D. S. and Van Horn, Carl E. 1975. *The Policy Implementation Process: A Conceptual Framework.*
Administration and Society 6, 4: 463.

In addition, availability of resources affects the economic, social, and political environment of the implementing jurisdiction in that it may create a need for participation and successful implementation of the program by private citizens and organized interest groups.

Third, the economic, social, and political environment of the implementing jurisdiction affect the character of implementing agencies, the dispositions of implementers, and performance itself. Environmental conditions affect the character of the bureaucratic structure as well as the level of political support an agency enjoys; they affect implementers' disposition through the mobilization of public support for a program. In other words, "environmental conditions may cause implementors to execute a policy without altering their personal preferences about that policy" (Van Meter and Van Horn 1975, 476). Environmental factors directly affect public service delivery irrespective of other forces at play; they facilitate or constrain performance.

Fourth, characteristics of implementing agencies, notably the nature of the communication network, the degree of hierarchical control, leadership style, and the agency's formal and informal ties to the policy-making or policy-enforcement body can affect the disposition of their personnel.

Finally, Van Meter and Van Horn suggest the likelihood of an interactive effect between interorganizational communication and enforcement activities and the characteristics of the implementing agencies. They point out that how enforcement and follow-up activities are conducted and the type of power used by superiors will be affected by the formal and informal relationship between the policy-making and implementing organizations.

There have been attempts, even before Van Meter and Van Horn's, to provide a framework for the analysis of the implementation process. Such attempts have been made by Bunker (1972) and Smith (1973). However, the attempts were neither elaborate nor adequate to cope with the dynamics of the implementation process. Similar efforts have been made in that direction by other scholars. So far, the most comprehensive framework of implementation process has been presented by Paul Sabatier and Daniel Mazmanian (1980).

Their framework, as presented at Table 2.3, identifies five major stages in the implementation process (as the dependent variables)—namely policy outputs of the implementing agencies, compliance with policy output by target groups, actual impacts of policy outputs, perceived impacts of policy outputs, and major revision in status, on the one hand—and three major variables (as independent variables)—namely the tractability of the problem, ability of status to structure implementation, and nonstatutory variables affecting implementation, on the other hand. The rest of the framework attempts to show how the independent variables affect one or more stages (dependent variables) in the implementation process (1980, 538–560).

In spite of these efforts, a fully developed theory of implementation has not been produced. In his examination of more than three hundred studies of implementation, O'Toole concludes:

Roughly half of the published studies in the field identified policy characteristics [especially clarity, specificity, and/or flexibility of goals and procedures, and validity of a policy's causal theory] as significant; approximately the same number claim that resources [financial and other] are crucial. Other frequently identified categories of variables include: implementing-actor or multi-actor structure, number of actors, attitudes and perceptions of implementing personnel, alignment of clientele, and timing [including the possibilities for learning among implementers] (1986, 189).

Thus, the artificial distinction between the top-down and bottom-up approaches has frustrated efforts at developing a theory of implementation that commands general agreement. In the circumstance, "researchers continue to work from diverse theoretical perspectives and to employ different variables to make sense of their findings" (O'Toole Jr, 1986, 182). However, the basic point remains: "It is ... a mark of immaturity of policy implementation research that these two perspectives have developed in relative isolation, with so little effort to incorporate the variables and insights of each in a more fully-developed empirical theory" (Lester 1987, 211).

## Figure 2.3
## Skeletal Flow Diagram of the Variables Involved in the Implementation Process

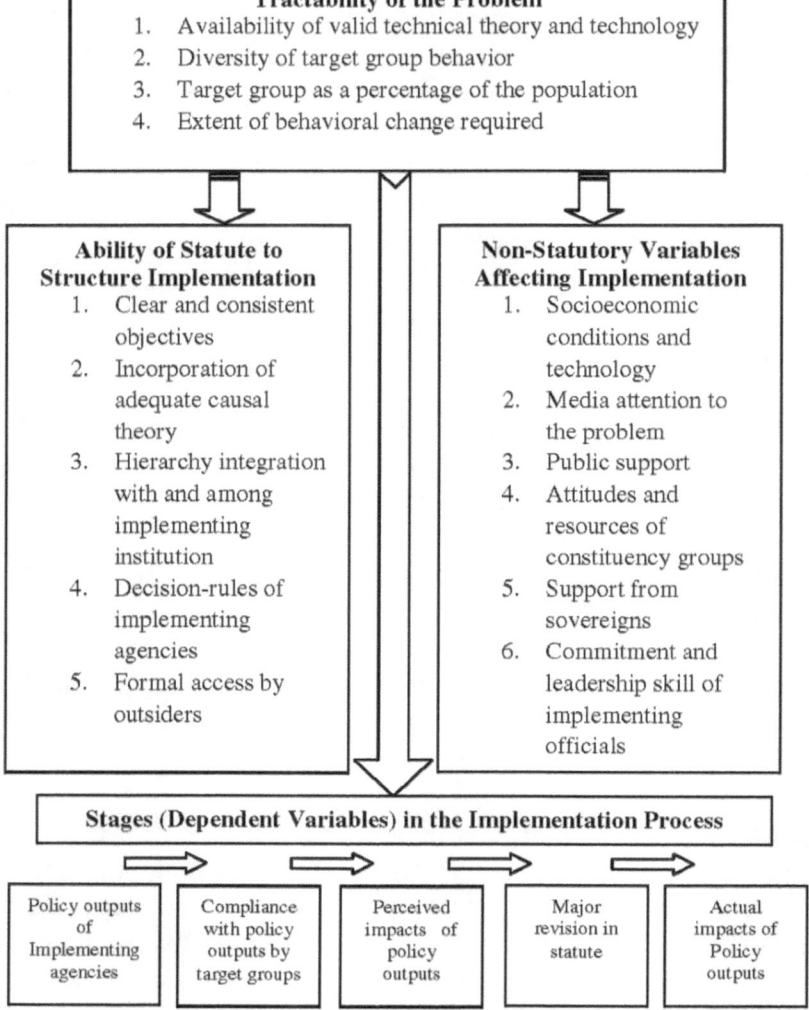

**Tractability of the Problem**
1. Availability of valid technical theory and technology
2. Diversity of target group behavior
3. Target group as a percentage of the population
4. Extent of behavioral change required

**Ability of Statute to Structure Implementation**
1. Clear and consistent objectives
2. Incorporation of adequate causal theory
3. Hierarchy integration with and among implementing institution
4. Decision-rules of implementing agencies
5. Formal access by outsiders

**Non-Statutory Variables Affecting Implementation**
1. Socioeconomic conditions and technology
2. Media attention to the problem
3. Public support
4. Attitudes and resources of constituency groups
5. Support from sovereigns
6. Commitment and leadership skill of implementing officials

**Stages (Dependent Variables) in the Implementation Process**

| Policy outputs of Implementing agencies | Compliance with policy outputs by target groups | Perceived impacts of policy outputs | Major revision in statute | Actual impacts of Policy outputs |
|---|---|---|---|---|

Sources: Mazmanian, Daniel and Sabatier, Paul (ed). 1981. *Effective Policy Implementation,* Lexinton: DC Heath, 542.

# Policy Makers–Implementers' Relationship

It seems that the basic factor influential in both perspectives is their perception of the policy makers–implementers relation and/or central-local relation. The top-downers see the relationship between policy makers and implementers as partners and as master–agent relation in which implementers, in most cases, simply execute the programs of the policy makers. On the other hand, the bottom-uppers, who see the relationship as that of bargaining, compromise, and conflict, regard implementation as a process of interaction between the central and local government, which is characterized by bargaining, compromise, and conflict.

This distinction is central to the understanding of some of the contentious issues surrounding the two approaches in the implementation literature. In Nigeria, elements of both approaches on central-local and/or policy makers–implementers relationships were manifested in the Second Republic. The relationship between the federal government under the National Party of Nigeria [NPN] and the state governments under the same party was based on partnership, while the relationship between the federal government and the states controlled by other parties (the Unity Party of Nigeria [UPN], Nigeria People's Party [NPP], Great Nigeria People's Party [GNPP], and People's Redemption Party [PRP]) was based on conflict, bargaining, and compromise. In other words, where the central and local governments are under the same political party platform, their interaction may not necessarily be of conflict, but essentially of partnership. On the other hand, where the central and local governments are under different political party platforms, their interaction may not be of partnership. It is not surprising, therefore, when the British Labour Government decided in 1965 to abolish the tripartite system of education that provided for three types of schools for children of different abilities, and to introduce a comprehensive secondary education so that all children of a given age would attend the same schools, irrespective of their abilities, only the Labour-controlled authorities supported the policy wholeheartedly; the conservatives did not (Blauch 1984, 19–32).

In Nigeria, the relationship between the policy makers and implementers at the federal level and their counterparts at the state level was based on a master–agent relationship (Ciroma 1980, 7). Although in his address to the federal permanent secretaries on October 22, 1979, the then-president, Alhaji Shehu Shagari, indicated that the relationship between the policy makers and implementers was based on partnership. The reality of the situation, and even the implication of his address, was not so. This is how he saw the relationship between the government and the career civil service:

> Members of Government and career Civil Servants should see one another as partners in progress. Progress in this context can only be defined as the execution of the programme on the platform of which the government received the mandate to govern. Whoever is not prepared to join fully in the prosecution of such programmes, be he a political appointee or a civil servant knows the honourable way out. There can therefore be no half measures.

Similarly, in his first address to permanent secretaries and the chief executive of parastatals of Sokoto State soon after his assumption of office, Colonel Garba Mohammed left no one in any doubt who was in charge:

> As the new Governor of Sokoto state, I decided to call on you as Permanent Secretaries and Chief Executives of various Government Parastatals to re-emphasize that you have an important role to play in the implementation of government policies and decisions. You are the principal channels through which governmental policies are translated into action. I must categorically affirm that this role should be carried out with thoroughness and speed. A situation whereby the implementation of government policies is slowed down due to unnecessary bureaucratic procedures will have no place under this administration. All matters under your consideration should be treated with despatch.... I will at all times demand dedication and commitment on all of you and where this

is not forthcoming, I will take firm and decisive action on the Permanent Secretary or Chief Executive involved … I expect smooth and cordial relationship between you and your Commissioners. The business of governance requires the spirit of team-work and understanding (unpublished).

The relationship between the federal and state governments was clearly demonstrated in the implementation of the federal government housing policy (1980–1983). In the policy document, the federal government decided to provide, in the first phase, one thousand units of houses in each of the states of the federation, irrespective of the political party in control in the states. However, in the process of implementing the policy, some state governments controlled by political parties other than the party controlling the federal government

became unwilling partners of the federal government. The governments of such states interpreted the entire arrangement as a means used by the NPN government to gain support from the electorate. Consequently, they refused to provide their own support for the project, and attempted to sabotage the efforts of the Federal Government (Dlakwa 1984, 146).

For example, in one such state, Bendel, the state governor, Professor Ambrose Alli, objected to the federal government involvement in the provision of housing in his state, and consequently all the one thousand housing units earmarked for his state had to be cancelled (Dlakwa 1984, 177–8). In this case there was no implementation. Similarly, having negotiated with the governor of Oyo State (controlled by a party other than the one at the center), without any success, the federal government decided to use its power to acquire some land and build some houses. Nonetheless, the governor, Chief Bola Ige, in retaliation, ordered the demolition of all the houses started by the federal government, which resulted in the destruction of about two hundred housing units, some of which were either partially or totally completed (Dlakwa 1984, 176). This invariably delayed or disrupted the implementation of the program. On the other hand, in states controlled by NPN, the federal government enjoyed the full cooperation of the state governments (Dlakwa 1984, 175).

Still, in spite of the confrontational attitudes of some state governments toward the federal government housing policy, Dlakwa concludes: "[N]o evidence exists to show that the performance ratio of the federal housing project was higher in the NPN controlled states than in the non NPN controlled states" (Dlakwa 1984, 184).

Under the military regimes (and most of Nigeria's post-independent political life has been under the military), the relationship between the policy makers and implementers at both the federal and state levels has been based on a master–agent relationship. Thus bureaucrats, who take an active part in the formulation of public policies, simply implement government policies. This has been the character of implementation in the Nigerian bureaucracy as a whole and Sokoto State bureaucracy in particular.

Yet, the implementation process is not just about the policy makers–implementers relationship or central-local relationship. It is essentially about how policies are communicated from one level of implementers to another (Nixon 1980, 135) and how they are monitored to ensure their implementation in accordance with their goals.

Although the focus so far has largely been on the top-down and bottom-up approaches, there are, nonetheless, other approaches in the implementation literature such as implementation game (Bardach 1977), implementation structure (Hjern and Porter 1981), resource exchange networks and implementation (Thrasher and Dunkerley 1982; Thrasher 1983), implementation through bargaining (Ingram 1977), legal structure and implementation (Sabatier and Mazmanian 1980), implementation as an organizational problem (Montjoy and O'Toole Jr. 1979), and implementation as evolution (Wildavsky and Majone 1978).

In addition, other implementation scholars have examined the contributions of various social science disciplines to understand implementation. Elmore, for example, has developed four organizational models of implementation: the systems management model, the bureaucratic process model, the organizational development model, and the conflict and bargaining model (1978). Similarly, Hogwood and Gunn have advanced four approaches to implementation: structural approaches, procedural and management approaches, behavioral approaches, and political approaches (1984). Furthermore, Lane, having reviewed the various approaches introduced in the implementation literature for over a decade, presented ten models of implementation: implementation as perfect administration, implementation as policy management, implementation as evolution, implementation as learning, implementation as implementation structure, implementation as outcomes, implementation as perspective, implementation as political symbolism, implementation as coalition, and implementation as responsibility and trust (1987). It is, however, not the intention of this study to discuss specifically these approaches, but to indicate that all the various approaches and their units of analysis are contained within the top-down and bottom-up approaches. In other words, the two approaches are dominant in the implementation literature.

Likewise, there have been some attempts at synthesizing the top-down and bottom-up approaches. The first to make such a bold attempt was Elmore (1985). He combines his previous work on "backward mapping" (a bottom-up perspective) (Elmore 1979) with what he terms "forward mapping" (basically a top-down perspective). "Forward mapping stresses what policy makers control; backward mapping stresses the marginal influence that policy exercises over decisions by individuals and organizations" (Elmore 1985, 68). Although Elmore has attempted to amalgamate the two grand approaches, he has nonetheless shifted toward the top-down approach. His concern is to aid policy makers to improve the chances of policy success. He contends that "in order to be good strategists, policy makers have to calculate the consequences of their actions from the point of view of the decisions they are trying to influence" (1985, 69). The attempt is remarkable at the practical level. However, it does not claim to provide a model of the policy process that can be used by social scientists to explain outcomes in a wide variety of settings (Sabatier 1986, 38).

The second and most ambitious attempt was developed by Sabatier (1986) in his attempt to synthesize the best futures of the two approaches, which he termed "advocacy coalition"—"i.e. actors from various public and private organizations who share a set of beliefs and who seek to realize their common goals over time" (Sabatier 1986, 39). Unlike Elmore, Sabatier's attempt to merge the top-down and bottom-up approaches is basically theoretical. His synthesis "is primarily concerned with theory construction rather than with providing guidelines for practitioners or detailed portraits of particular situations" (Sabatier 1986, 39). Furthermore, the synthesis adopts bottom-uppers' unit of analysis—a whole variety of public and private actors involved with policy problems—and shifts from policy implementation to policy change over periods of a decade or more.

The third attempt was advanced by Goggin et al. in their model of intergovernmental policy implementation. In short, they argued that implementation of any policy is dependent upon top-down and bottom-up types of variables (Lester 1987, 206–7). Their model is explicitly directed toward both theory development (like Sabatier's focus in 1986) and useful advice for policy practitioners (Elmore's focus of 1985) .

Although various syntheses have been put forward, Palumbo maintained, "[I]t remains to be seen whether or not such an amalgamation will work" (1987, 94). This is because unless the concept of implementation is explicated, any attempt to merge the two approaches will be ambiguous. So far the syntheses have either maintained a top-down or bottom-up approach in different names. Lester et al. contend that "a number of conceptual and methodological issues must be advanced before any of these approaches provide either an advance in theory development or useful advice for decision makers" (Lester 1987, 208).

# Implications for Empirical Research

At this juncture, the question is neither of choosing the top-down as opposed to the bottom-up approach, for they are not mutually exclusive (Wittrock 1982, 134). They are more or less the same thing but presented in different ways in order to ask different research questions: about policy (from the policy or policy makers down to the bureaucrats) or about implementers (from the bureaucrats up to the policy or policy makers). There can be no implementation without policy (which is the central focus of top-downers) so also an implementation process will not be complete without the implementers (which is the central focus of the bottom-uppers). In this respect a large number of empirical works using both perspectives have been produced. In all this, the critical variables in implementation process are the policy, the actors, the organization or organizations in which implementation takes place, and the political and socioeconomic environment in which implementation is conducted. Yet,

> The important issue is not whether the framework of analysis is right or wrong, but whether it is sufficiently clear to be controvertible. It is less important to agree on a single framework for analysing implementation problems than it is to be clear about the consequences of adopting one framework over another (Elmore 1979–80, 602).

This is because choosing any of the frameworks will determine the method of inquiry to be employed.

To this extent, it is pertinent, from the methodological point of view, to highlight the implication of choosing any of the perspectives discussed: First, an implementation perspective that does not restrict implementation to bargaining, negotiation, and conflict is capable of accommodating such phenomena in its analysis of implementation process, and not the other way round. Second, a study of implementation that starts from the bottom (bureaucrats) as its central focus of analysis cannot lead to identifying why a policy goes wrong, for it does not ask such a question in the first place. On the other hand, a study of implementation that starts from the policy, its objectives as its central focus, integrates the actors whose action it measures against the stated objectives.

Since the central concern of this book is the problem of policy implementation, the appropriate starting point of analysis is the policy, its declared or stated objectives, and the measurement and explanation of actors' performance against the policy objectives. This, undoubtedly, is the central conceptual and methodological focus of the top-downers.

# Chapter Three
# The Federation of Nigeria: Dominant Features and Challenges

The previous chapter indicates that Sokoto State is the focus of this book. With this in view, the current chapter seeks to provide insight into Nigeria, the country of which the state is an integral part. In examining the environment in which the bureaucracy operates, the chapter pays special attention to Nigeria's political evolution, development, economy, and infrastrure. The intention is to describe the context within which public policy is implemented in the country in general, and Sokoto State bureaucracy in particular.

**Figure 3.0**
**Nigeria's 19 States: 1976–1991**

Source: Davis, G. 1982, 3.

# The Republic of Nigeria: An Overview

The Britsh formally colonized Nigeria January 1, 1900, when the Union Jack was hoisted at Lokoja (then part of Northern Nigeria) in place of the Royal Niger Company, which had been in control of the area on behalf of the British government (Coleman 1958, 41). Before then, the colonial administration had already established itself in the southern part of Nigeria following the annexation of Lagos in 1861. The area covering modern-day Nigeria had a long and eventful history before the advent of colonialism. In the North there were the well-established Hausa states of Gobir, Zamfara, Kebbi, Kano, Zazzau, and Bornu, and in the South there were the Oyo Empire and the Benin Kingdom. In the nineteenth century an Islamic caliphate was established with Sokoto as its base. The new caliphate gradually became "one of the largest political communities in Africa, and certainly the most politically salient in Nigeria" (Paden 1986, 25 ). Of all the territories that were later to form the country of Nigeria, only the Sokoto caliphate had "a universal religion, a codified legal system, a lingua franca that had been reduced to writing, a Muslim literati, centralized political institutions with clearly defined leaders, and a sophisticated system of taxation" (Abdullahi 1977, 76). It replaced the Hausa states, which had been nominally Muslim for several hundred years, but which had started losing a sense of purpose and had in fact, started mixing the religion with indigenous religious and cultural practices (Paden 1986, 37). The caliphate lasted until 1903 when it was conquered by the British colonial forces under Frederick Lugard (later called Lord Lugard). He, Lugard, had not made any real effort to establish peaceful and friendly contact with the leadership of the caliphate (Nicolson 1968, 129).

In 1914 the southern protectorate and the northern protectorate (established in 1900) were amalgamated by Sir Frederick Lugard in order, among other things, to "give to the Southern Nigeria the benefit of the system of local rule which had been established in the North, where circumstances had allowed a far greater freedom in the development of a coherent policy of native administration than in the South" (Hailey 1951, 2). Lugard was made the first governor general of colonial Nigeria. Subsequently, two lieutenant governors were appointed for Northern and Southern Nigeria with their bases at Kaduna and Lagos, respectively. The two autonomous protectorates began to produce their separate budgets, maintain local police forces, run prisons and schools, and provide their own health services and other related basic functions (Ostheimer 1973, 22). In all this it was the traditional rulers who were effectively used as agents of indirect rule by the lieutenant governors to achieve the objective of colonial administration.

In 1939 Southern Nigeria was divided into two provinces, namely western and eastern provinces. The North, however, was not affected. In 1946 three provincial assemblies were created in the northern, western, and eastern provinces. In 1954 Nigeria adopted a federal constitution. Having been under colonial rule for sixty years (1900–1960), Nigeria was granted political independence in 1960 as a federation of three regions—north, west, and east—with Lagos as the federal capital. The independence constitution provided for a parliamentary system of government, based on the Westminster model. Furthermore, in 1963 Nigeria became a republic, and a new region, the Mid-West, was created, bringing the number of regions to four.

## Instability and Challenges of State Construction

However, in January 1966, the Nigerian military overthrew the civilian government (headed by the prime minister, Sir Abubakar Tafawa Balewa) and took over the leadership of the country. In July of the same year, a counter coup d'état brought Colonel (later General) Yakubu Gowon to power. A year later the four regional structures were dissolved and twelve new states were created: North-Western, North-Central, North-Eastern, Kano, Benue-Plateau, Kwara, Lagos, Western, Mid-Western, East-Central, South-Eastern, and Rivers. In May 1967 a civil war broke out between the federal military government and the secessionist forces in the eastern region (later to be called Government of Biafra). The war lasted thirty months. In the end the secessionist forces surrendered to the federal military government, and Nigeria once more became united, determined to accelerate the pace of its own development. Nevertheless, Gowon, like his predecessor, was overthrown in yet another coup d'état in July 1975, which brought Brigadier (later General) Murtala Mohammed to power. In 1976, General Murtala created an additional seven states, bringing the total number of states to nineteen, as shown in Figure 3.0.

In 1979, the military, having ruled the country for thirteen years (1966–1979), handed over power to a civilian-elected government of the National Party of Nigeria (NPN), with Alhaji Shehu Shagari as the first executive president. This second attempt at democracy (the first one was from 1960 to 1966) was short-lived, as on December 31, 1983, the Nigerian military intervened again in the politics of the

Second Republic, suspended some portions of the 1979 constitution, and banned all the political parties. The coup d'état brought Major General Muhammadu Buhari to power. A year and a half later, in August 1985, General Buhari was overthrown in a counter-coup which brought Major General Ibrahim Babangida to power as the president and commander-in-chief of the Nigerian Armed Forces. From then on, the regime made efforts to cope with the country's enormous socioeconomic problems. Of note is the measure taken by the regime to implement a structural adjustment program (SAP) designed specifically to revamp the country's ailing economy—an economy that had been in terrible shape since 1980.

As evidenced by the preceding account, Nigeria's political development failed for years to take a predictable path. From 1960 to date, Nigeria has been ruled by no less than twelve different heads of states, only three of whom were democratically elected. However, most Nigerians have not shown very much interest in the leadership of the country and in the installation of civilian over military regimes. The concern mostly has been whether the leadership is capable of improving their living standards, taking into account Nigeria's enormous human and natural resources, as amply demonstrated in the country's Second National Development Plan (1970–1974):

> The country is fortunate in having the resource potential in men, material, and money to lay a solid foundation for a socio-economic revolution in black Africa (Abba 1985, 7).

In spite of the country's wealth, most Nigerians are relatively impoverished and have little or no access to health coverage, housing, sanitation, water, and electricity supply (Kirk-Greene and Rimmer 1981, 66). Inequality in income distribution continues to widen. The various development plans and programs have made little impact on the people's standards of living.

It is important to appreciate that without political stability, it will be difficult for any Nigerian government to lay a solid foundation for socioeconomic development. To cope with the the mounting challenges, it is imperative to find out what has gone wrong in Nigeria's body politic.

As to be expected, several writers on Nigerian politics and history have cited different reasons for the persistence of the country's problems. At least four basic perspectives are discernible. Whereas some writers attribute the problem to ethnic chauvinism (Ostheimer 1973; Schwarz Jr. 1965; Schwarz 1968), others see it as leadership failure (Dudley 1973; Achebe 1983). Yet others trace the problem to the capitalistic nature of the Nigerian economy (Nafzigar 1983), while others submit that the problem is due to the disharmony between the political system and the sociocultural environment (Abdullahi 1984; Adamolekun 1985; Balogun 1983 and 2009; Bretton 1962; Tukur 1977).

Those who attribute the problem of political instability to ethnic chauvinism argue that the problem arises because of Nigeria's inability to attain nationhood as a result of marked ethnic differences and animosity. This was so even before Nigeria attained its independence. Diversity characterizes the relationship among the three ethnic groups in the country (Hausa/Fulani in the North, Yoruba in the West, and Ibo in the East). Ethnicity has been dominant in the thinking of some of Nigeria's nationalist leaders, colonial officers, and even among the elite of the present generation of Nigerians. For example, the late Chief Obafemi Awolowo, the leader of the opposition in the First Republic (1960–1966), and leader and presidential candidate of the Unity Party of Nigeria (UPN) during the Second Republic (1979–1983), had this to say during the nationalist struggle in the 1940s:

Nigeria is not a nation. It is a mere geographical expression.... The word Nigeria is merely a distinctive appellation to distinguish those who live within Nigeria from those who do not (Schwarz Jr. 1965, 3).

Similarly, Sir Hugh Cliford, a colonial governor of Nigeria, had this to say in 1920 on Nigeria:

a ... collection of self contained and mutually independent native states, separated from one another ... by vast distances, by differences of history and traditions and by ethnological, racial, tribal, political, social and religious barriers (Schwarz Jr. 1965, 3).

This ethnic animosity culminated in the January 1966 coup d'état, organized and executed by Ibo officers (from the eastern and midwestern regions) in the federal army. Those who lost their lives in the coup d'état included Alhaji Sir Abubakar Tafawa Balewa (the federal Prime Minister), Alhaji Sir Ahmadu Bello (the premier of the northern region), Chief Samuel Akintola (the premier of the western region), and seven army officers of the rank of lieutenant colonel and above. Of the seven, one was Ibo, two were Yoruba, and the rest were Northerners. Buttressing the argument that the coup had an ethnic overtone, critics cited the fact that the brutal slaughter of the federal prime minister was unjustified since he was known for probity. According to observers, the prime minister had been outstanding in placing the welfare of the country above personal or sectional interest, and in forging national unity (Frederick 1979, 218). Second, many of the army officers who were ruthlessly slaughtered were not culpable for the problems facing the First Republic, whether political or socioeconomic (Abdullahi 1977, 200). The exclusion of the premier of the eastern region and other Ibo army officers from the killings was perceived as a clear demonstration of the coup organizers' ethnic bias.

It is undoubtedly true that there is ethnic diversity and animosity in Nigeria. However, in order to cope with the problem right from the beginning, a federal constitution (acknowledging Nigeria's ethnic and linguistic diversity) was proposed for Nigeria (Azikiwe 1937; Awolowo 1947; Awa 1965). Thus, in 1954 Nigeria became a federation of three regions. In 1963, three years after its independence, another region (the Mid-West) was created out of the former western region, thus bringing the number of regions to four. Furthermore, in 1967 the regional structure was abolished, and instead twelve states were created. In 1976, seven additional states were created. This brought the total number of the states to nineteen. The metamorphosis continued, and in 1987 two new states were created. In a nutshell, Nigeria today is a federation of twenty-one states and the federal capital territory. In all this the intention is to cope with the problem of diversity in power sharing, in political and bureaucratic representation, and in resource allocation to all parts of the country (Collins 1980, 11).

However, with the collapse of the first republican government, a new thinking within this perspective began to emerge. Federalism was still appropriate for Nigeria; the problem as some observers felt, however, was the adoption of the parliamentary system of government, based on the Westminster model. It is argued that the Westminster model, even with some federalist modification, could not work effectively in Nigeria. The fact that it worked during the colonial regime was due to the application of the authoritarian version of the original model (Bretton 1962, 22). To this end, a presidential system was proposed, based on the American model, which makes it absolutely necessary for any future president to have at least one-fourth of all the votes cast in at least two-thirds of Nigeria's states. The objective is to ensure the acceptability of the president to the majority of Nigerians, unlike the situation that prevailed under the parliamentary system whereby the prime minister does not necessarily have to have national electoral mandate. The prime minister is able to form a government by first winning votes at a consituency level, and second by having party majority in the parliament. Based on this belief, the army, having ruled the country for thirteen years, produced a presidential constitution based on the American model and handed power to a democratically elected government.

Nonetheless, this experiment in the presidential system, like the one before it, was short-lived. These changes of government, which characterize the Nigerian body politic, are not just between the civilians and the military. The power struggle is even more intense within the military itself. Out of Nigeria's eight heads of state, from 1960 to 1987, only two were elected civilians. It is important to point out that, whereas under the civilian governments the principles governing the operation of federalism were maintained, under the military the system tends to move toward a unitary model in view of the military's bias toward hierarchy, unity of command, and discipline.

At this point it is appropriate to say that in its attempt to cope with the problem of political instability, Nigeria has experimented with various systems of government, leading to frequent transitions—

notably, from unitary goverment to federalism and vice versa, from the parliamentary to the presidential system, and from democracy to military dictatorship. Notwithstanding these changes, the problem has not been solved and probably cannot be solved from this perspective, for its diagnosis is inadequate.

This is not to trivialize the nature of ethnic diversity. The problem is not the diversity itself but, rather, its manipulation by the educated elite to promote personal or sectional socioeconomic and political interests at the expense of the majority of the ethnic groups. For example, during the Second Republic (1979–1983) the political elite in all the dominant ethnic groups subordinated their ethnic differences and competed for political power with the aim of fighting over what is fashionably called "the national cake."

The second perspective, on the other hand, argues that the problem is not with the political structure but is due, rather, to leadership failure (Achebe 1983). In particular, Achebe argues:

> The trouble with Nigeria is simply and squarely a failure of leadership. There is nothing basically wrong with the Nigerian character. There is nothing wrong with the Nigerian land or climate or water or air or anything else. The Nigerian problem is the unwillingness or inability of its leaders to rise to the responsibility, to the challenge of personal example which are the hallmark of true leadership (Achebe 1983, 1).

Similarly, in his interview with *Africa Report*, General Buhari insisted that:

> There is nothing fundamentally wrong with either the Westminster or the Presidential or American system.... The failure of both systems which have been tried in this country lies heavily on the operators, that is, the Nigerian politicians and the way they operated the system (Africa Report 1985, 8).

Buhari's assumption then is that with good leadership, Nigeria's problems would be solved. This assumption is gaining currency particularly among the army. The political crisis of the First Republic was attributed to the weak leadership of the federal prime minister, the flamboyant and uncompromising leadership of the northern premier, and the corrupt leadership of the western and eastern premiers. To solve this problem, therefore, a section of the military not only intervened in the political process, but also killed the federal prime minister and the northern and western premiers. Six months later, the leaders of the July 29, 1966, countercoup condemned the preceding military government as incompetent and as having failed to demonstrate an understanding of the Nigerian situation. Nine years later, when General Gowon was toppled, he was accused of running the affairs of the country without any sense of direction. However, when Brigadier Murtala Muhammed took over the leadership of the country, tremendous changes were noticed all over Nigeria and in all works of life. Within six months of his leadership, General Murtala created seven additional states (Sokoto State is one of them), which brought the total number of the states to nineteen. In the same vein, local government reform was undertaken, which led to the creation of a large number of local government councils throughout the country. The intention was to bring the government closer to the people. For the first time Nigerians unanimously acclaimed the vision and commitment of their leader, Brigadier Muhammed, for giving Nigeria a sense of direction in its internal policies and external relations. However, when he was overthrown, Murtala was accused of being too authoritarian. On the other hand, when Alhaji Shehu Shagari was overthrown by General Buhari, his leadership was accused of corruption, mismanagement of the national resources, and inability to resolve the growing crisis of confidence (Africa Report 1985, 4). Muhammadu Buhari, like Murtala, is acclaimed, although not by all, as another outstanding and highly principled leader Nigeria had after Murtala. When he was overthrown, Buhari was accused by General Babangida of being "too rigid and uncompromising in his attitude to issues of national significance" (Keesings Contemporary Archives 1985, 33956).

As the reasons given for the change of leadership vary, so do the style and the commitment of the leadership. In the light of this examination, Nigeria's problem may partly be attributable to its leadership. But the problem goes beyond that: from the weak, corrupt, and inefficient to purposeful leadership; from civilian to military leadership; and from reactionary to progressive leadership. Yet, despite trying out different leadership styles, Nigeria has not succeeded in solving its problems. To this extent, leadership does not provide an adequate explanation for Nigeria's multifaceted problems.

This leaves us with a third perspective, one that sees the problem as the crisis of a colonially planted capitalism. It argues that dependent capitalism is the fundamental factor of Nigeria's political instability. It indicates that capitalism, by its very nature, encourages the accumulation of private property, thereby enticing the political class, the bureaucracy, and the military to engage in corrupt practices and invariably creating miserable conditions for the poor who, by definition, are incapable of accumulating private property. In Nigeria the capitalist class has accumulated much property (legally and illegally) without investing it there, but has siphoned it off to the industrialized countries of the West. This process, it is argued, is being aided by the multinational companies whose subsidiaries operate within or outside the country. This system of production weakens the poor who are increasingly finding it difficult to improve their socioeconomic condition. Inflation is always on the rise, health services lack drugs, and the rural areas are not provided good drinking water. Thus, under these conditions, political instability is inevitable. It is understandable that most of the successive military regimes have pointed out that they came to power principally to improve the socioeconomic conditions of the people, which had been neglected. For example, at the time General Buhari took over power from President Shagari in December 1983, the country was witnessing its highest inflation record, and people's suffering had reached an alarming level. General Buhari attempted to reverse the situation by introducing stringent austerity measures and by detaining a large number of politicians (convicted and nonconvicted) (Keesings Contemporary Archives 1984, 33261–2), who had individually and collectively crippled the nation's economy. In spite of these measures, the living conditions of the people have not changed. This is not surprising, for under a dependent capitalist system, this perspective would argue, the socioeconomic condition of the people cannot be improved, even if a serious attempt is made.

Thus, in order to solve the problem, the capitalist system has to be changed (not just shift within the system) and be replaced by a socialist system. In other words, all private ownership of the means of production should be abolished, and private companies, whether owned by Nigerians or multinationals, should be nationalized. The objective is to ensure equitable distribution of the national resources and to assert the power of the proletariat in society.

This perspective, unlike the previous one, has raised a serious question regarding the relationship between the living condition of the people and political stability. It may, of course, be argued that political stability depends on economic factors and forces. However, Bretton argues:

> [I]n the poorer societies of the world, economic development takes place under the general control and supervision of political forces, that substantive and directional choices are made on political grounds, and that generally, in the decolonization process, the political kingdom precedes the economic one. Hence, regardless of the theoretical merits of a given economic development programme, the achievement of social stability depends initially, during the most critical stages, on the ability of the post independence political system to weather the storms released by decolonization (1962, 3).

Sound and elegant as the Marxist or neo-Marxist argument may seem, its explanation of the problems facing Nigeria is far from satisfactory. The military coups d'état of January 1966, July 1966, and February 1976 could not adequately be explained in "class conflict" terms. The factors that led to the changes were political rather than economic. Besides, there is no evidence to show that if a socialist government came to power in Nigeria, the problems would be solved. There are, for example, some socialist countries in Africa, notably Tanzania, Angola, and Mozambique, which are still struggling to solve their socioeconomic problems. That apart, unless the change is imposed in a revolutionary uprising, its acceptance by the majority of the people will be highly unlikely because some of its assumptions, such as "religion is the opium of the people," are incompatible with the sociocultural values of the majority of Nigerians, 95 percent of whom profess one kind of religion or another. Thus, any attempt to relegate their religious values will be resisted and is bound to fail.

Similarly, the assumption that the establishment of a socialist government would lead to the disappearance of class struggle is being challenged by powerful evidence. In the Soviet Union and China, the main socialist countries today, power conflict and the conflict of desires are posing serious problems to the political systems. To this extent it could be said that class conflict is only one dimension of conflict in society. Of course, a socialist government might lead to a better internal distribution of resources. Yet if Nigeria changed its economic situation from a mixed economy to socialism, it will still have to cope with the problem of dependency within the world capitalist market. Besides, Nigeria's economy depends heavily on the sale of few primary products, the prices of which are determined by the capitalist-dominated world market. Furthermore, it will have to cope with the problem of international confidence. The much needed investment would dry up if foreign investors had the slightest hint of expropriation of capital. This would in turn slow down the economy. Likewise, the enormous demands for democratic reforms today in the socialist Eastern Bloc countries, following the lead by the Soviet Union, are indisputably a testimony to the failure of socialism to cope with problems of socioeconomic and political development of those countries.

The Marxist or socialist perspective is thus limited in its analysis. It has failed to take into account the complexity of the Nigerian situation and the influence of the world capitalist market on the Nigerian economy and, to this extent, could not provide a relevant solution to the problem.

The fourth and final perspective under consideration attributes the problem of political instability to the disharmony between the sociocultural environment and the political system. This approach claims that the application of the alien values, which have no relationship whatsoever to Nigeria's precolonial political experiences, is the basic factor in instability. When people's values are alienated by a political system, they are unlikely to be fully committed to the system's survival or progress. As Ibrahim Tahir forcefully argues,

> [N]o state can really expect its citizens to be motivated to achieve development goals through values and procedures with which they absolutely have no ideological relationship (Tahir 1974; cited in Tukur 1977, 869).

Similarly, Balogun notes that at independence,

> [T]he political and administrative system handed over to the indigenous political and administrative elites was based on values totally alien to the elite (Balogun 1983, 84).

In the same vein, Adamolekun submits,

> [P]arliamentary government collapsed in Nigeria in January 1966 because the values and the norms appropriate for the successful functioning of the governmental system were either non existent or not sufficiently widely shared among the relevant actors in the governmental process (Adamolekun 1985, 9).

Instability, therefore, is inevitable since successive regimes in Nigeria have failed to appreciate the relevance of people's cultural values in coping with their own problems. The country is always in search of a viable polity, but always outside its sociocultural values. All the systems that have been attempted (parliamentary and presidential, civilian and military) have failed because they are not rooted in the people's values. "There are no philosophic links between the substantive historic past of Nigeria and the modern legal-constitutional system under which the country now operates" (Bretton 1962, 16).

To cope with the problem, Tukur (1977) in particular holds that the Sokoto caliphal experiences of the nineteenth century, which were based on Islamic political philosophy, should be relevant in transforming the Nigerian polity into a viable political system. The caliphate, which lasted for a century (1804–1903), had established sufficient social and political cohesion and a highly sophisticated system of administration. Such experience had undoubtedly facilitated the establishment of indirect rule by the British colonial forces in Northern Nigeria, unlike in Southern Nigeria where they encountered some initial opposition. Bretton argues:

> The social discipline primarily derived from Islam produced adequate stability and seemed to provide more effective means of law enforcement and general administration than the direct British intervention could have achieved at the time (Bretton 1962, 10).

This accent on conflict in values has raised a very important issue, notably the relevance of Nigeria's indigenous precolonial experience, particularly the Sokoto caliphate, in coping with present-day Nigeria's problem. The diagnosis of the Nigerian malaise is undoubtedly sound, and the solution it offers for it is relevant, appealing, and plausible. However, its underlying logic (that Nigeria's political instability is due to the application of alien political values) is questionable.

First of all, it should be established that all the so-called stable countries of the world experienced some kinds of political instability in their early history, their "uninterrupted" political values notwithstanding (Blitz 1965, 1). Furthermore, it should be pointed out that values (and political values in particular) are not static; they are developed and shaped by experiences and circumstances that, in turn, shape subsequent developments. To this extent, having been under formal colonial rule for sixty years (1900–1960), and having operated party politics for fourteen years (1952–1965), Nigeria's political values must have been developed and shaped by its colonial experiences. As a matter of fact, all the politicians of the First Republic were products of colonial experiences. They were all exposed to the Western values of politics and administration. They were trained, in most cases, in Britain and participated either at the federal, regional, or local bureaucracy. They formed political parties, conducted elections, and formed governments at federal and regional levels based on the Westminster model, even before independence. To this extent, their values must have been influenced by that historical epoch. The culmination of that value is the production of the independence constitution and the subsequent republican constitution that was purely a Nigerian product through the Act of Nigerian Parliament (Odumosu 1965, 41). At independence the politicians had the chance, if they had wanted, to change the system, but they did not. When the military came into politics they had the opportunity, if they wanted, to change the system but, like the politicians, they saw nothing wrong with it. They blame the "operators" rather than the system, which they fully participated in fabricating or creating. Furthermore, the 1979 constitution and the attempt at presidential democracy are further testimony to the incorporation of the Western democratic values into Nigeria's political values. If, however, the problem of political instability was due to incompatibility of the Westminster model with Nigeria's political value, how about the collapse of the presidential system? If the problem is about democracy, how about the military and counter-military coups d'état?

Inlight of the above analysis, it suffices to say that the problem of political instability is due primarily to the overambition of the military to rule in the face of the politically apathetic majority: military coups d'état against civilian politicians is usually greeted with enthusiasm; counter-military coups are equally welcome; and, still, any program for return to civil rule is often loudly applauded. This behavior, undoubtedly, demonstrates the problems of "immature" political culture and lack of attachment to civilian institutions (Abdullahi 1977, 184–5). However, this condition of apathy is created by the military itself in view of the constant military coups d'état, which make it impossible for effective political education of the population to be achieved. Once the military tasted political power, it would never step down completely; it may hand over power, but only temporarily.

The nature of political instability in Nigeria is very different from what happens in other countries, notably Latin American countries and a few African countries. Whereas political instability is characterized by violence in some countries, it is peaceful in Nigeria with the exception of the first and second military coups d'état and the subsequent civil war. Apart from the civil war, there are no other cases of rebellion or guerrilla activities. However, having discussed Nigeria's political instability, and in doing so highlighting the nature of the political system, it is appropriate to outline the country's political philosophy in order to have a general view of the political system.

## Political Philosophy

Nigeria's political development from independence, as shown above, has been characterized by regime changes. The changes, however, are not fundamental: the socioeconomic conditions of her people have not significantly changed, and the underlying political philosophy remains the same and has been influential in guiding and shaping public policies. The political philosophy is made up of the following strands:

1.  Secularism: Nigeria is a secular state. No state is allowed to adopt a state religion. As is conspicuously stated in the Nigerian constitution: "the Government of the Federation or of a state shall not adopt any religion as state religion" (1979, 14).
2.  Nigeria is a mixed economy. Her socioeconomic policies are neither socialist nor rabidly capitalist.
3.  Nigeria is a federation comprising quasi-autonomous states. Presently there are twenty-one states and the federal capital territory in the federation. Each of the states has its own bureaucracy, which is instrumental in initiating, formulating, and implementing state and federal government policies.

## Bureaucracy: Evolution and Development

As earlier indicated, Nigeria became a unitary state in 1914 when the northern and southern protectorates were amalgamated. At the same time, a unified bureaucracy was established for the country. However, the two protectorates developed separately in view of their distinctive traditional systems of government, customs, and ways of life. The bureaucracy was based on the legal–rational–authority model. The protectorates were divided into provinces. In the northern protectorate there were twelve provinces while in the South there were three. The use of provinces as administrative units continued even after independence until 1967 when the newly created states became the basic administrative unit.

The colonial bureaucracy was under the governor general (later to be called governor), who was accountable to the secretary of state for the colonies in the UK government in London. The latter (i.e., the colonial secretary) was responsible to the British cabinet and parliament for the administration of Nigeria. Under the governor general were the lieutenant governors of the northern and southern provinces. In 1939 the number of lieutenant governors rose to three following the division of the southern province into western and eastern groups of provinces. The lieutenant governors were thus responsible for the administration of the northern, western, and eastern provinces. Under them were the residents who were answerable for the administration of the provinces. To assist the residents, district officers were appointed to be in charge of the district administration. The residents and their district officers had considerable discretion and autonomy and were, in fact, seen as "the government" in their various areas of jurisdiction. Apart from their routine administrative duties, they served as heads of local police units and as prosecutors as well as magistrates. The residents and the district officers were effectively the backbone of the colonial bureaucracy. It was through them that colonial policies were pursued (Kingsley 1963, 307–13; Nwosu 1977, 43).

With the establishment of a secretariat in 1919 in Lagos, a chief secretary was for the first time appointed to head it (Nicolson 1969, 219). As the head of the colonial service, the chief secretary was essentially responsible for coordinating the entire service, which, apart from its vertical divisions (from central to provincial to district administration), was equally, functionally divided into departments (notably railway, medical, public works, agriculture, education, police, prison, and customs) (Nwosu 1977, 42). Whereas the provincial administrations were responsible for the hospitals, public works, forestry, agriculture, education, police, prison, marine, and customs (which was later transferred to the central government), the central government took charge of the railway, audit, treasury, posts and telegraphs, and judicial, legal, and survey departments. In addition, the directors of medical and sanitary, forest, and education services were retained at the center (Nicolson 1969, 192). These departments, under the chief secretary, were responsible for initiating, formulating, and implementing government policies and giving policy guidance to the provincial administrations (Nicolson 1969, 194).

However, in 1954, following the adoption of a federal structure in the administration of the country, the provincial bureaucracy was integrated into the regional civil services. From then on the regions' sphere of activities and that of the federal government were delimited (Nwosu 1977, 50). From 1957 to 1960, the federal government had no substantive head of service, the post of the chief secretary having been abolished and that of the federal prime minister created in 1957 (Nicolson 1969, 298). Nonetheless, it should be pointed out that the governor general remained the titular head of the civil service until independence. Other changes included the establishment of ministries in 1951. In 1959 (following the Newns committee recommendation), the hitherto autonomous departments were integrated within the ministries. The role and function of the permanent secretaries were defined and a machinery for the operation of the new integrated ministries introduced (Balogun 1983; Longe 1984, 5).

The function of the colonial bureaucracy is relevant to an understanding of the role of the contemporary Nigerian bureaucracy in the conduct of public affairs. Whereas some see the role of colonial bureaucracy as mainly maintaining law and order (Kingsley 1963), others see it as inducing development (Nicolson 1969). The general consensus leans toward the former (law and order) view of the bureaucracy (Tukur 1971; Nwosu 1977; Adebayo 1981; Balogun 1983). However, on closer examination, it is likely that the primary function of the colonial bureaucracy in Nigeria was not the maintenance of law and order as such. After all, law and order were being maintained even before the colonization of the country. With only nine political officers in Northern Nigeria in 1900, which had an estimated population of eleven million (Heussler 1966, 20), the colonial forces could not have maintained law and order without the active cooperation of the traditional rulers. The colonial administration had to use the traditional rulers as the agent of indirect rule in the administration of the country. To this extent, it is not enough to say that the colonial bureaucracy was basically concerned with the maintenance of law and order. One may even ask the following question: maintaining law and order for whom and for what? The basic function of the colonial bureaucracy can very much be understood in the context of the whole concept of colonialism, and this has been succinctly stated by Lord Lugard, the first governor general of colonial Nigeria:

> We hold these countries because it is the genius of our race to colonize, to trade, and to govern.... There will always be those who cry aloud that the task is being badly done, that it does not need doing, that it brings evil to subject races and breeds profiteers at home. These were not the principles which prompted our forefathers, and secured for us the place we hold in the world today in trust for those who shall come after us (Lugard 1922, 619; cited in Nicolson 1969, 7).

Seen from this imperialist perspective, colonialism was essentially concerned with the political and economic control of the colonized people and the imposition of Western values on them. The bureaucracy, understandably, was the instrument for achieving the colonialist objective and, in so doing, law and order had to be maintained within the framework of the British sense of justice. On the other hand, Nicolson argues that by 1900 there was not only the plan but also the will and means to develop Nigeria:

> One early sign was the raising of a loan of £255,000, in 1896, through the Crown Agents, to begin railway bridges between Lagos Island and Ebute Meta.... Chamberlain also took immediate steps to lay the bogey of the White Man's Grave by encouraging the establishment of two new schools of Tropical Medicine, at London and Liverpool, and by the appointment to the colony of Lagos of a Governor, Sir William MacGregor, who was not only a successful administrator but also a medical man with an impressive public health record and scientific interest. With this appointment, the appointment

of a former police officer, Moor, as High Commissioner for the 'unruly' Southern Nigeria, and the appointment of an exceptionally ambitious and energetic frontier soldier, Lugard, to the 'unpacified' Northern Nigeria, Chamberlain had clearly taken good care to get Nigeria off to a flying start in the twentieth century (1969, 18).

Based on this submission, the function of the colonial bureaucracy was the development of Nigeria right from the beginning. This, undoubtedly, is to defend colonialism at all costs.

Kirk-Greene, however, categorizes the work of the Nigerian bureaucracy up to independence into five phases: The first was the typically colonial one, that of law and order, of "pacification" or conquest. This can be said to have concluded by 1910. Then came the period of consolidation, say 1910 to 1925, when the administrative edifice was erected on the earlier foundations. The logical third phase, that of economic development, was severely checked by the world depression of the thirties, and no sooner had it recommenced after the slump had been overcome than the disruption of the 1939–1945 war intervened. The decade from 1947 can be labeled a period of urgent social and political development, merging into the fifth phase, that of transitional administration, a shrinking of the expatriate cadre and the deliberate training of Nigerian civil servants to assume the reins of office (1965, 216).

This view, endorsed by Balogun (1983, 67), sees the growth of the Nigerian bureaucracy as a straight-line development and a preconceived program: after the conquest, then consolidation; after the consolidation, then development programs; after the development programs, then handing over power and bureaucracy to Nigerians. These phases are presented as if the first colonialists had foreknowledge of the eventual breakup of the British territories. This, to say the least, is an oversimplification of the issue.

Contrary to the Lugadian and Nicolsonian extreme perspective on the role of the colonial bureaucracy, to the Kirk-Greenian and Balogunian moderate position, I want to argue that the role of the colonial bureaucracy was both exploitative and developmental, corresponding to the periods 1900–1946 and 1947–1960, respectively.

During the first (exploitative) phase, the bureaucracy was basically facilitating exploitation by providing some infrastructure in order to support and consolidate the colonial grip over the colonized peoples and to serve the interests of expatriate firms. In the first place, a direct taxation was imposed, first in the northern provinces, replacing the taxes being paid by Muslims, in accordance with the Quranic injunction (Lugard 1970, 172). The Muslim tax, called Zakat, is a compulsory alms payment by Muslims who have the means, and it is fixed in proportion to the nature of the property an individual possesses. The abolition of Zakat has once and for all destroyed the foundation of economic structure of the Sokoto Islamic community. The new single tax, based on income assessment, was not fixed and in most cases not equitably made, even at the level of senior British officers (Shenton 1986, 123). This created room for manipulation and served as an instrument of oppression in the hands of some unscrupulous district and village heads. Later, in the 1930s, after some resistance in the 1920s, direct taxation was finally imposed in Southern Nigeria. Direct taxation had absolutely forced people to either turn to wage labor or to produce cash crops for the need of the colonial regime (Coleman 1958, 57).

The bureaucratic efforts in agriculture were not for production of food crops but cash crops. The basic intention was to induce the colonized people to produce raw materials, notably cotton, groundnut, hides and skin, cocoa and palm produce, and rubber, which feed the industries of the metropolitan country, on the one hand, and by absorption in return of metropolitan manufactured goods, on the other (Nicolson 1969, 133).

Yet, in order to export these raw materials, it was necessary to provide transport, limited though it might be to ensure the free flow of the goods. It is not surprising, therefore, that the colonial government gave urgent and considerable attention to the development of communication and transport. Construction of railway lines started even before the date of the formal colonization of the country. By 1900, the Lagos–Ibadan line, covering 120 miles, was completed. The line reached Kano, in Northern Nigeria, in 1911, covering about 704 miles and, by 1926, an additional 600 miles were constructed, connecting Northern with Southern Nigeria. In the same vein, Lagos and Port

Harcourt harbors were developed (Coleman 1958, 55). Similarly, the construction of roads was pursued with vigor. Although there were no roads in 1900, by 1926 there were roads covering over six thousands miles. "The real significance of this development is that the roads were purposely constructed as feeders to railroad lines, so as to open up fresh districts to commerce" (Coleman 1958, 56).

The emphasis placed on transport and the enormous investment made to that effect were crucial, for the whole scheme of colonial exploitation depended on it. Decidedly, up to 1939, about 40 percent of the country's revenue was being expended on the construction and maintenance of communications and transport (Coleman 1958, 56). Without transport it would have been difficult and even uneconomical to convey the raw materials from the North to the coast. It is not by accident that the railway lines and roads were constructed from the coast to the northern interior, as there were no economic gains in building links between the East and the West.

Another important facility provided to some small extent during the pre-1947 period was Western medicine. However, it should be pointed out that the health facilities provided were essentially for the health of the British officials and European businessmen so that they would not die there unnecessarily (Nicolson 1969, 77). The establishment of the Liverpool and London Schools of Tropical Medicine has to be seen in that context; the schools were not established primarily to solve the problems of malaria and other tropical diseases among the colonized people, but essentially to find solutions to malaria, which had been killing the colonialists (Nicolson 1969, 18). It should be appreciated that it was the need and pressure of the capitalists in Liverpool and Manchester, which, among other things, compelled the British government to pay special attention to the development of communications, health measures, and trade in Nigeria and other West African countries; and, invariably, to appoint, through careful selection, governors with considerable knowledge of public health, railway, and port construction to see to the realization of these colonial objective (Nicolson 1969, 26).

Apart from health facilities, a Western type of education was provided, mainly by the Christian missionaries and primarily to convert the local people to Christianity and, in so doing, enabling them to know how to read and write in English and to be able to carry out minor clerical duties. Some of the products of this education were subsequently recruited into the colonial service and other private commercial firms whose expansion required the recruitment of more people and, by implication, the Western educated elites as accountants and clerical officers. It would be uneconomical to employ expatriate British officers for such jobs (Nwosu 77, 87). The provision of education, as with health services, was to help realize the colonial policy objective.

It is in the light of this that Western educated elites were deliberately excluded from taking important positions in the bureaucracy. They were regarded with suspicion because of their radicalism, which could not be accommodated into the colonial scheme (Coleman 1958, 410). They received lower salaries than their British counterparts (Nicolson 1969, 199). It should be pointed out that some of the Western educated elites were better qualified than some of the residents and district officers, but it was inconceivable at that time for a British colonial officer to work under a Nigerian when distinction was made between African and European posts. From 1900 to 1945, there was only one Nigerian resident, Dr. Henry Carr, who retired from the colonial service in 1924 and, from then until 1945, there was no Nigerian who attained such a level in the colonial bureaucracy. This was largely because of the deliberate victimization of a large number of qualified Nigerians, which necessitated their resignation from the service (Nicolson 1969, 262).

During the second phase (1947–1960), which I call the period of development, the British government had made deliberate efforts to develop Nigeria. In 1947 the colonial office drew up a consistent and conscious strategy of decolonization and development of her colonies, for it felt political progress in those colonies was inevitable (Pearce 1984, 86). This is not to minimize the importance of the effort made before 1947; in 1940 the British parliament passed the Colonial Development and Welfare Act and provided under it £120 million, of which £23 million was allocated to Nigeria. Subsequently, the colonial administration in Nigeria planned a ten-year development program (1946–1956) at the estimated cost of £55 million, to be financed by the £23 million Colonial Development and Welfare grant, £16 million from bank loans, and the balance of £16 million from locally generated revenue (Balogun 1983, 78). Although the program was interrupted in 1950, 1953, and 1954 due to a number of factors (not examined here), from 1947 up to independence, the British government had committed itself to a positive program of colonial development (Adebayo 1981, 120). Deliberate efforts were made toward socioeconomic and constitutional development and reforms of the public service. In particular, I will be concerned with the reform of the bureaucracy.

However, before doing so it is pertinent to say that the positive change of attitude of the British government toward Nigeria and her other colonies was not spontaneous. It arose out of internal and external pressures. Internally, a minor left-wing interest had become conscious of the exploitation of the colonized countries and the absence of development there, and consequently put pressure on the government for the development of the colonies and eventual self-government (Nicolson 1969, 250). Externally, the effect of the Second World War had increased the tempo of the nationalist struggle, thereby enhancing their effective demand for self-government. That apart, the United States, emerging from the world war as the strongest world power, supported the freedom of the colonial people as opposed to the threat of Soviet communism and, to that extent, put pressure on the British government for the urgent granting of independence to the colonized countries (Coleman 1958, 412). This, in brief, is the context under which the British government made an effort to develop Nigeria so that, even after independence, a relationship would continue to exist between the two countries. The most important agent for fostering this relationship is the bureaucracy. It is not surprising, therefore, that special attention was paid for the reform of the bureaucracy.

One of the remarkable reforms of the bureaucracy was the abolition, in 1945, of the distinction between "African" and "European" posts, following the Harragin Commission's recommendation, and the establishment of a new concept of "senior" and "junior" services with the same basic salary for both Africans and Europeans. However, in 1954, the distinction between the "senior" and "junior" services in both the federal and regional bureaucracies was abolished following the recommendation of the Gorsuch Commission, and a new structure was established based on the British pattern. The Gorsuch Commission observed that the rigid division of the service into two was grossly defective in view of the clear absence of an adequate middle manpower and, to that extent, recommended the reorganization of the service into five grades as follows: subclerical, clerical, executive, administrative, and superscale. The corresponding equivalent in the professional cadres would be: minor technical, technical, higher technical, professional, and superscale (Longe 1984, 4). This remained the basic structure of the bureaucracy until 1975, when it was abolished (following the Udoji Public Service Review Commission recommendation) and replaced by a unified grading and integrated structure and the recognition of the permanent secretary as the overall manager and chief executive of each ministry (Longe 1984, 8). Thirteen years later, in 1988, Babangida's administration introduced yet another civil service reform that basically abolished the distinction between administrative and professional cadres, made the post of permanent secretaries temporary, changed their nomenclature to directors general, made their position fully political in the sense that they leave the service with the government that appointed them (unlike the situation before), and made ministers (at the federal level) and commissioners (at state level) the chief executives of their ministries, a responsibility that used to be the permanent secretaries'. The president said in his 1988 budget speech:

Henceforth, holders of the [Permanent secretary] position will retire with the government which appoints them unless, of course, an incoming administration decides to re-appoint them. It follows that any officer who is offered the post of Permanent secretary may have an option whether or not to accept it (Newswatch Magazine 1988, 34).

Apart from the structural changes in the bureaucracy, efforts were similarly made to replace expatriate officers with qualified Nigerians, a process later to be called "Nigerianization." In light of that, a commission was appointed in 1948 under the chairmanship of the chief secretary, Hugh Foot (later Lord Cavadon), with Dr. Azikiwe as a member, to make recommendations on the recruitment and training of Nigerians for senior posts in the public service. The commission, having observed that there were only 172 Nigerians in the senior service (representing 10 percent of its strength), recommended, among other things, that no non-Nigerian should be appointed if suitable Nigerians were available; scholarships should be awarded to secondary schools and University College, Ibadan; and, in particular, special consideration should be given to the backward northern provinces (Symond 1966, 157). By 1952 the proportion of Nigerians in the senior service had risen to 19 percent. By 1955 the number had risen to 550, and by independence the figure had risen to 2,308 (Nicolson 1969, 297). However, these individuals were entirely drawn from the western and eastern regions and, by 1955, the North, with 55 percent of the country's population, provided only 1 percent of the entire federal civil service (Symond 1966, 158). This imbalance was fundamentally due to the nature of the colonial educational policy, which is discussed in Chapter Six.

It seems to me that the colonial bureaucracy had to some extent been transformed into an indigenous bureaucracy even before independence, in view of the deliberate Nigerianization policy that started in 1948. Although there had been some organizational, structural, and functional changes in the bureaucracy up to independence, the basic character of the bureaucracy—legal rational authority—had been maintained. Thus, the issue is not whether bureaucracy is a Western phenomenon that does not fit into the African way of doing thing, as Kingsley observes that "since the institutions of administration have been imported, since they are not African but European in origin, their ethos, structure, and functional character all reflect European more than African conditions" (1963, 303). The issue is, rather, whether the bureaucracy is relevant and appropriate to the needs and realities of the Nigerian situation. Of course, there were bureaucracies in Nigeria even before the advent of colonialism. Throughout history, different political systems have evolved their own bureaucracies in order to cope with their own peculiar circumstances. But, fundamentally, they perform the same functions: advising the government or sovereign in the formulation and implementation of public policies and putting these into effect. The emergence of the character of the contemporary Nigerian bureaucracy was inevitable, as even countries that had never been colonized are operating the same bureaucratic system. The essence of bureaucracy throughout the world today is legal rational authority.

In all this analysis one is not trying to justify colonialism from 1947 to 1960 and the bureaucratic system it brought. On the contrary, the attempt is to show that the modern Nigerian bureaucracy is development-oriented and hence suitable for the Nigerian situation, for it has been able, in spite of the dramatic changes of government since independence, to keep the people together and to provide a basis for continuity of government. In this respect, Collins observes: "The public services of the 'new states' continue to cope with a range of problems involved in promoting economic development and raising the levels of living of the broad masses of the citizenry (1980, 1).

# Chapter Four
# Sokoto State: Dominant
# Features and Challenges

**Figure 4.0**
**Sokoto State, 1976–1991**

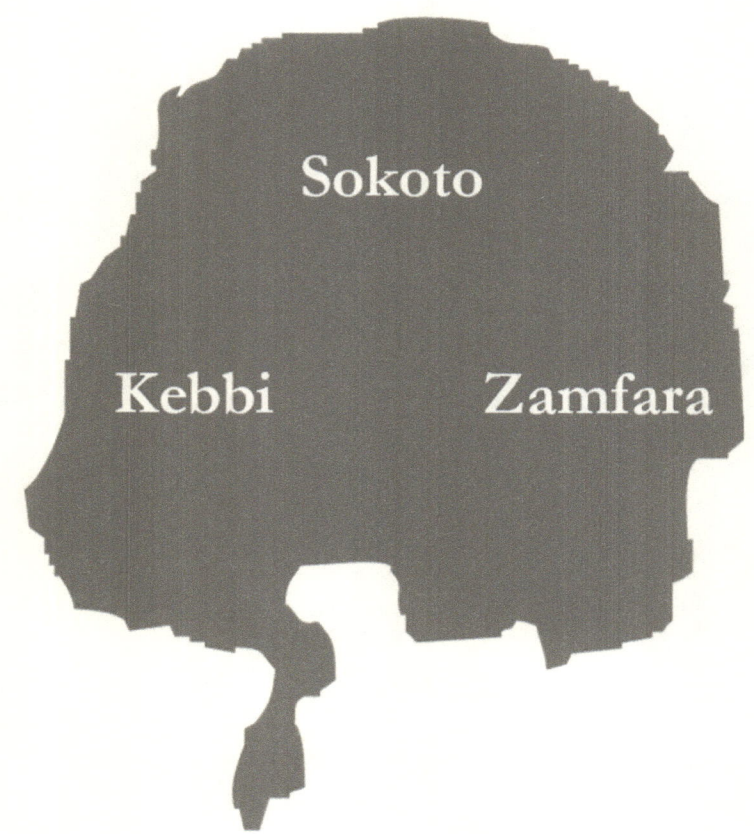

# Main Features

Sokoto State is located between latitudes 10 and 14 north of the equator and longitudes 3 and 7 east of the Greenwich Meridian. In other words, the state is situated in the northwest corner of Nigeria. It is bounded to the north by the Republic of Niger, to the east by Katsina State, to the southeast by Kaduna State, to the south by Niger and Kwara states respectively, and to the west by the Republic of Benin. It covers an area of 102,500 square kilometers, representing 11.7 percent of the total land area of Nigeria. It is therefore the second largest state in the federation.

Sokoto is also one of the hottest states of Nigeria. Its average annual low and high temperature range from 15.1°C to 31.1°C. It is characterized by two marked seasons. The dry season is typified by both cold spell, resulting from Harmattan winds that blow from the Sahara desert to the north between December and mid-February, and severe heat between February and April. The wet season is characterized by rain that lasts between May and October with intermittent heat. Thus there may be periods within the wet season when the state goes without rain. The average annual rainfall ranges from 553 mm. in the extreme north to 1155 mm. in the extreme south of the state. These climatic conditions have largely influenced the state vegetation.

There are two marked vegetation zones: the savanna zone, which covers much of the land area and which gets more rain, and the semi-desert zone, which receives less rain. While there are trees and long grass species in the savanna zone, fewer or hardly any tall grass species exist in the semi-desert zone.

There are three major land formations in the state, namely the High Plains of the east and southeast (366 m–700 m), the Sokoto Plains of the north and center (244 m–366 m), and Riverine Lowland of the Niger and Rima valleys (122 m–244 m). As there are differences in the land formation, so also the land fertility varies. Whereas the Sokoto Plains has ferruginous soil, the High Plains and the Riverine Lowland have good and fertile soil.

The state has five major rivers: Niger, Rima, Sokoto, Zamfara, and Gagara. Apart from these rivers, some of which sometimes become dry during the dry season, there exists large reservoirs of underground water, especially in the northern part of the state.

With a population of over 8 million Sokoto State is one of the most populous states in Nigeria. It has two dominant ethnic groups: the Hausa and the Fulani. Nevertheless, with intermarriages of Hausa and Fulani, the two groups have now moved toward forming one ethnic group: the Hausa/Fulani. There are, of course, other Nigerian ethnic groups in the state as well as people from other African and non-African states. Most of the non-African expatriates are in government employment, particularly in the teaching, engineering, and health services.

The official language in the state, as in all the states of the federation, is English, but Hausa is the lingua franca. Although the language is important in homogenizing the indigenous people, religion (Islam) is more important as a unifying factor among the people. Their attitudes and behavior are largely influenced by this religion.

Islam is a Divine Guidance for all fields of human life: spiritual or temporal, private or public, political or economic, social or cultural, moral or legal, and judicial. In other words, "Islam is not a mere collection of dogmas and rituals. It is a complete way of life" (Maududi 1955, 1). Schwarz Jr. observed:

> Islam is a total religion without the Christian concept of separation of secular and religious concern. There is no Quranic verse which separates secular from religious duties (Schwarz Jr.1965, 48).

Islam is an all-embracing ideology. It does not cater to the individual and neglect his role in the society. It does not concern itself with his private life to the detriment of his political role nor ignore the relationship of his state to other states (Qutb 1977, 3). In essence, Islam is the total submission to the will of God, the creator of the universe. To submit to God's will means to serve Him, to observe His wishes as they affect all fields of human life, within the framework of His Divine Guidance contained in the Qur'an, the revealed Holy Book of Islam, and the sayings and the deeds of

His Prophet, Muhammad (PBUH), as whatever he said or did was revealed to him by God.

Islam is simply based on three basic relationship: people's relationship to God, which is based on total submission and obedience to Him; people's relationship to their family, which is based on obedience to parents and love and kindness to all members of the family; and people's relationship to their neighbors, society, and their environment at large, which is based on unity, brotherhood, justice, fair play, and hard work to earn a living. Men have certain rights over their families (they are to be respected as the leaders of their families). Similarly, women have certain rights over their husbands (it is incumbent on the men to feed, clothe, and meet other financial obligation of their wives and children) (Wali 1984, 26). On the whole, Islam provides answers to three basic issues: the creation of the universe and what it contains; the purpose of human and nonhuman existence in the universe; and the question of life after death. It should be pointed out:

Islam does not tackle life's problems in fragments, for it does not set up an independent principle to solve each individual problem. It makes from its comprehensive theory an axis around which all other problems revolve. Thus, the different issues are linked, tightly or loosely, to the axis and the whole complex forms a unified religious outlook (Qutb 1977, 5).

In brief, Islam is believing in God (in His Oneness) as the Creator, the Sustainer, the Cherisher, and the Lord of the universe; believing in His Angels, Books (the Scroll of Abraham, Psalm of David, Scroll of Moses, Gospel of Jesus, and Qur'an of Mohammad), believing in His Messengers (some of them are Adam, Noah, Abraham, Moses, Jesus, and especially Prophet Mohammad); believing in the Hereafter, His unlimited knowledge; doing as much as one can what God commands to be done; and avoiding what God prohibits, as they are contained in the Qur'an and the Hadith of Prophet Mohammad, and as they are explained and interpreted by Islamic scholars generation after generation.

Ninety-nine percent of the indigenous population of Sokoto State are Muslims. But the state is secular, thereby limiting their freedom to practice their religion in accordance with its Divine Guidance. However, the government is aware of the importance of religion to the people and its application in the conduct of public affairs. As one of the governors of the state, Alhaji Usman Faruk, observed:

[I]n my work as the military governor of this state, I have come to realize something of the continuing power and significance of the traditions of the old Sokoto Caliphate. They are still very much alive and continue to mould the outlook of the people in a much more effective and, indeed, useful way than many of our newfangled notion of twentieth century (Usman 1979, 498).

Yet, it has not been possible to completely Islamize the state because of the secularization of Nigeria. This, nonetheless, is not to suggest that Islam is not being practiced in Sokoto, but to say that only certain aspects are being practiced, notably the conduct of marriage and divorce, distribution of inheritance, worship, teaching of Islamic education in schools, giving alms to the needy, and suspending official work during prayer times. Islam, undoubtedly, is an integral part of Sokoto culture.

## Political Evolution and Development

Sokoto State, created in 1976, has a long established history. The town of Sokoto was founded in 1809 by Muhammadu Bello, the son of Shaikh Usman dan Fodio, the leader of the Islamic revivalist movement of the nineteenth century in Northern Nigeria. It became the headquarters of the Sokoto caliphate. Muhammadu Bello became the second Amirul-Mu'mineen, the leader of the faithful (but later the title was changed to sultan), after the death of his father. The caliphate grew and expanded and, by the end of the nineteenth century, more than half of the land area of Northern Nigeria was under its influence. The caliphate, in the course of the nineteenth century, comprised the following emirates: Sokoto, Gwandu, Kebbi, Yauri, Zamfara,

Zaria, Kano, Hadejia, Kazaure, Katsina, Nupe, Daura, Adamawa, Bauchi, Katagum, Gwambe, and Ilorin (Paden 1986, 44). The caliphate contained a number of ethnic groups, notably Fulani, Hausa, Barebari, Nupe, Taureg, and Yoruba. It has been indicated earlier that the caliphate was the largest and the most politically significant precolonial community in Nigeria. It not only lasted for a century, but also established a highly sophisticated political and socioeconomic system based on the Islamic perspective. It had an organized form of taxation, possessed a separate judiciary of professional judges, and decentralized its power into administrative units, each under an emir (Campbell 1965, 115). Islam was the dominant force in guiding the official and private conduct of the society. However, this system was disrupted by colonialism through the imposition of secularism which, Tijani argues, "disrupted the balance that existed between belief and action in personal conduct at all levels of social life and social organization" (Tijani 1979, 274–5).

After the conquest of the Sokoto caliphate in 1903, following other areas north of the River Niger, which were not part of the caliphate (namely Borno and Benue-Plateau, between 1900 and 1902), the whole area was proclaimed the British Protectorate of Northern Nigeria. The word Nigeria was formally used in 1914 when the northern and southern protectorates were amalgamated under Lord Lugard, the first high commissioner of the northern protectorate. Lugard chose Lokoja, the former headquarters of the Royal Niger Company, to be his headquarters, but later it was moved to Jebba, to Zungeru in 1905, and finally to Kaduna in 1927.

Lugard, having realized the limitation of direct British administration of the northern protectorate, evolved a system of indirect rule on the following grounds. First, with only £136,000 as annual revenue at his disposal for all purposes at that initial period, and taking into account the vastness of the area, it was impossible for Lugard to engage the services of the required number of British personnel to administer the protectorate. Second, the area covered by the then-caliphate and Borno already had a highly organized system of administration. Hence, it was convenient to utilize the known system, with minor adjustments to reflect the British colonial expectation (Haily 1951, 48). However, it should be pointed out that the British colonial forces had adopted indirect rule in almost all their colonized areas. Yet, it was not until Lugard established the Northern Nigerian administrative system and duly subjected it to a thoroughgoing and skillful rationalization in his numerous post-retirement writings and speeches that the words "indirect rule" became a technical term conjuring up ideas of "native authorities, native administrations, native direct taxation, native treasuries, native authority police and prisons" operating at the lower level of local government (Okonjo 1974, xvii).

Anyway, for administrative expediency, the protectorate of Northern Nigeria was divided into twelve provinces, namely Adamawa, Bauchi, Benue, Borno, Ilorin, Kabba, Kano, Katsina, Niger, Plateau, Sokoto, and Zaria. After independence another province, Sardauna, was added. The larger provinces were further split into divisions. Each province was headed by a resident and, together with his assistants at the divisional level, the district officers, they ran the provincial administration. Initially, the role of the residents was advisory: to advise the emirs and not to usurp their functions. Later, however, they usurped the power to the extent that any important decision had to receive their approval (Haily 1951, 66). Among the larger provinces was Sokoto.

Sokoto province up to 1947 consisted of three divisions, but later the number was increased to four, namely Sokoto, Gwandu, Argungu, and Yauri. Whereas in the Sokoto province the Sultan was the sole native authority, in other divisions it was the emirs, each with its own council. The post of resident was changed before independence to provincial commissioner. This structure of the provincial administration under the northern regional government continued until 1967 when it was abolished, following the military coup d'état of 1966 and the establishment of a new twelve-state structure for the federation. Sokoto and Niger provinces were merged to form the North-Western State, with Sokoto as the capital.

Usman Faruk, chief superintendent of police, was appointed military governor of the North-Western State, and he appointed the members of his executive council. Similarly, the secretary to the military government was appointed primarily to coordinate the implementation of government policies and provide leadership to the civil service. Ministries and departments were created and permanent secretaries and heads of departments appointed to coordinate the activities of their ministries and departments respectively. Most of the civil servants in the new ministries and departments were seconded from the former northern regional civil service, which was abolished following the creation of the new states. However, ten years later, in 1976, the North-Western State was split into two, following the creation of additional states in the country, to become Sokoto and Niger States, respectively. The assets of the former state were divided between the new states.

Sokoto State, the focus of this study, inherited and consolidated, among other things, the politico-bureaucratic structure of the former North-Western State. In addition, nineteen local government councils were created throughout the state to bring government closer to the people. Colonel Umaru Muhammad, the first military governor of the state, was replaced in 1978 by Colonel Muhammad Gado Nasko as military administrator, to pave the way for handing over power to civilians in 1979. The military, therefore, having created and ruled the state for eight years (from 1967 to 1979), handed over power to a democratically elected government of the National Party of Nigeria (NPN) under the leadership of Alhaji Shehu Kangiwa and, later, Alhaji Garba Nadama, following Kangiwa's death. In spite of the changes, the bureaucratic structure remains basically the same. However, other minor changes were introduced. For example, the post of the secretary to the military government, previously held by one person, was split into two: secretary to the government, and head of the civil service. Furthermore, additional ministries and departments were created. The civilian government, nonetheless, lasted for only four and a half years (October 1979 to December 1983), due to the military intervention in the political process.

The military, unlike the civilians, reduced the number of ministries, primarily to save cost, and abolished the dichotomy between the office of the secretary to the government and the office of the head of the civil service. Instead, the previous post of the secretary to the military government was revived. The argument was that, in the absence of party politics, separating the function of the secretary to the government from those of the head of the civil service was not helpful in the overall performance of the government.

From 1984 to 1988, the state had three different military governors, namely Brigadier Garba Duba (January 1984 to August 1985), Colonel Garba Mohammad (August 1985 to September 1986), and Colonel Ahmad Muhammad Daku (September 1986 to date). Despite changes in leadership, the basic structure of the bureaucracy has been maintained. The differences, however, are the leadership styles of the governors and their perception of the state's problems. Whereas Brigadier Duba was concerned with policies for revamping the state economy through cuts in public spending (in view of the prevailing financial status of the state, which was in terrible shape as a result of mismanagement of the public resources by the ousted civilian government), Colonel Muhammad focused his attention on improving the standard of education in the state, which had also been in terrible shape. Colonel Daku, on the other hand, has been pursuing policies for accelerating the pace of the overall rural development of the state. In particular, he has been concerned with the provision of drinking water and feeder roads in the rural areas, within the general framework of the federal military government's rural development program.

# Economy of Sokoto State

The Sokoto State economy is part and parcel of the Nigerian economy, which is dominated by petroleum and agriculture. Toward the end of 1987, the minister of petroleum resources, Alhaji Rilwan Lukman, indicated that crude oil production and export has been the main engine of growth in Nigerian economy since the seventies, accounting for 20 percent of the country's GDP, 94 percent of export receipts, and 82 percent of government revenue (1987). But it has contributed little to employment. Agriculture (comprising fishing, animal husbandry, and farming), on the other hand, accounts for 65 to 76 percent of employment despite continuous exodus of the population from the rural to urban areas. Agriculture also accounts for 20 percent of the country's GDP (USA Dept. of Bureau of Public Affairs 1982,

6, 19). Agriculture, therefore, is the dominant occupation of most Nigerians.

In Sokoto State, agriculture, particularly farming, is the main economic activity, providing employment to 80 percent of the male population (Sokoto State Government 1987, 3). Unlike in most African countries, women do not actively participate in farming (Wali and Bio-Ong 1985, 121). This is because, as we have mentioned earlier, Islam has made it incumbent on men to feed, clothe, and take care of the other financial necessities of their wives (among other things). Thus it is unnecessary for women to take an active part in farming, which is too demanding in the absence of appropriate technology. However, women are engaged in other agricultural activities, such as animal husbandry. Farming is organized at three levels: subsistence, small-scale farming, and large-scale farming. Whereas the majority of the population is engaged in subsistence farming, few rich farmers are engaged in small-scale farming, while the state and the federal governments are engaged in large-scale farming through the Dansadau cotton production scheme and the Goronyo-Bakalori irrigation scheme (Wali 1984, 20). In spite of all this, there has not been much improvement in agricultural production. Most of the farmers, although they possess their own farming land on which they grow crops for subsistence and exchange, cannot afford the implements for improving their production.

Farming, though the main economic activity in the state, contributes very little to the state revenue. The government, therefore, depends largely on the federal government's subvention for execution of its programs. Its other sources of revenue include the small tax receipts from industrial and commercial enterprises, small-scale traders, contractors, and poll tax. Poll tax was introduced in 1904 by the colonial regime, abolished by the civilian government (1980–1983) and reintroduced by the military in 1984.

# Social and Infrastructure Services

## Health Service

Health services are provided by general hospitals, rural health centers, basic health clinics, dispensaries, and private clinics. These institutions are grossly inadequate to cope with the needs of the growing population. In 1987 there were only ten general hospitals, sixteen rural health centers, and thirty-seven basic health clinics in a population of 7 million, as shown in Table 4.1.

**Table 4.1**
**Number of Health Institutions and Population in Sokoto State**

| Local Government Areas | General Hospital | Rural H.C | Basic H.C | Population |
|---|---|---|---|---|
| 02. ARGUNGU | 1 | 2 | 5 | 463,000 |
| 03. B/KEBBI | 1 | 1 | 2 | 300,000 |
| 04. BODINGA | - | - | 2 | 161,000 |
| 05. BUNZA | - | 1 | 1 | 299,000 |
| 06. BAGUDO | 1 | - | - | 267,000 |
| 07. GWADABAWA | - | 1 | 1 | 620,000 |
| 08. GUMMI | 1 | - | - | 256,000 |
| 09. GUSAU | 1 | 1 | 1 | 532,499 |
| 10. ISA | 1 | 1 | 1 | 390,000 |
| 11. JEGA | - | 1 | - | 280,000 |
| 12. K/NAMODA | - | 2 | 6 | 480,000 |
| 13. SILAME | - | - | 1 | 296,000 |

| Local Government Areas | General Hospital | Rural H.C | Basic H.C | Population |
|---|---|---|---|---|
| 14. SOKOTO | 1 | - | 15 | 484,000 |
| 15. T/ MAFARA | 1 | - | - | 496,000 |
| 16. YABO | - | 1 | 2 | 460,000 |
| 17. WURNO | - | 1 | 2 | 507,000 |
| 18. YAURI | 1 | 1 | - | 181,000 |
| 19. ZURU | 1 | 1 | - | 321,000 |
| **TOTAL** | **10** | **16** | **38** | **6,944,499** |

Source: Wali, Mohammad A. 1984. *The Medicalization of Health in Sokoto State.* University of Liverpool M.A. Thesis; Ministry of Information, Sokoto 1987:50.

# Transport and Communication

There are four means of transport in the state: roads, railways, rivers, and air transport. Road transportation is the most important in Sokoto State, as in all parts of Nigeria. There is only one airport in the state, the capital town. The railway, which runs from Zaria in Kaduna State to Gusau and Kauran-Namoda in the State, covers only about two hundred kilometers. Similarly, the navigable rivers are very limited and concentrated in the south-western part of the state.

All the nineteen local government headquarters are linked by either trunk A, B, or C roads. However, the roads are far from being adequate. There are many areas that are not accessible to roads. So people often have to walk for a number of kilometers before they come to a road. This situation is common in most of the states in Nigeria and in most developing countries (Wali 1984, 21). The state government is, of course, aware of the problem and is making efforts to tackle it through its rural feeder roads program.

Unlike transportation services, telephone services (introduced in the 1950s) are very limited. Out of the eighty-four districts of the state, only eight are provided with telephone lines. They are: Sokoto (8,000 lines), Gusau (1,000 lines), Birnin Kebbi (240 lines), Argungu

(200 lines), Yelwa (200 lines), Yabo (100 lines), Talata-Mafara (200 lines), and Zuru (300 lines). Even then the services are limited to district headquarters only. On the whole, there were, by the end of 1987, 10,240 telephone lines in the state.

# Power and Water Supply

Like the telephone service, power supply is grossly inadequate. It is provided by two organizations: the National Electric Power Authority (later reconstituted into the National Power Holding Company of Nigeria) and the State Rural Electricity Board (REB). NEPA/PHCN is the main power supplier throughout the country; the role of REB, however, is complementary, supplying limited power to areas not yet connected to the national grid. Although most of the district headquarters are provided with electricity, those supplied by REB are not continuous because of its limited facilities.

Similarly, water supply is characterized by deficiencies not only in quality but also in quantity—"accessibility and reliability." Presently, there are four sources of drinking water in the state: water from wells, rivers, boreholes, and pipe-borne water. Whereas the urban and semi-urban towns have piped water, the supply of which is very inadequate and inaccessible to a large number of the people, the rural communities use wells and boreholes, many of which are not reliable. A continuous supply requires constant servicing that, in most cases, is lacking in view of the enormous cost involved. Besides, the volume of water in the wells dramatically reduces in the dry season, thereby making it difficult for the people to get drinking water. Under these conditions of scarcity the people cannot afford to be concerned about the quality of water (Wali 1984, 36).

In this chapter, an attempt has been made, not only to set the context of the study area, but also to examine some political and socioeconomic variables that may have a bearing in the implementation of public policy in the Sokoto State bureaucracy. These variables are discussed in greater detail in the subsequent chapters.

# Chapter Five
# The Policy Process and Implementation Constraints in Sokoto State Civil Service

Apart from the disagreement over the central focus or analytic concepts of implementation study, there are also divergent views about what constitutes an implementation problem. So far, implementation problems in the Third World have been attributed to either the structure of the bureaucratic organization (Maipose 1984) or the characteristics of the bureaucratic officials (Odunlami 1986; Mato 1986) or, recently, the policy characteristics and the politico-administrative context of the policy (Grindle 1980). All these may be termed the conventional explanation for the problems of implementation in the Third World.

The aim of this chapter is to find out whether or not the variables frequently mentioned have any relevance in the analysis of the implementation of public policy in the Sokoto State bureaucracy. In doing so, some of the assumptions under each of the variables will be presented and then examined against the empirical situation in the state.

## Organizational Factors in the Policy Process

It has been argued that the organizational structure of bureaucracies and their methods of operations in the Third World are themselves constraints in the implementation of public policies. The bureaucratic operations are seen to be characterized by long and complex chains of command, which in turn lead to delays, bottlenecks, and red tape. This invariably hampers the coordination process and hence affects the implementation of public policy. In his doctoral study of constraints on administration of rural development in Zambia, Maipose concludes, among others, that the structure of the government machinery and managerial procedures are incapable of facilitating rural transformation in Zambia (Maipose 1984). Similarly, in his doctoral study of public policy formulation in Benue State of Nigeria, Mato asserts that the bureaucratic structure is not designed to cope with the rural health problems (Mato 1986, 185). In the same vein, in his study of the implementation of the 1976 local government reform in Bendel State of Nigeria, Egonmwan concluded that the structures of the bureaucratic organizations responsible for the implementation of the reform were not compatible with its aims and objectives and thus constituted a serious implementation problem (1982, 3). Describing the bureaucratic operation in Nigeria, Asiodu notes:

> There is too much delay in the processes within ministries of the laborious minuting of matters, sometimes very urgent ones, from Assistant Secretary to Senior Assistant Secretary, thence to Principal Assistant Secretary, and to Deputy Permanent Secretary, and finally to Permanent Secretary, and sometimes beyond to the Commissioner/Minister, each one adding his thought. The question of delays is even more serious in matters requiring the concurrence of several ministries. Here the co-ordinating department, usually the Cabinet Office, becomes very important (Tukur 1970, 138–9).

This observation is typical of bureaucratic operation in Sokoto State. Besides, as Elmore observed:

> [W]e cannot say with much certainty what a policy is, or why it is not implemented, without knowing a great deal about how organizations function.... [T]he translation of an idea into action involves certain crucial simplifications. Organizations are simplifiers; they work on problems by breaking them into

discrete, manageable tasks and allocating responsibilities for those tasks to specialized units (1978, 187).

The assistant secretary (or a professional officer) submits a proposal or analyzes a problem and passes it to the senior assistant secretary, who agrees or disagrees with the view by adding his own comments, and passes it on to the next stage, and the process continues up to the permanent secretary, who weighs the strengths and weaknesses of each argument (if there are divergent views). The permanent secretary may also set aside preceding submissions if he has different views altogether, and, depending on the nature of the issue, he may advise the commissioner on the course of action to take. Yet another course he may follow is to pass the proposal back to the hierarchy, either accepting the proposal as a whole or a portion of it, or directing otherwise. A similar process takes place in other organizations. The point is, the bureaucratic operation is characterized by many decision points and filters. This is neither new nor strange to the bureaucrats. It is, as a matter of fact, the norm in any governmental bureaucracy. However, little attention has been given to the importance of such a process in four key areas: first, in the formulation of sound policies; second, in the training and enhancement of skills of the officers involved in the process; third, in the checks and balances it ensures; and fourth, in the facilitation of work at the top. Elmore (1979–80, 606) observed:

[M]ost policy analysts are ... trained to regard complex organizations as barriers to the implementation of public policy, not as instruments to be capitalized upon and modified in the pursuit of policy objectives.

The main question, therefore, is not the long decision chains and the involvement of many actors in any implementation process within a given bureaucratic setting, but whether rigorous analysis of a complex problem is facilitated by such an organizational structure.

The bureaucratic setup in Sokoto at the end of 1987 consisted of six broad structures: the military governor's office, the ministries and departments, the service commissions, the judiciary, the statutory boards and corporations, and the audit department, as presented in Table 5.1.

The military governor's office, which is under the overall direction of the secretary to the military government and head of the civil service (SMG/HS), and which is the nerve center of the state administration, consists of four departments: Government House, Administration and Political Affairs Department, Careers and Special Services Department, and Establishment and Monitoring Department. Each of the departments is headed by a permanent secretary. The number of key officers in these departments is usually not more than five: assistant secretary I or II, senior assistant secretary or principal assistant secretary, undersecretary or principal secretary, secretary, and permanent secretary. Other things being equal, the number of the key officers in each department may be eight or more. All the departments are responsible to the SMG/HS. The office as a whole, apart from specializing in some policy areas (appointment to the boards of government owned companies and parastatals), is responsible for the coordination of implementation of the overall government policies (West Africa Magazine 1989, 970).

The ministries, furthermore, which are staffed by career administrators and professionals, include the following: agriculture and natural resources, commerce-industry and cooperatives, education, finance and economic planning, health, housing, information and home affairs, justice, local government, social development—youth and sport, and works and transport. While commissioners are the chief executives of the ministries, permanent secretaries are the administrative heads and accounting officers. Unlike the ministries, the boards and the corporations are under the supervision of either the executive chairman, general manager, or executive secretary.

The boards consist of the following: Sokoto Urban Development Authority (SUDA), Hotels Management Boards, Water Board, Rural Electricity Board (REB), Islamic Preaching Board, Sokoto Agricultural and Rural Development Authority (SARDA), Pilgrims Welfare Board, Scholarship Board, Housing Corporation, Sports Council, and Health Services Management Board. The organizational hierarchies of these corporations are limited in view of the specialized and specific functions they perform. The heads of these organizations are responsible to their boards, which are appointed and constituted by the military governor.

Apart from the boards there are commissions, namely the Civil Service Commission, the Local Government Service Commission, and the Judicial Service Commission. Although the internal structures of the commissions are basically the same with those of the boards, their performance are service-oriented, and their establishment has constitutional sanction unlike the boards. Whereas the Civil Service Commission is concerned with the recruitment, promotion, and discipline of senior officers in the state service, the Local Government Service Commission is preoccupied with the recruitment, promotion, and discipline of senior officers in the local government service. Similarly, the Judicial Service Commission is concerned with the recruitment, promotion, and discipline of lawyers and other judicial officers.

## Table 5.1
## The Bureaucratic Setup In Sokoto State: 1987

**The Military Governor's Office**

i.   Government House
ii.  Administration and Political Affairs Department
iii. Careers and Special Services Department
iv.  Establishment and Monitoring Department

| Ministries | Commissions | Judiciary | Audit Department | Boards |
|---|---|---|---|---|
| 1. Agriculture and Natural Resources<br>2. Commerce-Industry and Cooperatives<br>3. Education<br>4. Finance and Economic Planning<br>5. Health<br>6. Housing<br>7. Information and Home Affairs<br>8. Justice<br>9. Local Government<br>10. Social Development—Youth and Sport<br>11. Works and Transport. | 1. Civil Service Commission<br>2. Local Government Service Commission<br>3. Judicial Service Commission | 1. High Court<br>2. Area Courts<br>3. Shari'a Court | | 1. Sokoto Urban Development Authority (SUDA)<br>2. Hotels Management Boards<br>3. Water Board,<br>4. Rural Electricity Board (REB)<br>5. Islamic Preaching Board<br>6. Sokoto Agricultural and Rural Development Authority (SARDA)<br>7. Pilgrims Welfare Board<br>8. Scholarship Board<br>9. Housing Corporation<br>10. Sports Council<br>11. Health Services Management Board |

The judiciary is basically concerned with the administration of justice. It is headed by the chief judge who is assisted by other judges and judicial officers. The internal administration of the judiciary is under the chief registrar.

The Audit Department is responsible for auditing government accounts, preparing audit reports, and liaising with the military governor's office in coordinating/following up audit queries. It is under the director of audit.

Apart from the state institutions, there are federal government institutions in the state. The bureaucratic features in the state, like other states in Nigeria, are characterized by the following:

1. Division of labor. This is based on functional specialization. There are intra- and inter-organizational divisions of labor. At the organizational level, each ministry or department divides its activities and assigns duties to specific offices or specified officers with a defined sphere of competence as enunciated in the ministerial or departmental schedule of duties. Likewise, activities are divided among the ministries, departments, and boards that have been mentioned earlier for specific functions. They operate as subsystems, each contributing its own quota for the realization of the overall system objective. This arrangement facilitates the tracing of responsibility.

2. Hierarchy. All the ministries and departments have clear chains of authority, and the duties of each officer is demarcated along the hierarchy. In other words, the ministerial offices are hierarchically organized from top to bottom. Each lower office is under the supervision and control of the higher one, from the permanent secretary (as in ministries) or general manager (as in the boards) to the office messenger. This essentially provides clear "directions, cohesion, continuity" and orderly operations of the organizations.

3. Formally enacted codes of conduct. Official conduct is guided by rules as enunciated in the state civil service rules, guide to procedures, financial instructions, stores regulations, and numerous establishment circulars issued

from time to time. This is to say that the operation of governmental organizations is not based on individual desires or predilections.

4.  Impersonality. Impersonality in the official relationship is to some extent maintained. The rules apparently apply to everybody. However, there are cases here and there where personal relationships in the organization tamper with the pattern of the official conduct, particularly on disciplinary measures, but not on the basic rules. This is largely due to the close personal relationship of the officers or familial relationship. This, nonetheless, does not invalidate the overall formalism that characterizes the organizational relationship.

5.  Merit. Recruitment to the organization is based on technical qualification for jobs requiring technical competence. Jobs, such as office cleaning and gardening, do not require "paper qualification." There are variations in the qualification requirements for entry into the different cadres of the state civil service. The service broadly comprises five cadres: administrative, executive, clerical, sub-clerical, and professional (accounting, engineering, stores, auditing, education, medicine, secretarial, social services, printing, commercial, nursing, and midwifery).

It should be further noted that for the administrative cadre, the basic entry qualification is a university degree in social sciences, but lately it is restricted to political science or public administration. Thus almost all the administrators are university graduates. In the executive cadre, the entry requirement is either by promotion from the clerical cadre or by professional qualification. The clerical cadre, furthermore, starts with a secondary school certificate. In the professional cadre, there is no common requirement. Whereas some start with a university degree, such as medical doctors and engineers, others require a diploma, which may be from a university, polytechnic, college of education, or an A-level institution. Still others require only a secondary school certificate. In the sub-clerical cadre, no formal education certificate is required. However, the government is now encouraging all the illiterate workers to be literate through the organization of adult literacy classes. Generally, a large number of officers in the high-level manpower are university graduates.

The ministries, the judiciary, and other departments are authorized to employ officers from grade level 1 to 6 (the salary structure in the state is based on grade level 1 to 16), while officers on 7 to 16 are employed by the state Civil Service Commission and the state Judicial Service Commission on the recommendation of the ministries, judiciary, and departments and posted to respective organizations. The boards and corporations enjoy a high degree of autonomy and so have the power to employ their staff without reference to the Civil Service Commission.

Employment in the civil service follows clear career paths. This entails the following:

1. Delineation of salary structures for the workers with grading of posts according to the qualifications required for appointment to the posts and the degrees of importance attached to the functions carried out. Fresh university graduates are employed on grade level 8, graduates of colleges of education on 7, graduates of A-level, national diploma on 6, secondary school leavers on 3 or 4. Officers on grade level 8 to 16 are regarded as high-level manpower, officers on 6 to 7 as middle-level manpower, and 1 to 5 as lower manpower. The total manpower strength of the state in 1977 was 8,388, and three years later, in 1980, it rose to 14,740 (Economic Planning Department 1981, 154). By the end of 1983, the figure had reached 23,224, but reduced to 16,932 in 1984 following the mass retrenchment of the civil servants in the year as a result of the military takeover of the government (Economic Planning Department 1985, 52).

2. Establishment of a pension scheme for workers at their retirement age. In the state, the age of voluntary retirement is forty-five, while the age of compulsory retirement is fifty-five.

3. Promotion on the basis of seniority in the service and on merit. Generally, officers who put in two years of

meritorious service are promoted to the next grade level. Officers who display exceptional ability are equally promoted irrespective of whether or not they put up two years of service. However, there are instances where officers stay for four years without promotion, for no fault of theirs, particularly in the teaching profession, which has the highest number of officers in the state service, or where officers are promoted without actually meriting such promotion.

4. Control and disciplinary measures for the workers. This is very essential. Without disciplinary measures it would be hard to operate any bureaucracy. There are a variety of disciplinary measures contained in the state civil service rules and circulars. They range from advising officers verbally and in writing, to warning and termination of appointment or dismissal from the service on account of gross misconduct or inefficiency in the discharge of official duties. However, there are avenues for seeking redress if an officer felt he was unjustly treated. Such avenues include the Civil Service Commission, the Local Government Service Commission, and the Judicial Service Commission.

All the ministries and the departments mentioned are based in the state capital, Sokoto. Nonetheless, few have branch offices in some of the local government headquarters. That apart, none of the organizations is completely autonomous; they are all interdependent in the implementation of public policies. For instance, if the Ministry of Education formulates a policy that involves construction of a school or classes, the Ministry of Works and Transport will be involved in the implementation process, either by directly executing the project or supervising its execution by a contractor or contractors. Similarly, the Ministry of Finance will be involved by releasing the funds required for the project. So will the Ministry of Local Government, particularly, when it comes to acquiring the land for the construction of the schools.The military governor's office, for its own part, will oversee the overall and satisfactory implementation of the project. The whole process, therefore, involves a high degree of coordination between and among organizations, interaction between and among actors involved in such processes, and checks and balances resulting from such coordination and interaction for any implementation of public policy. After all, the bureaucratic structure, as Weber argues,

> is, from a purely technical point of view, capable of attaining the highest degree of efficiency and is in this sense formally the most rational known means of carrying out imperative control over human beings. It is superior to any other form in precision, in stability, in the stringency of its discipline, and in its reliability. It thus makes possible a particularly high degree of calculability of results for the heads of the organizations and for those acting in relation to it. It is finally superior both in efficiency and is formally capable of application to all kinds of administrative tasks (Weber 1947, 337).

It should be noted that in some respects, the Sokoto State civil service is markedly different from Weber's ideal type. What is important is the rationality that characterizes the conduct of official business in the state and all the other states in Nigeria. Describing the bureaucratic characteristics in Kaduna State of Nigeria, Ngu says:

> The organization of a government department featured some of the major characteristics of Max Weber's Model. For example, appointments, promotions, processing of grievances and commands, and training on any of the posts, were based on qualifications, experience and expertise (1985, 139).

On Nigeria as a whole, Kingsley observed that "an inherited administrative structure and bureaucracy in the full sense of the term already exist at independence" (1963, 302).

In light of all this, it seems that the problem of policy implementation in Sokoto State cannot adequately be attributed to the bureaucratic organizational structure. Anyway, the organizations involved in any one implementation process may be large, the actors involved may be many, but that does not in any real sense constrain the implementation process as long as the actors are performing their duties effectively. This brings us to the second variable—the characteristics of the bureaucrats.

# The Bureaucrats and Their Ways

Others attribute the implementation problem to the character of the bureaucrats themselves. The common assumptions are that they lack dedication to duty, they lack a sense of urgency, and they are corrupt and prone to colluding with outside interests to defraud the government. These attributes are likely to constrain the implementation of public policies (Smith 1973, 246).

The allegations of bureaucratic crookedness gained currency in Nigeria when a military coup d'état was staged in July 1975. In order to cure what it perceived as a serious national malaise, the army carried out an unprecedented mass retirement and dismissal exercise in both the federal and states public services. The purge involved about 11,000 bureaucrats (Nwosu 1977, 81). The aim was principally to get rid of officials that were fashionably termed "the bad eggs." The new government was anxious to reconstitute an efficient, dedicated, committed, and responsive public service that was capable of facilitating speedy implementation of its programs, designed primarily to satisfy the yearnings and aspirations of the citizens of the country (Longe 1984, 12). Nine years later, in 1984, the military had cause again to doubt the commitment and efficiency of the bureaucracy. This further resulted in the purge and retrenchment of thousands of bureaucrats throughout the country. By the end of October 1984, the total number of the affected officers was estimated at between 150,000 and 200,000 (Adamolekun 1985, 215). In Sokoto State, in particular, 3,078 bureaucrats were affected (Economic Planning Department 1985, 39).

In his address to the Nigerian mass media, Nigeria's former minister of agriculture, Major General Nasco, asserted that the nation's past agricultural policies failed because of the lukewarm attitude of those charged with their implementation (Nigerian Observer 1988). That was neither the first time that such a claim was made by people at the political level nor observed by scholars. For example, Mato (1986, 25) asserted that the failures of the Universal Primary Education (UPE) and the Green Revolution programs in Nigeria were attributable to the bureaucrats since they were responsible for their planning and implementation. Likewise, in his doctoral study on the ineffectiveness of land-use policies in Nigeria, Odunlami (1986, 231) concluded, among other things, that the noncommitment or reluctance of the bureaucrats to carry out needed reforms was one of the major causal factors of failure of land policies in Nigeria. In this respect, Ngu observed, "achievements, failures and problem of government tend to be measured in terms of achievements, failures and problems of the public bureaucracy, even though it may not always be the case" (Ngu, 1985:3).

Yet the assertion of Major General Nasco is significant, coming from an experienced insider in the Nigerian administration. He, General Nasco, was once a military administrator of Sokoto State, former minister of trade and industry, agriculture, as well as a member of the Armed Forces Ruling Council of Nigeria.

Successive regimes in Sokoto State have realized that without an effective and committed bureaucracy, their policies, no matter how well intentioned, could not be successfully implemented. The regimes acknowledge the fact that their success is dependent on the commitment, dedication, and efficiency of the bureaucracy. It is not surprising, therefore, the military relied on the bureaucracy for its policy formulation and implementation. Balogun (1983, 65) attributes the influence of the bureaucracy under military regimes to the symbiotic relationship between the two. Whereas the bureaucrats provide the military with ideas, facts, and policy proposals for important decisions, the military protects and allows the bureaucrats the leverage to increase and widen their scope of power in policy-making and implementation. In any case, the dominance of the bureaucracy was inevitable since the people's representatives (the politicians) had been dislodged from the seat of power, having been accused of corruption. Under the military, the politicians became the object of attack and condemnation (Beinen and Fitton 1978, 48–9; Balogun 1983). In the circumstance, it became necessary for the military to have a different approach or style of administration from the previous regime it overthrew. To this extent, relying on its commissioners would symbolize a continuation of the previous practice, as the commissioners had stepped into the shoes of ministers who had been accused of corruption. It became obvious that there was no other competent group the military could rely upon for the administration of the country, in the absence of partisanship, than the bureaucrats who had the monopoly of relevant information for the conduct of public affairs. This pattern continued throughout the nine years (1967–1975) of Usman Faruk's government at the state level (in Sokoto), and General Gowon's regime at the federal level.

Before the overthrow of General Gowon's regime in 1975, the bureaucracy, at both the state and federal levels, had come under serious criticisms from the public. They were accused of corruption and mismanagement of public resources, and for advising the general not to hand over power to civilians in 1974, as he earlier promised in 1970. It is not by coincidence, therefore, that the first group outside the military to feel the pinch after the coup d'état was the bureaucracy. As earlier noted, mass purges in both the states and the federal bureaucracies were carried out. Most of Nigeria's problems at that time were attributed to the bureaucrats. In particular, they were accused of inefficiency and ineffectiveness in the conduct of public affairs (Beinen and Fitton 1978, 52). There were instances where senior civil servants were "drilled" in the state by the military for coming to office late (Balogun 1983). In some states, even the permanent secretaries were "drilled." For example, the *West Africa Magazine* reported:

> Arriving late for work earlier this Month, 31 civil servants found themselves locked out of their offices by the acting Governor Lt Col. Mark Etonyo. He had reported for work at Government House at 7.30 am and ordered that the main gates be shut. Most of the top civil servants did not report for duty by 8.00 am (1989, 17–23).

All this is understandable since there were no politicians to attack and castigate; the bureaucrats became the object of serious attack. Adamolekun observed, "Unlike the situation in 1966 when the civilian politicians were the sinners and the civil servants were largely regarded as the saints, this time around, most people regarded the civil servants as an integral part of the discredited regime" (1985, 144).

During this period, the military at the federal level no longer depended on the exclusive policy advice of the bureaucrats as was the practice. Rather, they sought the advice of other actors (Adamolekun 1985, 144), particularly academics in the universities and business leaders. This was manifested by the enormous support given to the regime by the academics. Some academics had joined government delegations to international conferences.

However, in Sokoto State, the military leadership under Colonel Umaru Muhammed, in spite of its toughness, relied on the bureaucracy for support in the areas of policy formulation and implementation. This pattern of relationship between the military and the bureaucracy continued until October 1979 when political power was handed over to politicians of the Second Republic.

From the time the civilians took over the leadership to the time they were overthrown ( i.e., 1979 to December 1983), the influence of the bureaucrats, particularly in the area of policy initiation and formulation, had been slightly eroded. Their advice on the implications of some major policies were in most cases rejected. Some of the top bureaucrats, by maintaining neutrality, were even accused of sabotaging the government's efforts and subsequently reassigned to other jobs. Some were posted to organizations where they would have less influence or where they would not be seen as posing a threat to the government's declared objectives. Unlike the military, the politicians, many of whom were former bureaucrats, came to power on account of programs they promised the electorate. They had supposedly clear vision of what they wanted to do and how to do it. Thus, they did not need to rely completely on the bureaucrats, particularly for policy formulation.

The influence of the bureaucracy began to reemerge from the time the military took over from the politicians in December 1983. This continued up to December 1987. They were now relied upon and involved in the initiation, formulation, and implementation of public policies because they were not the object of attack and criticisms. The objects of scorn were the overthrown politicians who, it is said, did not heed the advice of the bureaucrats. Thus, having taken over from the politicians, General Buhari asserted, "We believe that appropriate government agencies did give good advice but their advice was disregarded by the leadership" (Adamolekun 1985, 81).

The realization by the military of the sour relationship between the politicians and the bureaucracy had further reinforced its confidence in the bureaucracy. Whereas the politicians saw the bureaucrats as being unnecessarily technocratic and unappreciative of the political dimension of government policy, the bureaucrats saw the politicians as being flamboyant, interfering, and too political in their approaches to the execution of public policy.

Although the bureaucracy had asserted its influence during this period, the degree of the influence was limited compared to the previous periods. During the colonial period, the situation was quite different in that the bureaucracy was not only under foreign rule but was also the major driving force in the policy process. In contrast, the period 1966–1975 was the first experiment in the military rule. The military lacked expertise in politics and political leadership. It was thus inevitable, having dislodged the politicians, that it would rely on the bureaucracy. It was this reliance, more than any other factor, that contributed to the predominance of the bureaucracy in the policy-implementation process. Along with this, the period 1975–1979 saw the second experiment of the military leadership. Though the military was critical of the bureaucracy at the beginning, it had to reconcile the situation toward the end of the period. On the other hand, the periods 1984–1985 and 1985–1990 saw the third and fourth military experiments in government and, by implication, it had by then been more exposed to leadership. The military had become highly educated and well exposed. From the 1980s, therefore, the military began to play an important role in the initiation and formulation of major policies. For example, the education policy coined "Operation Move a Head" in Sokoto State, was to a large extent, conceived of by Colonel Garba Muhammed, the governor of Sokoto State (1985–1986).

# The Bane of Corruption and Policy Implementation

Still on the characteristics of the bureaucrats, apart from the issue of dedication to duty, bureaucratic corruption is another most widely discussed subject. Peil (1976, 49) observes, "Accusations of corruption have been frequent in Nigeria, both under the civilian and the military regimes." There is no doubt that corruption is widespread in government organizations in Nigeria and has exacerbated the economic condition of the country (Bolaji 1970; Anigboh 1985). In Sokoto State, in particular, a large number of the bureaucrats in the state are perceived as corrupt. This involves both the junior and senior officers. Some junior officers go to the extent of hiding clients' files containing important information and bringing them out only when they are bribed or promised some form of gratification. Corruption among the senior officers is characterized by conniving with contractors to inflate contracts, to certify works that are haphazardly executed, to certify receipt of goods not supplied, or to embezzle public funds. There were cases where officers claimed the salaries of "ghost workers" or where nonexistent houses were being "rented." In early 1987, some senior officers were compulsorily retired from the service following the discovery of their involvement in a series of corrupt practices, ranging from inflation of contracts to embezzlement of large sums of public funds.

The 1980 housing policy, which involved the construction of 240 housing units at the cost of N60 million (being the most expensive and an unjustified contract awarded in the history of the state: each flat cost N250,000), was not just to provide houses to the people (as the houses do not even fit their cultural peculiarity) but fundamentally to get a certain percentage from the contract. It was not surprising when the military took over power from the civilians in 1983, the new military governor, Brigadier Garba Duba, instituted a committee of inquiry to review how the contract and similar contracts were awarded (The New Nigeria 1984). The committee observed,

[C]ertainly housing is an important social service. However, the type of houses provided [the 240 D.U housing arrangement] are not the type one would expect to be built in this environment, considering the cultural and climatic conditions that prevail here. The houses … do not meet the requirement of the majority of the inhabitants of this area (Committee Report on Project Financed by External Loans 1984, 36).

Regardless of this, the houses were completed within two and a half years (1982–1984), but it took the subsequent administrations in the state over three years to decide what to do with the houses and how to repay the foreign loan involved in the project, for it was executed by a Korean firm, Messrs Hanyang Nigeria Ltd. As a matter of fact, there were more cases of corruption in the state between 1967 and 1975, and there were other factors at play.

The issue of corruption is not limited only to the bureaucrats. A few governors were implicated. In 1975 when General Gowon was overthrown, ten of his twelve military governors were found guilty of misappropriating millions of public funds and were accordingly dismissed from the service. Among the ten was the military governor of North-Western State (later to become Sokoto and Niger states), Usman Faruk (1967–1975). He, Faruk, was accused of sidetracking laid-down procedures for the award of contracts and of corruptly enriching himself. This led to the confiscation of his landed property. However, under another administration, he was exonerated and all his properties that were confiscated were duly returned to him. Similarly, the then civilian governor of the State, Dr. Garba Nadama (1981–1983), was accused of engaging in "corrupt practices and unlawful enrichment" and was subsequently jailed (Keesings Contemporary Archives 1984, 33262) and some of his property confiscated. Dr Nadama too, under another administration, was subsequently exonerated and released from jail.

It should be pointed out that the junior officers become involved in corruption largely because of economic hardship (their limited salaries could not cope with the perennial inflationary trend in the country on the one hand, and their enormous family obligations on the other). Like their senior colleagues, the junior officers are under pressure to meet the needs of nuclear and extended family members, unemployed friends and relatives, and the like. As for the senior officers, the quest for monetary gain is fueled not only by family pressures, but also by the urge to consolidate their power base and to prepare for their retirement. This is not something new; corruption exists in every bureaucracy. The difference, however, is that it is more widespread in some societies and bureaucracies than in others. Its gravity and methods vary depending on the prevailing circumstances (Huntington 1968, 59).

The reasons for corruption as highlighted above are only apparent. The root cause of corruption in Sokoto State and in other Muslim states in the country is the disconnection of the secular obligations from religious injuctions. Islam, the dominant religion in Sokoto, condemns corruption in all its forms. However, because the conduct of public affairs in the state is not based on the religion, Muslim bureaucrats engage in corruption (what their religion forbids) in order to support their relatives and friends (what contemporary society demands). The civil servants are thus caught between their religious teachings and the prevailing social norms. If the conduct of public affairs in the state is based on a sound religious foundation (in this case, Islam), corruption will largely be reduced. This is because the people's religious value will be harmonized with the prevailing philosophy of public administration. So far, studies of corruption in Nigeria have failed to understand and appreciate the problem of corruption in this context. It is not surprising when Ngu (1985, 29) observes:

> [T]he issues of corruption and maladministration have continued [since independence], to dominate public discussions in the Nigerian Press, the Mass Media and intellectual forums, with little or no hope for solutions.

He further argues that no regime in Nigeria, military or civilian, has been able to "stamp out" corruption, despite the various institutions for public accountability or administrative control devices (Ngu 1985, i). The Solution to the problem has always been to establish commissions of inquiry and tribunals that come up with wide-ranging recommendations. All these measures have failed and will continue to fail as long as the root cause of corruption is ignored.

Corruption has many ramifications, and many studies have confused it with maladministration (Ngu 1985, 12). Its manifestations that prove devastating for implementation of public policy are inflation of government contracts, stoppage or abandonment of projects (after a lot of money had been sunk into them), and embezzlement of public funds. In his argument on the relationship between corruption and the poor implementation of Nigeria's economic development plans, Anigboh (1985, 290) concludes:

To say that Nigerian Economic Development Plans have not succeeded in achieving their goals because of lack of proper implementation, as a result of pervasive corrupt practices in its different levels of government, will be an understatement.

In the same vein, Mato (1986, 89) attributes the poor implementation of health policy in Benue State of Nigeria to corruption:

[O]ften it was impossible to achieve what money was voted for, because there was massive corruption concerning contract awards. Contracts were for example, awarded for the building of seven new hospitals, one each, in Kwande, Vandeikya, Katsina Ala, Oju, Gwer, Okpoga and Ogun Local Government areas. By 1986 only the General Hospital at Katsina Ala was completed. Work was stopped on the other six since the state had no money to continue with the project.

It is true that corruption has done a lot of damage to the Nigerian economy. It siphons off money that ought to have been productively allocated to development projects. It also puts the money in the hands of those who specialize in conspicuous consumption rather than in investment and production. It is, however, equally true that changes in the national and international environment could cause inflation, which in turn could affect the cost of projects and, hence, spending more than anticipated. Arguing on this issue with respect to Kaduna State, Ngu (1985, 11)says:

[D]evelopment projects may fail to take off as planned, not necessary because funds voted for them have been converted for private use but for other variety of factors one of such factors may be that the funds voted for the projects have either been mismanaged or underestimated, which may imply lack of adequate skill or foresight by both project planners and managers.

Thus, excessive spending is not necessarily "caused" by corruption, as other factors might be at work. Similarly, the example cited by Mato on the completion of only one general hospital in 1986 (the project might have started in 1980) and the stoppage of the other six was not completely due to lack of resources. The point that Mato ignored was that when the politicians were overthrown at the end of 1983, most of the projects they started were stopped all over the country as it was felt that the projects were launched based on the cheap political calculations rather than on rational economic analysis. It was later, after the merits and otherwise of the various projects had been examined, that some projects were restarted. In Sokoto, the construction of a few projects initiated by the civilian administration (e.g., the History Bureau Office, some schools, and health centers) was halted by Brigadier Duba in 1984. The projects, however, resurfaced in 1985 with the inception of another military administration and were completed by 1988.

Although corruption is prevalent among the politicians, the military, and the bureaucrats, they are all aware of its negative effect on government popularity. It is significant that corruption is one of the reasons consistently cited for all military coups d'état in Africa (Anigboh 1985, 138). Thus, regardless of the pervasive nature of corruption, government, and public service, leaders are keen to ensure the success of any policy that they initiate. As for the politicians, they may be corrupt, but they still have interest in seeing to the success of any program they have formulated. It is this kind of success they hope to cite to convince the electorate of the wisdom in keeping them in or returning them to power. They have no better way of convincing the electorate than to show them their concrete achievements. For example, presenting his 1982 budget proposal to the Sokoto State Assembly on December 30, 1982, the civilian governor, Dr. Nadama, said on education:

> In September 1981 alone, 26 additional post-primary institutions comprising 17 Secondary Schools, including Science and Secondary Technical Schools, 4 Vocational Training Centres, 3 Commercial Secondary Schools and 2 Arabic Teachers Colleges were opened (1982 budget proposal, 4–7).

On health he continued:

> Three new clinics in Sokoto town have been commissioned. In addition, five more Health Clinics at Runjin Sambo, Shagari, Lolo, Gidan Haki and Takalafiya in Birnin Kebbi are nearing completion (1982 budget proposal, 4–7).

On agriculture he noted:

> In our efforts to improve food production in the state ... 480 metric tons of improved seeds had already been distributed to farmers free of charge (1982 budget proposal, 4–7).

The quest for public acclaim is not limited to civilians but is equally shared by the military. For example, in his 1987 budget speech to the people of Sokoto State, the military governor, Colonel Ahmad Daku, said on water supply:

> In order to improve water supply in the State capital, 15 bore holes were drilled at the cost of N1.8m. Similarly, contracts for the extension of Sokoto Water Supply Works have since commenced and the first phase is expected to be completed in April 1989 and will cater for the demand of the town up to 1997 (1987, 9).

On electricity, furthermore, he reported:

> Works on electricity supply on Bungudu, Zauro and Ambursa projects have been completed, while those of Durbawa, Gagi, Gwadangwaji and Dange are expected to be completed shortly (Daku 1987, 9).

As for the bureaucrats, they want to show their commitment and dedication to duty irrespective of who is in power. This is the only way to win the confidence of the government of the day. In his address at a public service seminar for senior public officers of the Imo State government of Nigeria in 1984, the then-secretary to the federal military government had the following to say on the role of the civil service:

> In its service to the various regimes the civil service has seen its role essentially as follows: a] To contribute to the formulation of Government policy. b] To advise Government on the full implication of policy options open to it. c] To execute Government policy once this is settled by the Cabinet or the Minister or Commissioner as the de jure chief Executive charged with the responsibility for the Government business of the Ministry. d] To provide continuity through reference to, or clarification of the basis of, past Government decisions and procedures, which are relevant to an issue under consideration. e] To protect the public interest and act as the custodian of public conscience. f] To play a leadership role both within the service and in the community as a whole (Longe 1984, 7).

From the discussion so far, it is evident that attributing poor implementation to the character of the bureaucrats is inadequate and is likely to overblow the importance of informal behavior in the policy process.

It appears both the organizational structure and the characteristics of the bureaucrats could not provide adequate explanation for the problem of policy implementation in Sokoto State. Recently, however, analysis of implementation problems in the Third World has shifted to consideration of the nature of policy itself and its context as the crucial variables in the implementation process (Grindle 1980). These variables, too, will be examined against the situation in Sokoto.

# Policy Content as the "Enemy Within"

The content of a policy comprises its scope, complexity, projected impact on social or economic relationships, and feasibility (Grindle 1981, 54). For any policy to succeed, it should be clearly stated and be responsive to the people's interest. Unfortunately, most of the Third World governments' policies are ambiguous and not responsive to the interest of the people and, therefore, hard to implement. Yet, seen from this perspective, policy content does not seem to be a crucial variable hindering the implementation process in Sokoto.

In the first place, most of the major policies formulated in the state, although without the active participation of the people, are in response to their aspiration. Yet, some of the policies are not effectively implemented. For example, the 1976 transport policy that, among other things, established the Rima Transport Service and SUDA Bus Service was essentially to facilitate transport services in the state at a cheaper cost. The people really supported the policy as manifested in their patronage of the services. However, by 1980 both services were grounded. Similarly, the 1980 Marriage Law was supported by the people, as its aim was to simplify the conduct of marriage. Nevertheless, by 1982, it was apparent that the law had failed in spite of the support it had initially enjoyed. In the famous Oakland Project in California, Pressman and Wildavsky (1973, xii) observed:

> Some programs are aborted because political agreement can not be obtained. Others languish because funds cannot be secured. Still others die because the initial agreement of local officials or private concerns is not forthcoming. All these conditions were met in the EDA employment program in Oakland, but the program could not be implemented in time to secure the desired results.

Of course, policies need to be formulated in response to people's demands and interests. However, the expression of the demand and interest is not a sufficient condition for its satisfaction (or implementation). Besides, irrespective of whether a state is democratic or totalitarian,

> policies are the products of someone's perceptions of needs, even if those needs are determined merely by what is necessary to maintain control. Government is concerned with either doing things to, taking things from or providing things for society, or part of it (Hill 1979, 46).

Policies have been formulated and implemented over the objection of the people. The Nigerian government structural adjustment program, which involved the devaluation of Nigeria's currency and obtaining IMF loan, was openly rejected by the majority of Nigerians, but it was effectively implemented.

Secondly, the issue of ambiguity in policy formulation has been blown out of proportion. Ambiguity, which is manifested in the multiplicity of conflicting goals and lack of definite statement about the means of achieving policy goals, is the dominant feature of policy formulation (Sabatier 1986, 29). Most of the discussions on policy ambiguity are limited to policies formulated by the legislature. Policies formulated by the executive, with the active participation of the bureaucrats, tend to be less ambiguous during the implementation stage. The point is that ambiguity does not constitute a serious problem of implementation in Sokoto, for the simple reason that the bureaucracy has a mechanism for resolving it. This could further be appreciated in understanding the process of policy formulation in the state.

Simply put, policy is first initiated from either the top or bottom. If it comes from the bottom (from an assistant secretary or a professional officer, as the case may be), depending, of course, on his values and perception of a given problem, it proceeds along the organizational hierarchy, each adding his viewpoint to the initial submission until the matter reaches the top (the commissioner, as in the case of ministries or the chairman, where he is the chief executive, as in the boards]. In the final analysis, the original idea may be accepted with or without any modification at the ministerial level. At this point, other things being equal, the commissioner will ask the permanent secretary to convert the idea into a memorandum (after he had informed the chairman of the state executive council, who is the military governor) for the consideration of the state executive council. Copies of the memorandum will then be distributed to all the members of the executive council, the military governor, all the commissioners, including the commissioner of police and attorney general, the secretary to the military government (who participates in all its meetings), and all the permanent secretaries for their scrutiny before the council meeting.

At the executive council meeting, the memorandum may or may not be accepted, or accepted with some modification. At this point, with the approval of the executive council, the memorandum becomes a policy and it then goes back to the initiating ministry for implementation and, in doing so, other ministries would be involved.

On the other hand, if the policy initiation comes from the top (the commissioner), usually in a form of statement of intention to the permanent secretary, the latter passes the idea down the hierarchy for generation of further information on the idea. It is subsequently returned to the commissioner as a proposal for his consideration. If the commissioner is satisfied with the detailed analysis of the idea he initiated, then he gives the go-ahead for the production of memorandum for the consideration of the executive council. Policy formulation, particularly for provision of social services, is relatively free from what Grindle (1981, 62) termed "parochial pressures of interest groups ... or individual demands."

The point here is that whether the initiation of policy comes from the top or bottom, the bureaucrats define and design it in a way to make it implementable. Thus they provide the essential input for policy formulation and anticipate the problems that are likely to arise at the implementation stage. When it is said that policy is made by the politicians for implementation by the bureaucrats, it does not mean that the bureaucrats do not take active part in policy formulation. It simply means that, before a proposal becomes an actual policy, it needs top-level political approval. It is this approval that authorizes the bureaucracty to implement the policy and registers the commitment of the political level to the policy's success. Thereafter the political leaders accept the responsibility for the policy's success or failure.

From the analysis of the policy formulation process, it is clear that bureaucrats take active part in it. Similarly, before a policy is formulated, it is subjected to serious scrutiny, which invariably minimizes the possibility of ambiguity. Besides, since the initiation and the formulation of public policies are largely made by the bureaucrats, the issue of policy ambiguity does not constitute a problem at the implementation stage. Even where it arises for obscure reasons, it could easily be accommodated since ambiguity cannot lead to abandonment of policies and it cannot lead to unnecessary delays in policy implementation. Policies, whether ambiguously or clearly stated from the start, undergo some redefinition and modification in the process of implementation. Besides, clearly stated policies have no guarantee of successful implementation (Elmore 1979–80, 604). Many studies have shown that even the best conceived policies tend to encounter problems at the implementation stage (Bardach 1977, 5). Recounting the experience in the formulation of Nigeria's development plans, Anigboh (1985, 157) recalls "despite the meticulous care taken to prepare the ... Development Plans, they have failed to achieved their set objectives."

Where bureaucrats are actively involved in the policy formulation process, the tendency is that ambiguity would not constitute any serious problem, since professionally qualified officials working on the policy would have anticipated the main constraints. In this connection, Montjoy and O'Toole Jr. (1979, 434) concluded, "To the extent that an agency has been successful in writing its own mandate, we would expect little resistance or distortion during implementation." To this end, policy content, as presented in the argument, does not pose a serious threat to implementation process in Sokoto.

# Policy Context: The Enemy Without

Associated with the policy content is the policy context or environment in which administrative action is pursued. In other words, policy context is concerned with the political context of administrative action (Grindle 1980, 5). This view assumes that implementation is an ongoing process of decision-making involving a variety of actors who may be intensely or marginally involved in the process depending on the content of the policy and the form in which it is administered. It also assumes that each actor may have a particular interest in the policy that may be in direct conflict with the interest of other actors in the process and the outcome of this conflict. The question of who gets what will be consequently determined by the strategies, resources, and power position of the actors involved. Grindle (1980, 12) sums it up as follows:

> What is implemented may thus be the result of a political calculus of interests and groups competing for scarce resources, the response of implementing officials, and the actions of political elites, all interacting within a given institutional context.

Thus, in order to ensure effective implementation, the support of political elites must be acquired, the compliance of bureaucrats responsible for implementing policies and the intended beneficiaries should be sought, and the opposition of those who may be harmed or ignored by the policy must be redirected to avoid their subverting it. This undoubtedly involves much bargaining, compromise, and even conflict (Grindle 1980, 12).

There are, of course, in Sokoto State pressures, competitions, conflict, and bargaining among and from contractors and businessmen (they are an interest group and constitute a segment of actors in the implementation process), but which have no direct effect on the subject of implementation. Rather, the pressures are exacted on both the political and bureaucratic officials to influence their decision in the award of contracts for either construction or supply of materials that may be part of the implementation package. These businessmen and contractors are either related to, friends of, or fronts for the political leaders and bureaucrats who, in turn, would endeavor to see that their candidates get the contracts. To this extent, therefore, a large number of the actors involved in the competition and conflict are primarily concerned to satisfy their interests, such as gaining contracts for themselves (in the case of the contractors) by bribing their way, or gaining contracts for their relations, fronts, or friends (in the case of the political and bureaucratic officials). Beyond this, they do not necessarily facilitate or hinder the implementation process. For them, the issue is not the subject of implementation, as far as interest articulation is concerned, but the contractual package it contains.

To this extent, the basis of the assumption on the policy context is limited in that the interest groups, most of whom are businesspeople, rely greatly on government patronage. The norm of their interaction in the implementation process is of support rather than conflict and bargaining.

It is not surprising that the number of contractors in the state has increased substantially since 1976. They shuttle from one office to another, from one ministry to another, seeking contracts. In so doing, they corrupt some political leaders and career civil servants. It should be noted that major contracts involving about N50,000 are awarded by the State Tender Board, whose membership comprises a few commissioners and permanent secretaries.

Like the arguments on the bureaucratic structure and characteristics of the bureaucrats, the policy content and policy context arguments are limited. Thus, the whole conventional approach is inadequate in explaining implementation problems in Sokoto State.

However, another variable that comes under policy content and that can seriously cause implementation problem is the causal effect built into the policy. In other words, as indicated in Chapter Two, unless policy is based on adequate theoretical understanding of the problem it sets to solve, no matter what is done, implementation can hardly succeed. I have verified this argument in my study of the 1981 Sokoto State health policy in which I showed that the medical approach taken by the government to solve health problems of the rural areas, which was earlier termed "medicalization of health," was not based on adequate theoretical understanding of the problem, and hence contributed to its failure (Wali 1984).

It was argued that the patterns of disease in the state are infectious and malnutritious, both of which are deeply rooted in the socioeconomic conditions of the people and, hence, beyond the competence of the medical profession. For example, malaria and dysentery (both diseases are rooted in poverty, unsanitary living, and bad drinking water) accounted for 70 percent of reported incidence of diseases in the state. However, in order to solve the problem, the state administration "adopted a medical approach, which sees health as an outcome of medical care—both hospital care and primary health care" (Wali 1984, 67). Adopting this approach without even adequate medical personnel and financial resources to maintain regular supply of drugs to the medical institutions is inappropriate. "[S]tructural measures such as ensuring accessibility by the people to good nutrition, adequate and clean drinking water, education and good sanitary measure" would have largely solved the problems (Wali 1984, 67).

Thus, adequate policy causal effect is necessary for any successful policy. Yet it has been pointed out earlier that even the best conceived policies tend to have problems during implementation. And besides, most policies tend to meet this condition, for both policy makers and implementers are becoming increasingly sophisticated to appreciate this problem. As Elmore observes:

> A reasonably broad consensus has developed among analysts of social policy that the inability of government to deliver on its promises derives only in part from the fact that policies are poorly conceived. In some instances, policies are based on poor and incomplete understanding of the problems they are supposed to address. But in the largest number of cases it is impossible to say whether policies fail because they are based on bad ideas or because they are good ideas poorly executed (1978, 186–7).

# Toward an Alternative Explanation of Implementation Problems in Sokoto State

The central argument of this book is that implementation problems in Sokoto State are attributable to four interrelated variables, namely governmental instability (constant change of governments and officials), governmental overload (an enormous increase in the volume of the government's activities), socioeconomic problems of implementers and infrastructural inadequacies. These variables may stimulate one another. Some have argued, as examined in Chapter Three, that the problem of Nigeria's political instability is attributable to the socioeconomic problems of the country. On the other hand, some have contended that the continued socioeconomic problems of the country are largely due to the governmental instability. Overload could give government too many things to do so that it ends up doing little or nothing and so causes or perpetuates socioeconomic problems and governmental instability. The four variables, interacting at the same time, constitute the main implementation problems in the Sokoto State bureaucracy. The argument is further developed in Chapter Seven.

# Chapter Six
# Education Policy: The Context

The last chapter examined the factors helping or militating against the successful implementation of public policy. In following up the chapter's conclusions—other factors besides those frequently cited provide more plausible explanations for implementation successes and failures—the current chapter narrows down the argument to a review of the education policy formulated by the government of Sokoto State and implemented by the state civil service. The chapter begins by examining the backdrop to the enunciation of the policy, and particularly, the status of Western education in Nigeria and in Sokoto State. The chapter thus describes the context within which the education policy reviewed in this book ("Operation Move Ahead") was formulated.

## Western Education in Nigeria

Sokoto State, although the most peaceful in Nigeria (African Concord Magazine 1988, 2:3), is one of the most backward in terms of Western education. Some of the reasons for this are traceable to its delayed contact with Western education. Western education, it must be recalled, began in Nigeria during the colonial period but it did not expand rapidly to cover the entire country. As a matter of fact, up to 1945, the colonial government did not pay special attention to the education of Nigerians in spite of the repeated pronouncements between 1925 and 1935 for development of education by the colonial office's Advisory Committee on Native Education in Africa (Coleman

1958, 125). By 1939, only 12 percent of the Nigerian children of school age (350,000 out of 3,000,000) were receiving Western educational instruction. In 1918, education was allocated 1 percent of the total budget. It rose to 4.3 percent in 1939 (Coleman 1958, 126).

The first major attempt to transform colonial education was made in 1946, following the inauguration of a ten-year development plan for Nigeria. The education component of the plan focused on the extension of facilities for secondary and teacher training education (The Nigeria Handbook 1954, 115). Halfway through the plan period, the education expenditure rose in 1951–1952 to 16.9 percent as shown in Table 6.1. This phenomenal rise was attributable to, among other things, the regionalization of education in 1952 following the adoption of a federal constitution in 1951. By 1958, western and eastern regional governments were spending 50 percent of their budgets on education, while the northern regional government was spending 25 percent (Ogunsheye 1965, 128). The northern regional government could not compete with the western and eastern regional governments on allocation of resources to education, as there were more pressing problems to contend with in the North than in the South. In terms of land area, the North is more than half of the southern regions put together. It had more people to take care of than in the South. Besides, in spite of the annual grant-in-aid it received from the British treasury up to 1913, when it was finally stopped, and the local revenue it generated, the total northern regional government revenue and expenditure could not match those of its southern counterparts (which never received grant-in-aid to balance their budgets and which, up to 1913, had the monopoly of the custom duties—an important source of colonial revenue) (Carland 1985, 119). See Tables 6.2 and 6.3, respectively.

## Table 6.1
## Educational Expenditure in Nigeria: 1918–1952

| Year | Education | Total Expenditure | % of Total Expenditure |
|------|-----------|-------------------|------------------------|
|      | £         | £                 |                        |
| 1918 | 45,747 | 3,459,774 | 1 |
| 1923 | 100,063 | 6,509,244 | 1.5 |
| 1925 | 116,301 | 6,136,487 | 1.8 |
| 1929 | 263,457 | 6,045,621 | 4.3 |
| 1933 | 237,732 | 6,898,816 | 3.3 |
| 1936 | 231,983 | 6,585,458 | 3.5 |
| 1939 | 282,820 | 6,576,835 | 4.3 |
| 1951–1952 | 8,324,000 | 49,131,000 | 16.9 |

Source: Coleman, James S. 1958. *Nigeria: Background to Nationalism.* Berkeley: University of California, 126.

Thus, the limited allocation of resources to education by the northern regional government was partly due to financial reasons (Fafunwa 1974, 174).

## Table 6.2
## Northern Nigeria, Revenue and Expenditure: 1901–1913

| Year | Local Revenue | Grant-in-aid | Expenditure |
|------|---------------|--------------|-------------|
|      | £             | £            | £           |
| 1901–2 | 4,424 | 280,000 | 298,519 |
| 1902–3 | 16,316 | 290,000 | 389,391 |
| 1903–4 | 53,727 | 405,000 | 498,986 |
| 1904–5 | 94,026 | 405,500 | 520,546 |

| 1905–6 | 110,544 | 320,000 | 498,260 |
| 1906–7 | | 315,000 | |
| 1907–8 | 143,005 | 295,000 | 498,302 |
| 1908–9 | 178,444 | 290,000 | 540,644 |
| 1909–10 | 213,436 | 237,000 | 566,843 |
| 1910–11 | 274,989 | 275,000 | 565,760 |
| 1911–12 | 348,366 | | 827,939 |
| 1912–13 | | 156,000 | |

Source: Graham, Sonia F. 1966. *Government and Mission Education in Northern Nigeria 1900-1919*. Ibadan: University of Ibadan Press, 172; Carland, John M. 1985. *The Colonial Office and Nigeria, 1898-1914*. London: Macmillan, 119, 129–30.

## Table 6.3
## Southern Nigeria, Revenue and Expenditure: 1905–1913

| Year | Revenue | Expenditure |
|---|---|---|
| | £ | £ |
| 1905–6 | | 550,233 |
| 1906–7 | 1,088,717 | 1,056,290 |
| 1907–8 | 1,459,554 | 1,217,336 |
| 1908–9 | 1,387,975 | 1,357,763 |
| 1909–10 | 1,361,891 | 1,648,684 |
| 1910–11 | 1,933,235 | 1,592,282 |
| 1911–12 | 1,956,176 | 1,717,259 |
| 1912–13 | 2,235,412 | 2,110,498 |
| 1913 | 2,668,198 | 2,096,311 |

Source: Carland, John M. 1985. *The Colonial Office and Nigeria, 1898–1914*. London: Macmillan, 103, 114.

# Educational Disparity in Nigeria

The educational disparity between Northern and Southern Nigeria was evident in all respects, even before the launching of the ten-year plan. In terms of children's enrollment in government schools, while the North had a total enrollment of 527 out of a population of 9 million by the end of 1914, the South had 5,757 (Lugard 1970, 125). As for the overall enrollment in primary schools in both the government and mission schools by the end of 1913, the North had 1,131 while the South had 35,716 (Fafunwa 1974, 109). Similarly, during the same period, while the North had no single secondary school, the South had eleven, all but one being mission schools; only King's College was owned by the government (Fafunwa 1974, 109). The situation continued and, by 1934, the North, with a population of 11 million, had a school enrollment of only 10,000 compared to the South, which had 178,000 with a population of 9 million (Symonds 1966, 137). In 1943, only 1.7 percent of school-age children attended schools in Northern Nigeria, while 17.7 percent attended in Southern Nigeria. Similarly, during the same period, there were thirty-four secondary schools (thirty for boys and four for girls] with an enrollment of 8,110, but only one (which was for boys only) in the North (i.e., Katsina Teachers Training College) (Ogunsheye 1965, 127). It was founded in 1921 and remained the only full-fledged secondary school for the whole region for thirty-one years.

However, by 1947, there were five secondary schools in the North (only one was owned by the government while the rest were mission schools) with a total enrollment of 271, representing 2.5 percent of the total secondary school enrollment in the country. At the same time, there were eleven middle schools, all owned by the Native Authority (later to be called Local Authority or Local Government) with an enrollment of 1,855 boys and 74 girls, and 1,221 primary schools (owned by the government, Native Authority, mission and private) with an enrollment of 54,036 boys and 14,867 girls (Haily 1951, 41). Ten years later, in 1957, the secondary and primary school enrollments had risen to 6,197 and 186,297, respectively. By 1974, the figures for primary schools had reached 1,024,110 while those of secondary schools stood at 105,209, as shown in Table 6.4.

## Table 6.4
## Primary and Post-Primary Schools and Enrollment in
## Northern Nigeria 1947–1974

| | Primary Schools | | Post-Primary Schools | |
|---|---|---|---|---|
| Year | Schools | Enrollment | Schools | Enrollment |
| 1947 | 1,232 | 70,962 | 5 | 271 |
| 1948 | | 81,827 | | |
| 1949 | 1,383 | 95,598 | | |
| 1950 | 1,456 | 108,735 | | |
| 1951 | 1,535 | 107,561 | | |
| 1952 | 1,693 | 122,145 | | |
| 1953 | 1,777 | 143,809 | | |
| 1954 | | 154,000 | | 2,500 |
| 1955 | 1,824 | 168,500 | 60 | 5,213 |
| 1956 | 1,931 | 185,484 | 62 | 6,246 |
| 1957 | 2,080 | 205,769 | 83 | 7,069 |
| 1958 | 2,204 | 230,000 | 86 | 8,098 |
| 1959 | 2,340 | 250,912 | 97 | 9,246 |
| 1960 | 2,600 | 282,849 | 106 | 12,388 |
| 1961 | 2,584 | 316,264 | 107 | 13,556 |
| 1962 | 2,568 | 359,934 | 118 | 16,923 |
| 1963 | 2,625 | 410,706 | 126 | 20,312 |
| 1964 | 2,684 | 452,319 | 140 | 24,615 |
| 1965 | 2,743 | 492,829 | 144 | 28,061 |
| 1966 | 2,714 | 518,864 | 132 | 29,396 |

| 1967 | 2,733 | 506,818 | 158 | 32,222 |
|------|-------|---------|-----|--------|
| 1968 | 2,804 | 555,727 | 165 | 37,362 |
| 1969 | 3,001 | 601,104 | 191 | 44,061 |
| 1970 | 3,317 | 667,983 | 238 | 52,593 |
| 1971 | 3,758 | 767,473 | 270 | 64,564 |
| 1972 | 4,225 | 854,466 | 298 | 76,495 |
| 1973 | 4,410 | 925,308 | 318 | 89,112 |
| 1974 | 4,557 | 1,024,110 | 324 | 105,209 |

Sources: Coleman, James S. 1958. *Nigeria: Background to Nationalism*. Berkeley: University of California Press, 134; Nigeria Year Book 1959, 127; Annual Abstract of Statistics 1970, 1972; Kirk-Greene. 1966. *Government and Mission Education in Northern Nigeria 1900–1919*. Ibadan: University of Ibadan Press, xiii; Hailey 1951, 41; Ozigi and Ocho 1981, 32, 36, 52, 60, 66, 78, 133–5; Agu, Augustine O. 1986. *The Implementation of Universal Primary Education in Nigeria: Nation, States, and Schools*. Harvard University, 9; Social and Economic Progress in the Northern Region of Nigeria 1955, 38.

The increases in the number of schools and enrollment, as evidenced by Table 6.4, did not in any way challenge the southern lead in Western education, as shown in Table 6.5, where universal primary education was achieved since the late 1950s. This was still not achieved in the northern states twenty-eight years after the country's independence in 1960. Boorer (1985, 48) blames it all on the North's "conservatism":

[T]he North is more conservative, reactionary and has been less willing, in an historical context, to accept western education. Although the situation is now subject to substantial change, the education system in the North of Nigeria has lagged behind the development of Southern Nigeria, both in terms of quantity and quality.

## Table 6.5
## Primary and Post-Primary Schools and Enrollment in
## Southern Nigeria, 1947–1974

| | Primary Schools | | Post-Primary Schools | |
|---|---|---|---|---|
| Year | Schools | Enrollment | Schools | Enrollment |
| 1947 | 4,984 | 538,391 | 43 | 9,657 |
| 1955 | 10,866 | 1,489,675 | 277 | |
| 1956 | 11,768 | 1,722,038 | 521 | 155,237 |
| 1957 | 13,586 | 2,242,104 | 719 | 186,833 |
| 1965 | 12,234 | 2,419,913 | 1,305 | 193,379 |
| 1966 | 12,193 | 2,507,117 | 1,269 | 193,605 |
| 1969 | 6,981 | 1,433,914 | 430 | 109,544 |
| 1970 | 11,577 | 2,845,580 | 970 | 271,769 |
| 1971 | 11,566 | 3,120,714 | 997 | 291,801 |
| 1972 | 10,313 | 3,536,731 | 13,964 | 337,288 |
| 1973 | | 3,726,425 | | |

Sources: Annual Abstract of Statistics 1970, 149–50; Annual Abstract of Statistics 1972, 148; Annual Abstract of Statistics 1974, 151–2; Nigeria Year Book 1959, 127; Annual Report on Nigeria for the Year 1947, 47; Agu 1986, 10; Coleman, James S. 1958. *Nigeria: Background to Nationalism.* Berkeley: University of California Press, 134; Agu, Augustine O. 1986. *The Implementation of Universal Primary Education in Nigeria: Nation, States, and Schools.* Harvard University, 9–10.

The disparity is not limited to only primary and post-primary education. It is evident in university education, too. By the 1973–1974 academic session, out of the existing six universities in the country—namely Ahmadu Bello University Zaria (ABU), University of Benin, University of Ibadan (UI), University of Ife (now Obafemi Awolowo University), University of Lagos, and University of Nigeria Nsuka (UNN)—only one, ABU, was in the North. Out of the total university enrollment of 20,469, ABU had 5,880 students, representing 28.7 percent of the enrollment.

In 1975, seven new universities were established in the country, which brought the total number to thirteen. The new universities are Bayero University Kano, University of Calabar, University of Jos, University of Ilorin, University of Maiduguri, University of Port-Harcourt, and University of Sokoto. Out of the thirteen universities, six were situated in the North. Correspondingly, out of the total enrollment of 48,928 in 1978, northern universities had 14,287 students, which represented 29.2 percent of the national figure. Six years later the enrollment figure had more than doubled. In the 1984–1985 session, total enrollment in the federal universities stood at 104,032, out of which 37,950 students (representing 36.5 percent) were enrolled in the northern universities. It is necessary to emphasize the fact that the data do not provide adequate information on the number of students from the North and South who are studying in the southern and northern universities, respectively. All the same, it is common knowledge in Nigeria that there are more students from the South who study in the North than the other way around.

Anyway, by the end of 1988, there were twenty federal universities and seven state universities in Nigeria. Ten of the federal universities are located in the North while the seven state universities are all situated in the South. None of the northern states has a university of its own. All these have a bearing on the number of graduate output of the universities, as shown in Table 6.6.

# Reasons for the Educational Disparity

There are reasons for the educational disparity between the North and the South. The underlying factor is, in fact, history, not "northern conservatism." It should be noted that Western education started almost a century earlier in the South before coming to the North. It was first introduced by Christian missionaries around the coastal areas in 1516, but no significant impact was made until the 1840s when another batch of missionaries arrived and began some missionary work (building churches and schools) at Badagry and Abeokuta (Coleman 1958, 94). Specifically, it was in 1842 that the first primary school was built at Badagry by the Wesleyen Methodist Missionary Society; four years later, in 1845, the Church Missionary Society (CMS) also came to Badagry and opened a school and in 1846 opened another one at Abeokuta (The Nigeria Handbook 1954, 108). In that very year, the United Presbyterian Church of Scotland opened a school in Calabar and another one in 1847 at Bonny. It was not until in 1855 that two schools were opened in Lagos and Ogbomosho by the Southern Baptist Convention from the USA (Onabamiro 1983, 178–9). Since then the missionaries were in direct control of education until 1898 when the government began to participate in it. Even then, up to 1948, the missionaries controlled 99 percent of the schools and accounted for 97 percent of student enrollment, mostly in the South (Coleman 1958, 113). The government's first effort at providing Western education in the North was made in 1905 with the opening of a small school in Sokoto mainly to teach the children of the chiefs (Lugard 1970, 123). Four years later, in 1909, a primary school was opened at Nasarawa in Kano for education of children from the various provinces in the North. In 1913 two additional schools were built at Sokoto and Katsina provinces, and by the end of 1914, the number of the schools had risen to seven, together with two village schools at Birnin Kebbi and Badeggi with an average attendance of 507 (Lugard 1970, 124).

In contrast, during the same period, there were, in the South, 54 government schools (including King's College) with an enrollment of 5,757. This is apart from the mission and private schools whose enrollments were estimated at 41,343 (Lugard 1970, 123). This time gap is undoubtedly not easy to redress by any standard.

Second, unlike in the South, Western education, as a deliberate colonial policy, was initially not encouraged in the North, except in the non-Muslim areas of the Middle Belt. The colonial administration was anxious to retain the support of the traditional rulers and felt that preserving the cultural and religious values of the northern people was the best option (Haily 1951, 40). Lord Lugard, the first high commissioner of Northern Nigeria, had this to say on noninterference in religion (Orr 1911, 294):

There will be no interference with your religion nor with the position of the Sarkin Muslimi as the head of your religion. The English Government never interferes with religion; taxes, law and order, punishment of crime, these are matters for the Government, but not religion.

### Table 6.6
### Outputs of the Northern and Southern Universities:
### First Degree Graduates 1961/2 TO 1981/2

| Year | Northern | Southern | Total |
|------|----------|----------|-------|
| | | | |
| 1961–2 | 25 | 258 | 287 |
| 1962–3 | 55 | 415 | 470 |
| 1963–4 | 87 | 670 | 757 |
| 1964–5 | 112 | 866 | 978 |
| 1969–70 | 257 | 609 | 866 |
| 1971–2 | 454 | 1,530 | 1,984 |
| 1976–7 | 1,355 | 4,468 | 5,823 |
| 1977–8 | 1,973 | 5,787 | 7,760 |
| 1978–9 | 2,269 | 7,017 | 9,286 |
| 1979–80 | 2,673 | 6,964 | 9,637 |
| 1980–1 | 1,119 | 4,807 | 5,926 |
| 1981–2 | 3,333 | 5,318 | 8,651 |
| Source: Compiled from Statistics of Education in Nigeria, 1985. | | | |

However, the promise by Lord Lugard not to tamper with the Muslim religion was a ruse, especially since the fundamental policy of the colonial administration was to challenge the very basis of Islam by separating the religious from the secular. The colonial government did tamper with the people's religious values by limiting the authority of Muslim leaders to only religious affairs while it maintained the political and economic control of the people. It thus introduced secularism and put to an end centuries of Islamism in Northern Nigeria (Jalingo 1980, 351).

Lord Lugard initially prohibited Christian missionary activities in the Muslim areas of the North, but the decision was later reversed. From 1920, restriction on missionary activities began to be lifted, and by the 1930s they became fully established, consolidated, and spread in all important Muslim towns (Ozigi and Ocho 1981, 53). In Sokoto town, the Anglican Church became the first missionary church to be established (in 1923).The Anglicans also established the first mission school: St. Paul's Anglican Primary School. Even as early as 1903, the Church Missionary Society (CMS) was allowed to open a school in Nupe land of Niger Province, and in 1905 another mission school was opened at Zaria (Coleman 1958, 136).

It should be pointed out that the first mission school in the North was established by the CMS in 1865 at Lokoja, and it remained the only one up to the beginning of the twentieth century (Fafunwa 1974, 101). Anyway, by 1913, there were forty-three mission schools in the non-Muslim areas, and by the end of 1914 the number had risen to fifty-eight with a total enrollment of 1,682 (Lugard 1970, 124). The intention was to "establish a barrier against the further spread of Islam" (Graham 1966, 59). While there was only one mission school in the North in 1920 that received a government grant, by 1947 the number had reached 167 (Ozigi and Ocho 1981, 32). In 1933, about half of the total government expenditure on education went to the missions and other private agencies as grants (The Nigeria Handbook 1933, 180).

Others offer a different explanation for the limited spread of Western education in the North: Western education was slowed down in the North to cope with its radicalizing influence. Education was seen to be the main radical force in the South, and radicalism in the North would prove uncontrollable. Colonial education in the North, as they argued, was meant to serve a dual purpose: supporting and maintaining the ruling class by making them better rulers, on the one hand, and producing staff for the requirement of the Native Administration and lower cadre of the civil service, on the other.

Ogunsola shifts the blame on the colonial education administrators. He argues that the educational approach of the first director of education in the North, V. H. Vischer, was very irrelevant, for he insisted on the teaching of local crafts to the exclusion of modern machinery. This was at the time when the North was being exposed to modern means of transportation. The director of education failed to prepare Northern Nigerians for overseas examinations and diplomas knowing full well that the Northern Nigerian government would not employ any Nigerian who had not possessed those very overseas diplomas. To this end, Ogunsola submits:

> By denying the Northern Nigerians this type of education [referring to School Certificate type] and allowing Southerners with those same certificates to come to the North for employment, while they lived in segregated areas, was unfair to the Northerners who were made to look educationally inferior (Gulma 1983, 74).

It is not surprising, therefore,

> Sir Hugh Cliford, the Governor, affirmed in 1920 that the northern provinces had not produced a single native who was sufficiently educated to fill the lowest clerical post in the Government department (Egerton 1922, 266–7).

By 1951, with 54 percent of Nigeria's population, the North had only one university degree holder (Abdullahi 1977, 110). Ten years later, in January 1961, it had only one permanent secretary in the northern regional civil service (Kingsley 1963, 311).

Third, there was a resistance to Western education in the Muslim areas of Northern Nigeria (Nicolson 1969, 243). For instance, Major Burdon, who established the first government (small) school in the North, had problems trying to persuade the sultan and other important officials in the province to send their children to the school he had established in Sokoto in 1905 (Graham 1966, 59).

Throughout the first year of its existence, the school recorded an average attendance of only four pupils per session. The story was the same in all other Muslim areas. There were two reasons for this. First, Muslim parents were suspicious of the schools (Graham 1966, 29). They had found out that the mission schools were primarily concerned with converting people to Christianity (Fafunwa 1974, 71), as was manifested in the Christianization of the larger part of Southern Nigeria and the pagan areas (including the larger part of the Middle Belt) of Northern Nigeria. Thus, the northern parents were reluctant to send their children to Western-type schools. By 1920, there were about 800,000 Christian converts in Southern Nigeria and over 19,000 in the Middle Belt of Northern Nigeria, comprising large elements from Benue/Plateau province, as shown in Table 6.7. "The whole strategy of Christian missions in Africa," as Roome observes, "is viewed in relation to Islam" (Coleman 1958, 93). At the Lucknow World Missionary Conference held in 1910, it was resolved:

> We are strongly of opinion that concerted action among missionary boards and organizations is necessary, in order thoroughly to co-ordinate the forces now at work in Africa, and to regulate their distribution in such a manner as to provide a strong chain of mission stations across Africa, the strongest link of which shall be at those points where Moslem advance is most active (Coleman 1958, 93).

**Table 6.7**
**Number of Christian Converts in Northern and Southern Nigeria: 1900–1953**

| Region | Number of Christian Converts | | | Christian Converts as % of Total Population |
|---|---|---|---|---|
| | 1900–10 | 1920 | 1952–53 | |
| Western | 17,700 | 260,500 | xx | xx |
| Eastern | 18,500 | 514,395 | 3,915,500 | 50 |
| Northern | few | 19,200 | 558,000 | 3.3 |

Source: Coleman, James. S. 1958:95. *Nigeria: Background to Nationalism.* Berkeley: University of California Press.

Northern Nigeria, undoubtedly the most highly Islamized area in tropical Africa, was, and still is, the target of Christian penetration (Coleman 1958, 93). It was not by coincidence that by 1925 there were sixty-two Christian missions in the North (whose contact with Christianity was recent) compared to the sixty-two and fifty-two missions in the western and eastern regions, respectively, both of which had been in contact with Christianity for centuries (Coleman 1958, 95). The Christian missions in the North were so preoccupied with strategies for converting Northern Nigerians to Christianity that they "created for a long time among the people a dislike for western type schools in general and Christian schools in particular (Fafunwa 1974, 105).

Of greatest significance is the fact that Muslims had a well-developed system of Islamic education, even centuries before the advent of colonialism (Ozigi and Ocho 1981, 1–13). There were, in 1903, 25,000 estimated Islamic schools in the North with 250,000 pupils (Lugard 1970, 123). By 1947, the estimated figure had risen to 400,000 (Haily 1951, 41). In comparison, the absence of resistance to Western education in the South was "because they had no other developed system of education" (Lugard 1970, 123).

Thus the importance of education, whether Western or Eastern, is not new to the Muslims of the North. Their religion, Islam, has made it compulsory to every male and female to seek knowledge, wherever it may be and from whoever possesses it. Education is essentially a religious matter for Muslims (Graham 1966, 66). But what they resisted was the use of education as a means of converting people to Christianity. As aptly noted by Graham (1966, 29), " the missionaries were evangelists first and educationists second."

To this extent, Fafunwa (1974, 71–2) concludes:

Muslim education in Nigeria was retarded not because the muslims were unprogressive or because their religion was opposed to formal education but because "education" in those days tended to mean Bible knowledge, Christian ethics, Christian moral instruction, Christian literature, some arithmetic, language and crafts—all geared to produce Christians who could read the Bible.

The assumption that "Islam has played a significant role in slowing down the growth of the western education provision in the Northern states" (Bunza 1984, 141; Boorer 1985, 2; Agu 1986, 113) can therefore not be substantiated. Rather, it was the Christianization of education that played a dominant role in the initial slowing down of educational development in the Muslim North. It is clear that with the apparent separation of Christianity from education, concerted efforts were made by both Muslim parents and the northern regional government in sending children to Western-type schools, even though the approach and character of the education system was not rooted in an Islamic educational system. For example, in Sokoto, the Province Educational Development Fund (SPEDF) was established essentially to raise funds, through donations and levies on people of the province, to enlighten the public about the importance of Western education, and to build post-primary institutions (Gulma 1983, 18).

All these not withstanding, the uneven educational development between the North and the South continued until today. Highlighting this disparity at a meeting of the National Council on Education in 1974, the then Federal Commissioner for Education, Chief Abdul Eke, had this to say:

> So wide is the gap that, roughly speaking, for every child in a primary school in the northern states there are four in the southern states; for every boy or girl in a secondary school in the north there are five in the south. And for every student in a post-secondary institution in the north there are six in the south. (West Africa Magazine 1974, NO 2962, 326).

The extent of this gap is shown in Table 6.8.

Yet, within the northern states (Bauchi, Benue, Borno, Gongola, Kaduna, Kano, Katsina, Kwara, Niger, Plateau, and Sokoto) there are significant differences, as shown in Table 6.8. The differences, however, are attributable to the varying level of Christian missionary influence. Generally, Kwara, Plateau, and Benue states are educationally more advanced than the rest. Of the remaining, Sokoto State seems to be one of the backward, if not the most backward (Bunza 1984; Gulma 1983; West Africa Magazine 1974, NO 2962, 326).

Although Table 6.8 shows that absolute enrollment figures in Sokoto State in 1981 were higher than in Bauchi, Borno, Gongola, Niger, and Plateau, that was not withstanding, taking into account that Sokoto is bigger than any of the other states in terms of its size and population. It is the second most populous state in the North after Kano, and the third in the whole country. This is based on the National Population Bureau estimate of 1978 presented in Table 6.9.

## Table 6.8
## Post-Primary Schools and Enrollment in Nigeria, 1976–1983

### Southern States

| States | 1975–76 | | 1976–77 | | 1977–78 | | 1978–79 | | 1979–80 | |
|---|---|---|---|---|---|---|---|---|---|---|
| | Sch | Enroll | Sch | Enroll | Sch | Enroll | Sch | Enroll | Sch | Enroll |
| Anambra | 109 | 70928 | 147 | 89201 | 202 | 108003 | 270 | 148933 | 398 | 164714 |
| Bendel | 167 | 93463 | 165 | 103510 | 190 | 121715 | 210 | 140137 | 291 | 214311 |
| Cross River | 113 | 52585 | 121 | 66586 | 159 | 81297 | 207 | 105393 | 2555 | 133394 |
| Imo | 157 | 94935 | 174 | 121331 | 244 | 169101 | 297 | 227844 | 377 | 260044 |
| Lagos | 121 | 65214 | 102 | 80093 | 107 | 88711 | 88 | 95221 | 133 | 160637 |
| Ogun | 108 | 48006 | 109 | 51488 | 155 | 55555 | 127 | 58641 | 163 | 79876 |
| Ondo | 245 | 77084 | 273 | 85444 | 276 | 90596 | 267 | 95200 | 267 | 149785 |
| Oyo | 281 | 119937 | 317 | 135446 | 311 | 156652 | 349 | 176763 | 394 | 216739 |
| Rivers | 70 | 39510 | 80 | 40690 | 106 | 60100 | 114 | 62146 | 116 | 87614 |

**Northern States**

| States | 1975–76 | | 1976–77 | | 1977–78 | | 1978–79 | | 1979–80 | |
|---|---|---|---|---|---|---|---|---|---|---|
| | Sch | Enroll | Sch | Enroll | Sch | Enroll | Sch | Enroll | Sch | Enroll |
| Bauchi | 27 | 11303 | 18 | 11134 | 23 | 12131 | 34 | 15811 | 56 | 21677 |
| Benue | 66 | 20012 | 82 | 31300 | 88 | 43562 | 171 | 61219 | 196 | 63055 |
| Borno | 25 | 11686 | 25 | 13138 | 32 | 15124 | 33 | 17709 | 69 | 25000 |
| Gongola | 30 | 13189 | 35 | 14082 | 40 | 15860 | 47 | 25294 | 56 | 31197 |

**Northern States**

| States | 1975–76 | | 1976–77 | | 1977–78 | | 1978–79 | | 1979–80 | |
|---|---|---|---|---|---|---|---|---|---|---|
| | Sch | Enroll | Sch | Enroll | Sch | Enroll | Sch | Enroll | Sch | Enroll |
| Kaduna | 45 | 27308 | 48 | 34447 | 55 | 47238 | 63 | 53948 | 89 | 53368 |
| Kano | 44 | 15926 | 47 | 22714 | 55 | 29959 | 55 | 34551 | 58 | 38282 |
| Kwara | 83 | 33255 | 91 | 39021 | 93 | 47596 | 88 | 59083 | 118 | 73496 |
| Niger | 27 | 10777 | 28 | 12268 | 31 | 14638 | 31 | 16071 | 41 | 22110 |
| Plateau | 52 | 17576 | 56 | 20917 | 62 | 26630 | 64 | 33753 | 91 | 41671 |
| Sokoto | 48 | 16097 | 47 | 18902 | 47 | 23962 | 52 | 29260 | 83 | 45458 |

**Southern States**

| States | 1980–81 | | 1981–82 | | 1982–83 | | 1983–84 | |
|---|---|---|---|---|---|---|---|---|
| | Sch | Enroll | Sch | Enroll | Sch | Enroll | Sch | Enroll |
| Anambra | 507 | 173122 | 631 | 207002 | 447 | 201490 | 461 | 200188 |
| Bendel | 651 | 285486 | 713 | 387572 | 719 | 410277 | 724 | 426477 |
| Cross River | 306 | 193568 | 307 | 171808 | 324 | 189712 | 361 | 182094 |
| Imo | 431 | 299271 | 465 | 314836 | 467 | 294884 | 468 | 284191 |
| Lagos | | | | | | | | |
| Ogun | 333 | 119372 | 349 | 147172 | 351 | 171598 | 351 | 191826 |
| Ondo | 495 | 192167 | 517 | 271192 | 523 | 317672 | 502 | 312400 |
| Oyo | 650 | 257192 | 747 | 387276 | 806 | 573504 | 776 | 590017 |
| Rivers | 161 | 84751 | 258 | 100639 | 244 | | 267 | 99220 |

## Northern States

| States | 1980-81 | | 1981-82 | | 1982-83 | | 1983-84 | |
|---|---|---|---|---|---|---|---|---|
| | Sch | Enroll | Sch | Enroll | Sch | Enroll | Sch | Enroll |
| Bauchi | 75 | 29206 | 80 | 41490 | 80 | 57757 | 81 | 32232 |
| Benue | 318 | 61711 | 296 | 90169 | | | 295 | |
| Borno | 75 | 51564 | 87 | 68013 | | | 106 | |
| Gongola | 89 | 43495 | 107 | 60624 | 150 | 72405 | 150 | 100095 |
| Kaduna | 103 | 75896 | 105 | 84040 | 169 | 132259 | 169 | 183158 |
| Kano | 77 | 57489 | 82 | 60090 | 229 | 91437 | 233 | 101112 |
| Kwara | 204 | 103659 | 306 | 112343 | 347 | 134441 | 362 | |
| Niger | 47 | 29889 | 61 | 32779 | 148 | 59802 | 63 | 80481 |
| Plateau | 105 | 52335 | 142 | 66160 | 219 | 92486 | 222 | 96920 |
| Sokoto | 96 | 65075 | 124 | 79770 | 229 | 79716 | 178 | 110215 |

Sources: Bunza, Mustapha M. 1984. *Growth and Development of Higher Education in Sokoto and Niger States of Nigeria*. University of Wales; Gulma, A. Abubakar. 1983. *The Growth and Development of Grade II Teachers' Colleges in the Sokoto State of Nigeria, 1970–1980*. University of Wales; West Africa 1974, No. 2962, 326.

# Effects of the Educational
# Backwardness in Sokoto State

Presently, Sokoto State lacks sufficient indigenous manpower in the fields of medicine, science, and engineering to run its institutions effectively. To this end, it recruits skilled manpower within and outside Nigeria to work as teachers in schools, as doctors in hospitals, and as engineers in construction and allied organizations. Out of the total recruitment made between 1979 and 1984, 12 percent and 35 percent were other Nigerians and expatriate officers, respectively (Economic Planning Department, Sokoto 1985, 9). By the end of 1984, out of the total ministerial staff strength of 16,932, the state had on its staff 1,165 Nigerians from other states, particularly southern states that have qualified manpower in the relevant fields. In addition, 1,242 expatriate staff were recruited mostly from Britain, Canada, India, Pakistan, Philippines, Egypt, Sudan, Ghana, and Srilanka. See Table 6.10.

That apart, the state, like other states in the North, was, until recently, not well represented in the country's federal public service. This is in spite of the fact that the constitution dictates that appointments to the federal public service should be made in such a way as to ensure that all component parts of the nation are accommodated, thereby refelecting the federal character of the country. In other words, all the constituent parts of the country should be represented in the federal public seervice. The constitution specifically stipulates that:

The composition of the Government of the federation or any of its agencies and the conduct of its affairs shall be carried out in such manner as to reflect the federal character of Nigeria and the need to promote national unity, and also to command national loyalty thereby ensuring that there shall be no predominance of persons from a few states or from a few ethnic or other sectional groups in that government or in any of its agencies (Constitution of the Federal Republic of Nigeria 1999, 16).

Out of the total number of 255,881 civil servants in the federal public service at the end of 1987 (Office of the Head of Service of the Federation 1988), only eighty-four who are residents in the federal capital are from Sokoto State.

### Table 6.9
### Estimated Population of Nigeria's Nineteen States, 1978

| Regions | States | States | Estimated Size of Nigera, Percentage | Estimated Population Percentage |
|---------|--------|--------|------------------|------------------|
| 1963 | 1967 | 1976 | | |
| Northern Region | North-Western | Sokoto | 11.7 | 6.5 |
| | | Niger | 7.1 | 1.6 |
| | North-Eastern | Borno | 11.7 | 4.3 |
| | | Bauchi | 7.2 | 3.5 |
| | | Gongola | 10.5 | 3.8 |
| | North-Central | Kaduna | 7.7 | 6.0 |
| | Benue-Plateau | Benue | 5.2 | 3.5 |
| | | Plateau | 5.9 | 3.0 |
| | West-Central | Kwara | 6.7 | 2.5 |
| | Kano | Kano | 4.7 | 8.3 |
| Eastern Region | East-Central | Anambra | 1.9 | 5.1 |
| | | Imo | 1.3 | 5.3 |
| | South-Eastern | Cross River | 3.9 | 5.0 |
| | Rivers | Rivers | 2.0 | 2.4 |
| Western Region | Western | Oyo | 4.0 | 7.5 |
| | | Ogon | 1.9 | 2.2 |
| | | Ondo | 2.2 | 4.0 |

| Mid-West Region | Mid-Western | Bendel | 4.1 | 3.6 |
|---|---|---|---|---|
| | | | | |
| Federal Capital Territory | Lagos | Lagos | 0.4 | 2.3 |

Source: Panter-Brick, K. (ed). 1978. *Soldiers and Oil: The Political Transformation of Nigeria.* London: Frank Cass, 358; Kirk-Greene, A. H. M. and Rimmer, Douglas. 1981. *Nigeria since 1970: A Political and Economic Outline.* London: Hodder & Stoughton, 10.

**Table 6.10**
**Expatriates and Other Nigerians on the Service of Sokoto State Government, 1980–1984**

| Year | Sokoto Indigenes | Other Nigerians | Expatriates | Total |
|---|---|---|---|---|
| | | | | |
| 1980 | 12,475 | 819 | 1,078 | 14,372 |
| 1981 | 14,077 | 918 | 1,107 | 16,102 |
| 1982 | 18,076 | 1,217 | 1,582 | 20,875 |
| 1983 | 20,236 | 1,071 | 1,917 | 23,224 |
| 1984 | 14,524 | 1,165 | 1,242 | 16,932 |
| Source: Economic Planning Department, Sokoto 1985, 52. | | | | |

Besides, one hardly finds indigenes of Sokoto State working in the government institutions of other states. As a matter of fact, there is no single, professional indigene of Sokoto State working in the public service of any of the southern states. This is because, as mentioned earlier, the southern states are not in short supply of manpower.

The whole phenomenon is attributable to, among other things, the age-long disparity in Western education between the northern and southern states on the one hand, and the proximity of the southern states to the seat of the federal government on the other. Up to 1920, not a single northerner was employed as a clerk by the Nigerian government because education in the North, at that time, was practically the exclusive preserve of the ruling class. The children of the ruling class were given just sufficient education to prepare them for positions in the Native Administration (Symonds 1966, 137). Even by 1955, as indicated in an earlier chapter, the North, with 55 percent of the country's population, accounted for only 1 percent of the entire federal civil service.

Similarly, apart from the University of Sokoto, the state does not fill its quota in other federal universities and polytechnics, including the Kaura-Namoda Polytechnic, which is sited in the state. Furthermore, the state does not fill its quota even in the institutions to which it pays subventions (Institute of Administration of Ahmadu Bello University and Zaria and Kaduna Polytechnic) for provision of additional opportunity to its indigenes. The state government had given grants of N700,000, N700,000, N350,000, N600,000, and N800,000 to Kaduna Polytechnic in 1977–1978, 1978–1979, 1979–1980, 1981, and 1983, respectively. This phenomenon is attributable to the following reasons: First, many of those who are qualified for university admission or admission into polytechnics or colleges of education prefer to go to the University of Sokoto, Sokoto Polytechnic, or Sokoto College of Education due to their limited financial resources. Going to other institutions that are far away from Sokoto may only add to their hardship in view of high transport and living expenses. Besides, by being far away, individuals from poor backgrounds who need financial assistance most may find it hard to obtain it at the opportune time.

**Table 6.11**
**Number of Sponsored Students to Universities, Polytechnics, and Other Institutions of Learning by the Sokoto State Scholarship Board, 1985/6–1987/88**

| Institutions | 1985–1986 | 1986–1987 | 1987–1988 |
|--------------|-----------|-----------|-----------|
|              |           |           |           |
| ABU          | 371       | 372       | 311       |
| BUK          | 58        | 73        | 65        |

| UNISOK | 1,221 | 1,330 | 1,244 |
|---|---|---|---|
| SCASS | 225 | 189 | 129 |
| FSASS | -- | 29 | 37 |
| SOK POL | 435 | 422 | 476 |
| KAD POL | 249 | 468 | 501 |
| FED POL KAURA | 35 | 55 | 56 |
| COL OF ADMIN | 59 | 39 | 27 |
| COL OF AGRIC ZURU | -- | 192 | 309 |
| OVERSEAS | 61 | 57 | 49 |
| OTHERS | 171 | 75 | 88 |
| TOTAL | 2,885.00 | 3,301.00 | 3,292.00 |

KEY: ABU = Ahmadu Bello University, Zaria; BUK = Bayero University, Kano; UNISOK = University of Sokoto; SCASS = State College of Arts and Science, Sokoto; FSASS = Federal School of Arts and Science, Sokoto; SOK POL = Sokoto Polytechnic, Birnin Kebbi; KAD POL = Kaduna Polytechnic, Kaduna; FED POL KAURA = Federal Polytechnic, Kaura-Namoda; COL OF ADMIN = College of Administration, Zuru; COL OF AGRIC ZURU = College of Agriculture, Zuru.

However, it should be pointed out that the state government, through its scholarship board, provides scholarships to any state indigene who gains admission to any higher institution of learning in the country. Yet the late payment of the award hinders its effective utilization. In some cases, some students get their awards at the end of the academic year. This undoubtedly makes it difficult for students from poor backgrounds to pursue their educational dream or, when at school, to concentrate on their studies. There were cases where students had to turn down their admission into educational institutions because they could not pay their registration fees. It is, therefore, the children, brothers, and sisters of well-to-do bureaucrats who make effective utilization of scholarship awards, particularly from 1981 to date.

This is because, for one, they are supported by their parents or relations before payment of their awards are made and, for another, they are more qualified for university admission due to their advantaged positions. Students from privileged families enroll at good secondary schools, notably the federal government colleges located in all the states of the federation (two are sited in Sokoto State) and the urban secondary schools in the state (Committee Report on Infrastructure in Sokoto State 1986, 10), notably Sokoto, Gusau, Birnin Kebbi, Argungu, Yauri, and Zuru. Nevertheless, it should be pointed out that the State Scholarship Board does not discriminate in the award of scholarships to the state indigenes.

As a matter of fact, there were some years in which the board could not exhaust its allocation of the awards. In 1976–1977, the board budgeted N700,000 for scholarships and in the following year it was increased to N1.700 million, but could only spend N1.2 million in that year. There have been increases since then till today, as shown in Table 6.12. In the 1986–1987 academic year, the board sponsored 3,301 students to various institutions of higher learning within and outside Nigeria at the cost of N3.500 million. It proposed to spend N6.420 million in the 1988–1989 session (1988 Recurrent and Capital Estimate of the Government of Sokoto State of Nigeria). In short, there are more financial allocations to scholarship awards than there are qualified applicants to avail themselves of the benefit.

Potential undergraduates and diploma and A-level students usually obtained admissions between August and September. Still others had to wait till late admissions in November, while the academic year, in most of the higher institutions, was scheduled to begin between September and October. Yet, the disbursement of the awards by the scholarship board most frequently started in March, causing an interval of five months. That had been the practice from 1982 until recent years.

**Table 6.12**
**Estimates and Expenditures by the Sokoto State Scholarship Board, 1976–1988**

| Year | Estimates | Expenditure |
|------|-----------|-------------|
|      | N         | N           |
|      |           |             |
| 1976–7 | 700,000 |  |
| 1977–8 | 1,700,000 | 1,275,000 |
| 1978–9 | 2,000,000 | 2,000,000 |
| 1979–80 | 1,700,000 | 1,700,000 |
| 1980–1 | 1,300,000 | -- |
| 1981–2 | 4,500,000 | 4,500,000 |
| 1982–3 | 4,000,000 | 4,000,000 |
| 1983–4 | 4,750,000 | 3,450,800 |
| 1984–5 | 2,700,000 | 2,700,000 |
| 1985–6 | 3,000,000 | 3,000,000 |
| 1986–7 | 4,700,000 | 3,500,000 |
| 1987–8 | 3,500,000 | 4,200,000 |
| 1988–9 | 6,420,000 | -- |

Source: Computed from the Sokoto State Government Budget Estimates: 1976–88 and file records of Sokoto State Scholarship Board.

Before 1982, there was no problem of late disbursement of award. The scholarship board had agreements with some higher institutions of learning, which most of the potential candidates from Sokoto State preferred (notably Ahmadu Bello University, Zaria, Bayero University, Kano, University of Sokoto, University of Maiduguri, and Kaduna Polytechnic) for loaning feeding allowances to its sponsored students as soon as they arrived in their institutions.

## Table 6.13
## Number of Students Sponsored by the Sokoto State
## Scholarship Board 1976/77–1987/88, and Number of Awards

| Year | Male | Female | Total |
|------|------|--------|-------|
|      |      |        |       |
| 1976–7 | 374 | 55 | 429 |
| 1977–8 | 624 | 93 | 717 |
| 1978–9 | 813 | 180 | 993 |
| 1979–80 | 1,114 | 222 | 1,336 |
| 1980–1 | 1,128 | 740 | 1,868 |
| 1981–2 | 2,505 | 432 | 2,937 |
| 1982–3 | 2,676 | 464 | 3,140 |
| 1983–4 | 2,700 | 603 | 3,303 |
| 1984–5 | 2,628 | 582 | 3,210 |
| 1985–6 | 2,429 | 456 | 2,885 |
| 1986–7 | 2,813 | 488 | 3,301 |
| 1987–8 | 2,833 | 459 | 3,292 |

Later the scholarship board would repay the loans on behalf of its sponsored students to the institutions and pay the remaining maintenance allowances directly to the students, mostly in December. Although the students were not given their scholarship allowances in time, they still felt relatively contented since they were given feeding allowances on time. However, the arrangement was interrupted by the institutions in 1981 for some reasons. First, the institutions were facing financial problems following their enormous expansion in the face of limited financial grants from the federal government. Second, some state governments were not honoring their obligations to the institutions. Their students were given loans by the institutions, but the states were not making reimbursements as and when due. To this end, the higher institutions found it impossible to continue with the loan agreement. In the circumstance, students went to the higher institutions without any transport, feeding, or any allowance from the scholarship board until after a long process of interviews.

Before scholarships were awarded, potential candidates had to apply and be interviewed by the board of the scholarship. Applications for scholarships were submitted from August (when admission letters were being released) until December, and at times beyond that. Since admission offers were not made at the same time by all the institutions, and since there were late admissions, the scholarship board found it appropriate to start interviewing the candidates from January, when it was assumed that most admissions would have been released and therefore most scholarship applications would have been submitted.

The main purpose of the interview was to certify that all the applicants were indigenes of the state. Every state had its own provision to cater for the educational needs of its indigenes. However, educational priorities differed from one state to another. While some states offered scholarships to their indigenes (all the northern states), others did not (the southern states). Still there were variations, even among the northern states. Whereas the award of scholarship was very competitive in some northern states (notably Kwara, Plateau, and Kaduna), it was not in others, particularly in Sokoto. Since scholarships were not awarded in some states, and where it was awarded it was subject to keen competition, some potential candidates from the "hard" states tended to impersonate or pretend they were indigenes of the "soft" states (like Sokoto) by faking their birth certificates and other relevant data. This was all in an attempt at obtaining the Sokoto State scholarships. To this extent, in order to prevent cases of impersonation on the one hand, and to check corruption among the officials of the scholarship board on the other, thorough interviews were conducted by the members of the board before scholarships were awarded. Yet the problem was not just getting the award (since it was automatic once one got admitted). The problem was getting the money on time. This was a major concern among students from poor backgrounds. It was this late payment of the scholarship award that was making it difficult for the awards to be effectively utilized. This also affected the degree to which the state utilized its quota in the higher institutions. It is not surprising, therefore, that candidates from poor backgrounds preferred to go to colleges of education where, financially, they were sure of getting their allowances on a timely basis, but had to wait up to six years before they got a degree, while their counterparts who went straight to university obtained their degrees within four years.

Second, apart from the problem of scholarship disbursement, there is the general perennial problem of poor performance in the state colleges and secondary schools, as shown in Tables 6.14 and 6.15.

**Table 6.14**
**Examination Results—GCE "O" Level: Secondary Schools in Sokoto**

| Year | Candidates | Number of Passes | Percentage of Passes |
|------|-----------|------------------|---------------------|
|      |           |                  |                     |
| 1979 | 1,454 | 285 | 19.05 |
| 1980 | 2,113 | 675 | 31.95 |
| 1981 | 1,903 | 240 | 12.61 |
| 1983 | 3,387 | 393 | 11.60 |
| Source: Ministry of Education, Sokoto. | | | |

**Table 6.15**
**Examination Results—Teachers Grade II: Teachers Colleges**
**in Sokoto**

| Year | Candidates | External subjects | Number of Passes | Percentage |
|------|-----------|-------------------|------------------|------------|
| 1982 | 5,283 | English | 1,402 | 26.5 |
|      | 4,820 | Arithmetic | 2,146 | 44.5 |
|      | 5,437 | Education | 963 | 17.7 |
| 1983 | 6,601 | English | 4,348 | 65.9 |
|      | 5,778 | Arithmetic | 4,172 | 72.2 |
|      | 6,673 | Education | 1,943 | 29.1 |
| 1984 | 6,571 | English | 2,525 | 38.4 |
|      | 6,083 | Arithmetic | 1,562 | 25.7 |
|      | 7,326 | Education | 1,904 | 26.0 |
| Source: Ministry of Education, Sokoto | | | | |

This makes it hard for the state to fill its quota in the federal higher institutions of learning and invariably in the federal civil service. Without good results from secondary schools, university admission is impossible; and without relevant university qualifications, opportunity for employment in the federal service is limited.

Based on the realization of this situation, the state government established in 1976 the State College of Art and Science (SCAS). The aim was to provide A-level and remedial courses for ambitious students who were unsuccessful in their secondary school final examinations. Attendance at the college would enable them to make up for their previous failures and prepare them for entry into universities or any other higher institution of learning (Sokoto State Government Budget Estimates 1976–77, 6).

Apart from SCAS, other higher institutions (there are nine post-secondary institutions, including two by the federal government), such as Sokoto Polytechnic, College of Education, Sokoto, Kaduna Polytechnic, Federal School of Arts and Science, Sokoto, and Federal Polytechnic, Kaura Namoda, provide, in addition to their regular courses, remedial and introductory courses basically to prepare students for further education. In 1986, the rector of the Federal Polytechnic, Kaura, Alhaji Ja'afar Ango, reported in an address that about 63 percent of Sokoto State students in his institution, the highest in the country, were studying introductory courses (The New Nigeria Tuesday 25 February 1986, 9). That, indisputably, was a critical situation. Similarly, universities in the northern part of Nigeria, namely University of Sokoto, Ahmadu Bello University, Zaria, Bayero University, Kano, University of Maiduguri, University of Jos, University of Ilorin, University of Technology, Bauchi, and University of Technology, Yola, provide one to two years of preliminary courses for direct absorption to a three-year degree course.

All these remedial courses are unnecessary if secondary school performances are good. The poor performance in secondary schools has been attributed to a number of factors. Some observers maintain that the problem of poor results in the post-primary institutions in the state is due mainly to the bad conditions in the primary schools. They argue that children with a bad educational background from primary schools could hardly perform well in secondary schools. It is common knowledge in the state that a large number of pupils in their final year in primary schools, particularly in the rural areas, could neither read nor write simple sentences, even in the native language: Hausa (Committee Report on Infrastructure in Sokoto State 1986, 8). This is also true in other parts of Nigeria, as observed by several writers. In particular, Junaidu (1987, 106–7) noted:

In Nigeria, for instance, even before the expansion of education in the 1970s, cognitive achievements were so poor that some pupils left the primary vii grade without becoming functionally literate.

Under this situation it is difficult or impossible to expect such pupils to do well, if, as usually happened, they found themselves in secondary schools. Thus, in order to cope with the problem, the conditions at the grass roots (primary schools) should be improved.

There were in 1976, when Sokoto State was created, 732 primary schools with a total enrollment of 136,977. Within the 1976–1977 academic session, the number of schools had risen to 1,771 and enrollment to 206,177. Nine years later, in 1984–1985, the figures had risen to 2,552 and 717,744, respectively, as shown in Table 6.16. Despite the increase in the enrollment it was still below 55 percent of the school-age children, and below the national average—78 percent (Directorate of Budget Sokoto 1987, 3). That apart, enrollment in some schools in the rural areas are below 40 percent capacity while some schools in Sokoto town have oversized classes with over fifty children in a class handled by a single teacher (Committee Report on Infrastructure in Sokoto State 1986, 8).

# Focus of Education

As the problems of education change across different historical epochs, so also does the immediate focus of education. In the early colonial period, education was meant to produce clerks and artisans to serve in low-level colonial jobs. From 1946 when the colonial government launched a ten-year development plan for Nigeria up to independence, the aim was to prepare the people to take over the control of their country. At independence, the intention was to provide universal education. At the regional level it became a matter of competition between the western and eastern regions, while the northern region was trying to catch up with the two regions. In 1976, the most ambitious education attempt in Nigeria was made at the federal level—to provide Universal Primary Education (UPE) throughout the country. By the end of the 1970s serious emphasis was placed on a shift from the arts, humanities, and social sciences to natural sciences and technical education. The intention was to prepare the country for the challenges of technology and place the country among the technologically developed. This shift is apparent in the subjects being studied by the Sokoto State-sponsored students, as shown in Table 6.17.

**Table 6.16**
**Primary Schools, Enrollment, and School-Age Population (6–11) in Sokoto State, 1976–1986**

| Year | Primary School-Age Population (6–11) | Schools | Enrollment | Enrollment Ratio % |
|------|------|------|------|------|
| | | | | |
| 1976–77 | | 1,771 | 206,177 | |
| 1977–78 | | 2,692 | 301,542 | |
| 1978–79 | | 3,167 | 397,401 | |
| 1979–80 | | 3,865 | 446,185 | |
| 1980–81 | 1,225,494 | 3,867 | 564,129 | 46 |
| 1981–82 | 1,256,520 | 3,939 | 644,657 | 51 |
| 1982–83 | 1,288,328 | 4,038 | 684,030 | 53 |
| 1983–84 | 1,320,938 | 4,038 | 705,777 | 53 |
| 1984–85 | | 2,509 | 717,744 | |

Source: Ministry of Education, Sokoto; Statistics of Education in Nigeria 1980–84, 1985.

**Table 6.17**
**Sokoto State-Sponsored Students: Course of Study**

| | 1985–1986 | 1986–1987 | 1987–1988 | Total |
|------|------|------|------|------|
| Arts | 6091 | 1881 | 315 | 3,112 |
| Sciences | 1,0711 | 4411 | 675 | 4,187 |
| Social Science | 1,205 | 672 | 302 | 2,179 |
| Total | 2,885 | 3,301 | 3,292 | |

The focus of education in Sokoto today is to catch up first with the rest of the northern states and then southern states. The strategy to adopt in pursuit of this objective is ensuring the production of sufficient indigenous staff in all relevant fields. This strategy would further ensure the State's representation in the federal government establishments and fill its quotas in the universities and other institutions of higher learning (Mohammed 1986). To achieve this, standards at both primary and secondary schools have to be improved.

Successive administrations in the state have realized this situation and, in order to cope with it, have given education top priority in its share of the state annual budgets, as shown in Table 6.18.

### Table 6.18
### Educational Expenditure in Sokoto State, 1976–1988

| Year | Total Expenditure (N) | Educational Expenditure Nigerian Naira (N) | % of Total Expenditure |
|---|---|---|---|
| 1976 | 208,631,037 | 49,464,642 | 24 |
| 1977 | 291,759,520 | 101,949,350 | 35 |
| 1978 | 269,667,651 | 67,746,820 | 25 |
| 1979 | 283,873,069 | 79,733,135 | 28 |
| 1980 | 274,198,720 | 67,982,920 | 25 |
| 1981 | 612,843,920 | 128,431,030 | 21 |
| 1982 | 642,480,040 | 117,013,645 | 18 |
| 1983 | 583,718,991 | 123,381,380 | 21 |
| 1984 | 354,320,120 | 63,427,927 | 18 |
| 1985 | 337,208,950 | 59,873,230 | 18 |
| 1986 | 407,284,000 | 67,793,230 | 17 |
| 1987 | 434,520,550 | 92,048,005 | 21 |

| 1988 | 910,865,840 | 127,279,970 | 14 |
|---|---|---|---|
| Sources: Budget Speeches of Governors of Sokoto State 1976–88; *Sokoto State Government Budget Estimates 1976–1988.* | | | |

In his maiden speech to the people of Sokoto State on Tuesday, September 10, 1985, outlining the priority of his administration, the then-military governor of the state, Colonel Garba Mohammed indicated that improvement of standard of education was his first priority. According to the governor:

> this administration will pay greater attention to Education, Agriculture and Integrated Rural Development, Water Supply, Health and the issue of unemployment. We are all aware that Sokoto State is one of the educationally disadvantaged states. It is therefore the determination of this administration to see that the situation is reversed (1985).

Soon afterward, the military governor visited some primary and post-primary institutions in the various local government areas of the state. The visits offered him the opportunity to realize the gravity of the situation. His impression formed part of his 1986 budget speech to the people of Sokoto State:

> From what I saw during these visits, I am further convinced that unless urgent actions are taken and immediately, we will continue for a long time to become backward in education. In addition, all the investment made in that area so far stands to be a complete waste, unless we undertake a major salvage operation not only in terms of saving physical facilities, but also the ethos of teaching as a profession. The state government has therefore set out to redeem the situation, and will count on the support of the citizens of this state to achieve these objectives.

It is within this context that Operation Move Ahead was formulated and launched "to improve education in Sokoto, to increase admission of its indigenes into institutions of higher learning, and place them better in the scheme of things in the country" (The New Nigeria Tuesday 25 February 1986, 9). Two days earlier, the same paper came out with a story captioned "The Governor launched Operation Move Ahead with a view to bringing back sanity and discipline into education administration in the State" (The New Nigeria Sunday 23 February 1986, 16).

# Chapter Seven
# The Implementation of Education Policy: "Operation Move Ahead" as a Case Study

The last chapter traces the development of Western education in Nigeria and, in doing so, highlights the disparity in between the former northern region and southern region (western and eastern regions]. Besides stressing that this disparity has been perpetuated until today, the chapter identifies the factors responsible and describes the context within which the state's educational policy was formulated. The focus of the present chapter is on a specific educational policy, Operation Move Ahead. The chapter traces the origin of the policy and examines the problems encountered during its implementation.

## Operation Move Ahead: The Policy

The objectives of Operation Move Ahead were highlighted by the military governor himself on January 25, 1986, on the occasion of the graduation ceremony of the State College of Arts and Science, Sokoto. According to the governor, the policy was enacted with a view to:
1. rehabilitate the whole educational structure with special emphasis on primary education,
2. reorganize the administrative apparatus at the headquarters of Ministry of Education and the zonal offices,

3. provide effective and dedicated leadership in all educational institutions,
4. restore the interest of the rural populace in Western education, and
5. reverse the deplorable trends of massive failures in the state and national examinations.

# Policy Targets

Besides outlining the policy's strategic or development objective, the governor identified the targets by which the success of the policy was to be measured. He declared:

I am directing the Ministry for Local Government and Ministry of Education to intensify efforts so that we have at least 1.2 million pupils actually attending primary schools by 1990.... [W]e are determined to completely change the present situation where (students in post-primary) schools in the state score less than an average of 20 per cent in the WASC examinations, to more acceptable level of 70 per cent or even better in the next year or two. It is expected that these ... schools will produce enough qualified young boys and girls who will fill the state quota in institutions of higher learning, and various federal establishments (Mohammed 1986).

# Policy Strategies

In order to achieve the objectives of the policy, the following causal links were incorporated into the policy:
1. renovating the existing primary schools to make them more conducive to learning,
2. removing unproductive officers in the Ministry of Education and its zonal offices and replace them with dedicated and responsible officers,
3. posting suitable, interested, senior officers no matter how high their salary grade levels to head primary schools,

4. boosting the morale of teachers by ensuring regular promotion to deserving ones,

5. establishing magnet schools from the existing schools to admit brighter pupils who could be prepared for higher academic excellence,

6. evolving basic skills and proficiency targets for every class in the educational structure so that promotion from one class to the next is dependent on scoring at least 50 percent of the targets,

7. mounting massive campaigns toward girls' education, and

8. involving village and district heads in the affairs of primary education so that they ensure good attendance of pupils in schools within their areas of jurisdiction (1986 unpublished).

As noted in a previous chapter, public policy contains both its goals and the means, which serve as the causal linkages for realizing them. In this connection, the assumption of the education policy, Operation Move Ahead, is that if the policy means (1–8) are implemented, the policy goals will be realized. In addition, the policy has indicated the main organizations responsible for the implementation of the policy, namely the Ministry of Education, the Ministry for Local Government, and the military governor's office. However, the financial requirement of the policy was not stated in the policy document. It was at the implementation stage that the cost implications were spelled out. Thus, provisions were made for the implementation of the policy with effect from the 1986 budget and subsequent budgets.

## The Implementation Process

The policy, as pointed out earlier, came from the top—the military governor, Colonel (later Brigadier) Mohammed, and the commissioner of education, Dr. Mustapha Bunza—and was passed down to the permanent secretary and to the directors of Ministry of Education who communicated the policy down to their zonal officers and principals of post-primary schools in Sokoto. Similarly, the policy was communicated to secretaries of local governments by the Ministry of Local Government through the ministry's hierarchy.

The Ministry of Education, under the overall supervision of the commissioner of Education, Dr. Bunza, was reorganized into two major departments: secondary and primary education and science, technical and teacher education. Each department was to be under a permanent secretary. Accordingly, two permanent secretaries were posted by the Secretary to the Military Government and Head of Service (SMG/HS), Alhaji M. B. Alkali, to take charge of the two new departments: Alhaji Yahaya Maigari for Secondary and Primary Education Department, while Alhaji Yahaya Abdulkarim was to head the Science, Technical and Teacher Education Department. Further, the post of coordinating director was established for coordinating some of the activities of the two departments. The former director of planning in the Ministry of Education, M. M. Madugu, who was one of the three most senior officers in the ministry, was appointed to the post. The other two, Alhaji Hamidu Bage and Alhaji Abdullahi Kamba, were reassigned to the posts of chief inspector of education for the Departments of Science and Secondary-Primary Education, respectively. The two departments were further divided into a number of divisions, each under a director, as shown in Figure 7.1.

The divisions under the Department of Secondary and Primary Education were: Junior Secondary and Primary Education (under Sani Ashafa), Senior Secondary Education (Idris Illo), Inspectorate Services (Abdullahi Kamba), Planning and Statistics (Musa Nagayya), and Extension and Support Services (Abdullahi Yusuf Gada).

The divisions under the Department of Science, Technical and Teacher Education were inspectorate services (under Hamidu Bage), teacher education (Ibrahim Maru), science and technical education (S. H. Hashimi), and Higher Education (Muhammed Attahiru).

It was the Department of Secondary and Primary Education that was directly concerned with the implementation of Operation Move Ahead. The Division of Primary Education had the responsibility for improving the quality and standard of primary education in the state. In particular, it had to see to the implementation of Operation Move Ahead, as it affected the improvement of primary education.

Many officers, including those in the ministry headquarters, zonal offices, and schools, were reshuffled to assume new responsibilities. Some secondary school principals were brought to the ministry to take up administrative duties. Alhaji Abubakar B. Bawa was posted to head the Division of Primary Education as its director. Under him were the chief education officer, principal education officer, and education officer.

While all these were going on, some officers, whose continued stay in the ministry was found to be unproductive, were compulsorily retired in order to bring in committed officers for the execution of the program. Among the officers affected were a director, a chief education officer, a principal education officer, a school principal, and a librarian.

After this first level of implementation in which the broader framework for the implementation of the program was set out, the second level of implementation began. Eleven days after the policy was enunciated, on February 6, 1986, the coordinating director of the Ministry of Education, M. M. Madugu, was directed by the permanent secretary, Alhaji Yahaya Maigari, to communicate the policy document to all the zonal

**Figure 7.1**
**Ministry of Education: 1986 Reorganization**

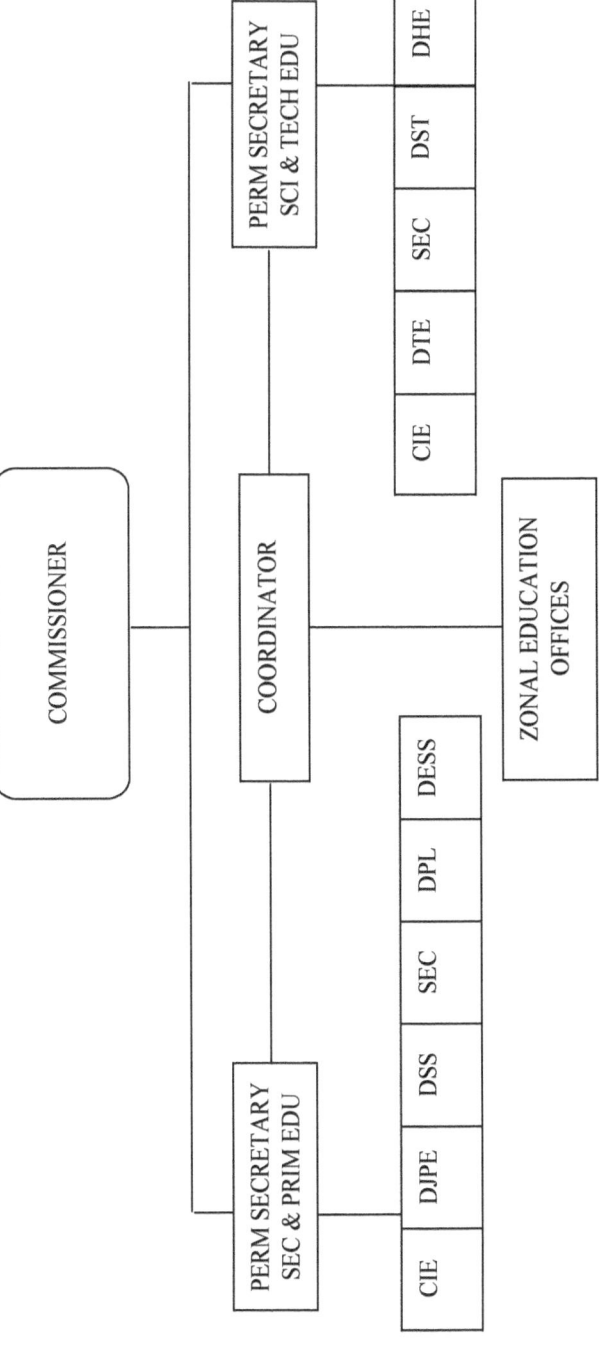

Key: CIE = Chief Inspector of Education; DJPE = Director of Junior and Primary Education; DSS = Director of Senior Secondary Schools; SEC = Secretary; DPL = Director of Planning; DESS = Division of Extension and Support Services; DTE = Director of Teacher Education; DST = Director of Science and Technical Education; DHE = Director of Higher Education.

officers and principals of post-primary schools for implementation purposes. In the circular, M. M. Madugu (1986) wrote:

> I am directed to send to you a copy of the speech of the Military Governor of Sokoto State, Col. Garba Mohammed, at the third graduation ceremony of the State College of Arts and Science, Sokoto, for your study and action on the policy statements contained in the speech.
>
> You will note that key policy announcements were made at the ceremony on the main objectives of the State Government on improving the various aspects of education in the State, and the operational strategies planned for the attainment of the desired goals and objectives.
>
> As one of the major implementers of educational policies, you are required to carefully study the ... objectives outlined together with the points made on the programme of action drawn for the implementation of this policy. This, it is hoped, will enable you to be fully prepared to participate more actively with a greater sense of commitment in the implementation exercise.

The first task of the zonal offices was to approach school principals under their zones to assess the number of post-primary institutions that needed to be rehabilitated. The zonal education officers in conjunction with the school principals and the Ministry of Works zonal engineers assessed the schools' requirements and submitted estimates for rehabilitation of such schools to the Chief Inspector of Education (CIE) in the Ministry of Education in Sokoto. The CIE made some adjustments to the estimate and forwarded it to the permanent secretary for his consideration. The permanent secretary, in turn, endorsed the CIE's proposal to the commissioner for his approval. The commissioner, having approved the proposal, returned it to the permanent secretary, who passed it down the hierarchy for information and further action. The ministry now, having identified its detailed financial requirements for the rehabilitation of 127 post-primary schools, forwarded its request to the State Tenders Board for the award of contract for the execution of the work.

Tenders for the repairs of the schools were invited. Many contractors now began to pay frequent visits to the ministry and the State Tenders Board, shuttling between one office to another and making spirited efforts to secure government contracts. At this stage, contractors were brought in in the implementation process. Their participation, however, was not directed at the goal of the program, but basically at how to determine the extent of the contractors' involvement and calculate the costs. In the end, the contracts, which involved carrying out repairs on school buildings, erosion control, rectification of storm damages, and other related matters, were awarded at the cost of N7,415,341.00, and the rehabilitation exercise was executed on 127 schools as required.

Similar contracts were awarded for the supply of textbooks; exercise books; agricultural, science, home economics, and sports equipment; and other teaching material at the cost of N7,124,275.50. The equipment and material were subsequently distributed to all post-primary institutions.

During the same period, 187 kits of introductory technology equipment were received from the federal government and distributed to all the appropriate schools.

At the level of primary schools, the rehabilitation process involved the participation of the Ministry of Education, the Ministry of Local Government, the local governments themselves, and the federal government. The Ministry of Education was concerned with quality control in the area of primary education; the Ministry of Local Government was responsible for control of local government finances. Local governments were also in charge of the management and running of primary schools. The federal government's role was ensuring proper utilization of its financial assistance.

Unlike the rehabilitation process of the post-primary schools where the Ministry of Education was the only main actor, the rehabilitation of primary schools involved the participation of all the three layers of government: federal, state, and local government.

Before the launching of Operation Move Ahead in 1986, a program for improving the condition of primary schools to reach the standard of model primary schools had already started in 1984. However, the first model primary school was established in the 1970s to cater to the children of expatriate and other indigenous officers. The school was run by the Ministry of Education. With the high performance of the school, as a result of its better teaching staff and equipment, demand arose for establishing similar schools in other parts of Sokoto. In light of this, three additional model schools were established at Dorawa Road, Secretariat Road, and Wurno Road. Due to their remarkable performance, the schools provided most of the candidates admitted from the state to federal government colleges in the country.

Realizing the exceptional performance of those schools, Dr. Bunza, the commissioner of education, initiated a program for modeling some schools throughout the state along the same lines. Modeling constitutes renovating the physical facilities (school buildings), equipping them with adequate desks, chairs, textbooks, exercise books, and other essential teaching apparatuses, and providing them with qualified teachers and dedicated head teachers.

Thus in 1984, thirty-eight primary schools, two in each of the then-nineteen local government areas, were remodeled to make them more conducive to learning. The rehabilitation involved 456 classrooms at the cost of N2.8 million. In 1985 an additional 95 schools, consisting of 570 classrooms, were remodeled at the cost of N4.50 million. With the launching of OMA, 300 additional schools were remodeled in 1986, 91 in 1987, which brought the total by the end 1987 to 492, as shown in Table 7.1

On February 6, 1986, the permanent secretary of the Ministry of Local Government instructed the chief inspector of local government, Alhaji Idris Musa Wara, to issue a circular to all local governments, zonal engineers, and zonal inspector of education, who were members of the state committee appointed earlier to study the requirements of each of the three hundred schools to be rehabilitated, and authorized them to start work on repairs of the schools in their zones. Each school was to cost no more than N10,000.00. Apart from the refurbishing of the 300 model schools, 2,010 other schools were also improved at the cost of N1000.00 each, as shown in Table 7.2. The contracts for the rehabilitation of the schools were awarded by the respective local government committee responsible for the rehabilitation process.

Similarly, contracts for the supply of furniture with all the required school materials to the rehabilitated schools were awarded to six main contractors: Sokoto Furniture Factory, Muhammadiya Metal Factory, Niger Furniture Factory, Toro Furniture Factory,

### Table 7.1
### Model Primary Schools Completed Each Year, 1984–1987

| Year | Schools |
|------|---------|
| 1984 | 38 |
| 1985 | 95 |
| 1986 | 300 |
| 1987 | 91 |

### Table 7.2
### Number of Schools Rehabilitated and Their Cost, 1986

| L/GOVT | Model Schools | Other Schools | Expenditure (Naira) |
|--------|---------------|---------------|---------------------|
| 1. Anka | 11 | 76 | 186,000.00 |
| 2. Argungu | 19 | 128 | 318,000.00 |
| 3. Bodinga | 16 | 112 | 272,000.00 |
| 4. Bagudo | 13 | 86 | 216,000.00 |
| 5. Bunza | 13 | 85 | 215,000.00 |
| 6. B/Kebbi | 12 | 81 | 201,000.00 |
| 7. Gummi | 14 | 91 | 231,000.00 |
| 8. Gwadabawa | 23 | 158 | 388,000.00 |
| 9. Gusau | 22 | 149 | 369,000.00 |
| 10. Isa | 18 | 121 | 301,000.00 |
| 11. Jega | 12 | 81 | 201,000.00 |

| | | | |
|---|---|---|---|
| 12. K/Namoda | 22 | 147 | 367,000.00 |
| 13. Silame | 13 | 86 | 216,000.00 |
| 14. Sokoto | 14 | 90 | 230,000.00 |
| 15. T/Mafara | 16 | 107 | 267,000.00 |
| 16. Wurno | 17 | 116 | 286,000.00 |
| 17. Yabo | 19 | 134 | 324,000.00 |
| 18. Yauri | 10 | 57 | 157,000.00 |
| 19. Zuru | 16 | 105 | 265,000.00 |
| **Total** | **300** | **2,010** | **5,010,000.00** |

Ibrahim Furniture Factory, and Gusau Trading Company. The number of local governments and schools supplied with furniture by each of the contractor is shown in Table 7.3

The rehabilitation process cost N13 million in 1986. Out of this amount, N3.6 million came from the federal government. That was outside its normal budgetary allocation to the state. The amount was a special financial assistance to the state, as other states too were given such financial assistance to enable them to cope with the appalling condition of primary schools all over the country. The remaining N10 million came from the state-local government joint account.

After the initial rehabilitation process had been implemented, the federal government sent its representatives to verify how its contribution of N3.6 million to Sokoto State was utilized in the rehabilitation of primary schools. The representatives of the federal government, having seen the rehabilitation work and the amount of money spent so far on the program, became satisfied that the federal government contribution was judiciously utilized.

In addition to the amount spent on the rehabilitation process, local governments were instructed to commit 50 percent of their locally generated revenue to the improvement of primary education by remodeling more schools. This instruction encouraged the local governments to intensify their efforts on revenue generation in order to meet their educational needs.

When the implementation process was going on, another important strategy for improving the quality of education at the grass roots and restoring interest of some parents in Western education was conceived—namely, the introduction of the Mobile Classroom. The project was first introduced at Bado Ukku-Ukku, a village in the outskirts of the Sokoto metropolis by the wife of the military governor, Mrs. D. L. Mohammed.

Mrs. Mohammed is a well-known head teacher in Kaduna State where she established and ran a multipurpose educational institution, which comprised nursery, primary, and secondary wings. With a husband who was equally interested and committed to the improvement of education in Sokoto State, Mrs. Mohammed took delight in visiting some schools in Sokoto.

During one of her school visits, she came to Bado Ukku-Ukku Primary School, where to her surprise and disappointment found the school almost empty and attendance record very poor. The pupils and their parents seemed uninterested in Western education. She took this as a challenge, and the issue was discussed with the officials of Ministry of Education and Local Government with a view to encouraging the indigenes of the area to send their children to school. Soon afterward, officials of both Ministries of Education and Local Government visited the local elders of Bado Ukku-Ukku and discussed with them the problem of poor attendance of their school and solicited their cooperation for improving the situation. They were also invited to attend the first launching of Mobile Classroom in the village. Hence, on August 6, Mrs. Mohammed established a Mobile Classroom at Bado Ukku-Ukku with initial intake of forty-five children.

The mobile unit is a bus equipped with cupboards, writing desks, and the following four units:

1.  Teaching Material Unit: chalk, portable blackboard, blackboard dusters, two meter sticks, scissors, poster cardboard, rubber balls, jump ropes, writing pens, pencils, sharpeners, erasers, color pencils, color markers, crayons, copybooks, scrap paper, and typing paper.

2. First-Aid Unit: first-aid manual, junior aspirin, soap, antiseptic, disinfectant, plasters, bandages, elastic bandages, cotton, wool, and towels.
3. Maintenance and Repairs Unit: hammer and nails, two large jerricans filled with water, two plastic basins, soap, disinfectant, insecticide, safety pins, sewing kit, four brooms, two dust cloths, and one pair of utility gloves.
4. Canteen Unit: plastic cups, cooler containing bottles of pre-mixed squash, and student snacks in plastic bags.

The unit was transported to certain areas in Sokoto and its outskirts where children seemed not to be interested in Western education. Lessons were provided in different fora: either in a village square, under a shady tree, on a sidewalk, and, where available, in an existing classroom. The subjects taught included beginning English, beginning math, beginning social studies, arts and crafts, and physical education.

**Table 7.3**
**Furniture Supplied to 300 Modeled Primary Schools**
**in Sokoto State, 1986**

| Suppliers | L/Govt | Sch | Class room | Four seat | Three seat | Two seat | Teach set | H/M set | Cup b/d |
|---|---|---|---|---|---|---|---|---|---|
| | | | | | | Supplied to: | | | |
| Sokoto Furniture Factory | 8 | 112 | 672 | 2,240 | 3,136 | 4,480 | 672 | 112 | 672 |
| Muhammadiya Furniture Factory | 6 | 94 | 564 | 1,880 | 2,632 | 3,760 | 564 | 94 | 564 |
| Niger Furniture Factory | 2 | 30 | 180 | 600 | 840 | 1,200 | 180 | 30 | 180 |
| Toro Furniture Factory | 1 | 23 | 138 | 460 | 644 | 920 | 138 | 23 | 138 |
| Ibrahim Furniture Factory | 1 | 19 | 114 | 380 | 532 | 760 | 114 | 19 | 114 |
| Gusau Trading Company | 1 | 22 | 132 | 440 | 616 | 880 | 132 | 22 | 132 |
| Total | 19 | 300 | 1800 | 6000 | 8400 | 1200 | 1800 | 300 | 1800 |

As pointed out, introducing the concept of Mobile Classroom was not part of the original "Programme of Operation Move Ahead." Nonetheless, since the idea was useful in sparking parents' interest in Western education and increasing enrollment (and hence in conformity with the policy objectives of the program), it was incorporated into the program. In other words, a new strategy was conceived during the implementation process. In this case, however, the formulation of the new strategy was to facilitate the realization of the same goal and not to change or modify it. Thus, the policy was not reformulated, as in a number of policy case studies, but its scope of strategies was extended.

Earlier on, the secretary to the government, Alhaji M. B. Alkali (1985), had issued a circular for recruitment of special headmasters no matter how high their grade levels. He stated:

The State Government has recently made a policy statement to declare its determination to improve the standard of education. Proposals for the attainment of this objective at all levels of education are being worked out and will be put in force immediately.... [I]t is realized that primary education holds a crucial place in any attempt to improve the standard of education. The role of teachers is of particular significance. The success or failure of primary education is largely dependent on the commitment of primary teachers, particularly headmasters. In order therefore to ensure that primary schools are provided with the right leadership, the State Government has decided that serving officers with the right qualification, no matter how high the present grade level, will be allowed to opt for headmastership, and will retain their grade levels and any other benefits as personal and be eligible to regular promotion as and when due.... Furthermore, retired headmasters, principals or teachers of proven competence and leadership ability can also be considered for appointment and, depending on suitability, will be placed on a special grade level.

Following the issuance of the circular, many serving and retired officers applied for the post, among whom one hundred were employed and posted to different primary schools. The position of headmaster in any school is important, for "the climate within a school is a direct result of the philosophy of those in charge" (Agu 1986, 165). In her study of UPE schools in some states in Nigeria, Agu confirms that the headmaster is the critical person in the school improvement program (1986, 165–8).

An orientation course was also arranged by the Division of Extension and Support Services (DESS) for three hundred head teachers of primary schools and sixteen assistant inspectors of education. The aim was to improve the skills of the participants and sensitize them to the goals of the new education program and their role in the overall implementation process. In July 1986, the division organized a workshop for one hundred principals of post-primary institutions on guidance and counseling and emphasized the importance of enlightening the students to choose appropriate courses for their chosen career.

As part of the strategy to mobilize some people to develop interest in the new education program, traditional rulers from the district, village, and ward levels were requested by their respective local governments to participate in the supervision of primary schools in the areas of their jurisdiction. That was not, of course, the first time that traditional rulers had been involved in the supervision of primary education. They had been involved since the introduction of Western education. But their role in that direction had diminished in view of a number of reforms, including the 1976 local government reform. The government now wanted to revive their traditional role, which was considered crucial, for they were closer to the parents than any other officials. Their participation would undoubtedly encourage undecided parents to show interest in Western education and thereby to send their children to schools.

The program was given adequate publicity by the state radio and television stations purposely to orient parents, teachers, and educational planners to the objectives of the new policy. The program was called in the local language (Hausa/Fulani) *gaba-dai-gaba-dai* ("move ahead"). The policy became so popular within a few months of its official launching that even some officials from other states of the federation visited Sokoto State to find out the details of the policy with a view of adopting it in their states.

At the level of post-primary schools, twelve senior secondary schools were selected and converted to magnet schools. They were adequately staffed and provided with additional science and elementary technology equipment, laboratories, workshops, libraries, textbooks, and exercise books to make them more conducive for learning. Selection of pupils to the schools was based on an aptitude test conducted by the West African Examination Council (WAEC) in conjunction with the Ministry of Education. The schools and their locations are presented in Table 7.4.

## Table 7.4
## Magnet Schools

| Schools | Location | Local Government |
|---|---|---|
| 1. Sultan Bello Secondary School | Sokoto | Sokoto |
| 2. Kanta College | Argungu | Argungu |
| 3. Government Secondary School | Gwandu | Birnin Kebbi |
| 4. Government Secondary School | Anka | Anka |
| 5. Government Secondary School | Kamba | Argungu |
| 6. Government Secondary School | Mahuta | Zuru |
| 7. Government Secondary School | Gwadabawa | Gwadabawa |
| 8. Government Secondary School | K/Namoda | K/Namoda |
| 9. Government Secondary School | Koko | Bagudo |
| 10. Government College | Sokoto | Sokoto |
| 11. Government Girls' College | Sokoto | Sokoto |
| 12. Government Science Secondary School | Gusau | Gusau |

The schools were to provide the needed ground for training students, particularly in the sciences, who would be able to pass the School Certificate Examination as a prerequisite for direct entry to universities. Through this, the state would be able to fill its quota in the higher institutions of learning.

After the first and second levels of implementation had been accomplished, the third level began. The inspectorate directorate of the two departments were provided with three new Peugeot 504 Estate Saloons by the military governor's office. The purpose was to enable the inspectorates to carry out regular inspections of schools. In line with this, the chief inspectors of education and their zonal education officers mounted regular visits of all the rehabilitated schools, both primary and post-primary. The schools were inspected twice in 1986 and the inspectors' reports on the general atmosphere in the schools and their performance were very encouraging. Apart from the inspectors' visits, the two permanent secretaries in the Ministry of Education, Alhaji Yahaya Maigari and Alhaji Yahaya Abdulkarim, paid a number of unscheduled inspection visits to some schools in order to see for themselves what had been happening in terms of both teacher and student performance and the needs of the schools. These unscheduled visits had put the school principals and teachers on the alert to always be up-to-date with their work.

The organizations that were actively involved in the implementation process are the Ministries of Education, Local Government, and Finance, and the military governor's office. Of these organizations, the Ministry of Education was the main organization responsible for the program, and its traditional orientation was in conformity with the policy goals.

Most of the Ministry of Education's departments are in one way or another involved in the implementation process. Specifically, the Departments of Primary and Secondary Education, Inspectorate Division, and zonal offices were involved.

Similarly, at the Ministry of Local Government, the Inspectorate Division was involved through its liaison with local governments, which implemented the policy at primary-school level. At the Ministry of Finance the disbursement of money was carried out through the local government joint account committee.

In the military governor's office, the Department of Administration and Political Affairs was involved in the implementation process. These departments constituted what the bottom-uppers called implementation structure. However, contrary to the bottom-uppers' assumption, the members of the implementation structure were not furthering any other interest apart from the interest of the policy. In other words, the implementation structure had no other interest to pursue apart from the interests of the organizations it represented.

The relationship among the organizations responsible for the implementation of the policy was not based on conflict. It was based on coordination and cooperation. A state committee comprising officials of the Ministries of Education, Local Government, and Works was established to monitor the rehabilitation of the 300 model primary schools and improvement of the 2,010 primary schools.

However, in 1987, a conflict arose between the Ministry of Education and the Ministry of Local Government over who should be the sole controller of primary education in the state. Traditionally, primary education had been under the control of the Ministry of Local Government. Nevertheless, some states of the federation changed such arrangement and created school management boards to be responsible for primary education. In light of this development, the Ministry of Education now wanted the responsibility for primary education transferred to it. The Ministry of Local Government, on the other hand, rejected vehemently the proposal. This caused a strained relationship between the two organizations. Yet, it should be noted that this conflict was not directly related to the implementation of OMA. In other words, the conflict was not based on disagreement over the objective of or strategy for implementing the policy, but rather on the control of primary education as a whole as it was practiced in other states of Nigeria.

The relationship between the Ministry of Local Government and local governments was based on a master–agent relationship. The Ministry of Local Government controlled the finances of the local governments, appointed their secretaries, and ensured their in-service training program.

On August 7, 1986, the military governor, Colonel Garba Mohammed, in his address on the occasion of the nineteenth meeting of the principals and directors of schools and colleges of basic and preliminary studies, reiterated his commitment to the goals and implementation of Operation Move Ahead when he said:

> Since my assumption of office, I have severally and in definite terms indicated that it is the intention of this government to pursue positive policies that will help to raise the standard of education in the State. Toward this end, we have launched Operation Move Ahead which represents our strategy for educational development in this State. Broadly, the programme entails the restructuring of the entire education approach at both primary and post primary levels in order to make it more effective and responsive to the needs of our immediate environment. As a starting point, we have undertaken physical improvement of a large number of primary and post primary institutions as well as provided necessary teaching equipment and material. Recently, science and technical equipment have been procured and distributed to all our science institutions so as to provide a sound base for the development of education. It is our view that if the standard of education is to be improved, concerted and consistent efforts have to be made first and foremost in raising the standard of education at primary school level. A significant element in this direction is the need to have competent and resourceful headmasters to provide responsible leadership. We have therefore embarked on appointment of Special Headmasters who are officers of considerable experience and proven integrity and are capable of instilling discipline and providing committed leadership. Such Special Headmasters are placed on enhanced salary position as a personal right (Governor's Office Sokoto 1986).

## The Policy Causal Effects

What are the policy causal effects of the implementation process on the policy goals? As for primary school enrollment, it

## Table 7.5
## Primary Schools and Enrollment, 1984/5 to 1988/9

| Year | Number of Schools | Enrollment |
|------|-------------------|------------|
| 1982–3 | 4,038 | 684,030 |
| 1983–4 | 4,040 | 705,777 |
| 1984–5 | 2,552 | 717,744 |
| 1985–6 | 2,452 | 724,625 |
| 1986–7 | 2,455 | 608,302 |
| 1988–9 | 2,458 | 723,124 |
| Source: Ministry of Education, Sokoto, 1989. | | |

decreased from 724,625 in the 1985–1986 academic session at the start of the policy to 608,308 in 1986–1987 and then rose to 723,124 in 1988–1989, as shown in Table 7.5.

In 1986, the year of the launching of the program, about ten thousand children who had earlier dropped out returned to schools. Parents had shown interest in the program. In all the remodeled schools, parents showed readiness to buy the new school uniforms for their children, even though the new uniforms were more expensive than the usual school uniforms, as required by the schools.

The number of schools, however, decreased since 1984–1985. This was a result of the merger of some schools that were built between 1979 and 1983, but which could not be adequately maintained. By the end of 1983–1984 there were 4,040 schools, but by the end of 1984–1985 the number was reduced to 2,552, and to 2,452 in the 1985–1986 session.

It is hard to assess the performance of the remodeled schools. This is because the State Common Entrance Examination could not be used as a basis for assessing pupils' performance. It is only partially used to select students for admission to federal government colleges in the country. Yet, it is generally believed that since remodeled schools were better equipped than even many junior secondary schools, their products would be better qualified than those in the non-modeled schools. The former had better qualified teachers. Over 50 percent of their teachers were qualified. Their head teachers were either qualified Grade I teachers (NCE), qualified Grade II teachers, or special head teachers. Moreover, the experiences of the performances of the older model schools are testimony to the relevance of the modeling process. Some studies in Britain and in the Third world have shown that schools have effect on children's performance (Agu 1986, 63).

The performance of the post-primary schools in general did not show any remarkable improvement. Out of the 2,738 students from 41 senior secondary schools under the Department of Primary and Secondary Education who sat for GCE "O" Level Examination in 1988, three years after the program had been launched, only 515 had actually passed, which represents 18.8 percent, as shown in Table 7.6. Similarly, out of the 1,263 students from 15 science and technical secondary schools under the supervision of the Department of Science, Technical and Teacher Education who sat for the GCE "O" Level Examination in 1988, only 315 passed, which represents 25 percent, as shown in Table 7.7. Even the performance of the magnet schools (selected from both departments of the Ministry of Education), which were established basically to improve performance, was no better than the other secondary schools, as presented in Table 7.8. Out of 1,012 students of the 12 magnet schools who sat for their 1988 exam, only 265 passed, which represents 26 percent. The situation is not different from the results of the Teachers Grade II Examination, as shown in Table 7.9

## Table 7.6
## 1988 "O" Level Examination Results, Some Senior Secondary Schools in Sokoto State

| Schools | Number of Candidates | Number of Passes in 5 Subjects | % Passes |
|---|---|---|---|
| 01. ARMY DAY S S SOKOTO | 133 | 78 | 58.6 |
| 02. GOVT. GIRLS S S ILLELA | 33 | 16 | 48.8 |

| | | | |
|---|---|---|---|
| 03. NANA GIRLS S S SOKOTO | 55 | 26 | 47.2 |
| 04. GOVT. GIRLS S S ZAGGA | 46 | 11 | 23.9 |
| 05. GOVT. S S TURETA | 134 | 28 | 20.8 |
| 06. GOVT. GIRLS SS MORIKI | 63 | 13 | 20.6 |
| 07. GOVT. DAY S S JEGA | 15 | 3 | 20 |
| 08. GOVT. S S D\GARI | 120 | 22 | 18.3 |
| 09. GOVT. S S TANGAZA | 131 | 23 | 17.5 |
| 10. GOVT. S S ILLO | 29 | 4 | 13.7 |
| 11. GOVT. S S ZURU | 44 | 5 | 11.3 |
| 12. GOVT. S S GUMMI | 75 | 6 | 8 |
| 13. GOVT. S S SHUNI | 12 | 0 | 0 |
| 14. GOVT. S S GANDI | 15 | 0 | 0 |
| Source: Ministry of Education Sokoto 1989. | | | |

However, the statistics may not be telling the whole story. Most of the students who graduated in 1988 might not have received qualitative background primary education in the first place; they might not have received adequate training in the junior secondary education in the second place. It will be demanding too much on the policy to expect the students in their second or final year of senior secondary education to perform remarkably well.

## Assessment of Operation Move Ahead's Impact

There have been some successes in the implementation of OMA that could be identified at the various stages of implementation. During the first level of implementation, the Ministry of Education was reorganized, which led to the establishment of a new pattern of behavior and the provision of new services. Although, as Larson hypothesized (1980, 10), the reorganization did not show significant improvement in the coordination of the day-to-day bureaucratic operations, it had nonetheless succeeded in reorienting the implementers toward the objectives of the new education policy (i.e., OMA). This certainly facilitated the implementation of the policy.

Similarly, the second level of implementation—which involved the rehabilitation of schools, appointment of special head teachers, and involvement of traditional rulers in the running of primary schools—had all been fully executed by the end of 1986. The third level of implementation, which was basically the supervision of the rehabilitated schools, had also been successfully carried out twice in 1986.

# Personnel Changes and Policy Slowdown and Reversal

All these have to be maintained in order to achieve the overall policy goals. But after barely ten months of the implementation of Operation Move Ahead, the initiator of the policy, Colonel Muhammed, was redeployed to the general staff headquarters in

**Table 7.7**
**1988 "O" Level Examination Results, Science and Technical Secondary Schools in Sokoto State**

| Schools | Number of Candidates | Number of Passes in 5 Subjects | % Passes |
|---|---|---|---|
| 01. GOVT. SCIENCE S S. YABO | 64 | 41 | 64.06 |
| 02. KANTA COLLEGE ARGUNGU | 52 | 31 | 59.62 |
| 03. GOVT.TECH COLL R/ SAMBO | 79 | 43 | 54.43 |
| 04. GOVT. GIRLS COL SOKOTO | 55 | 27 | 49.09 |
| 05. GOVT. SCIENCE S S. YAURI | 69 | 33 | 47.83 |
| 06. GOVT. SCIENCE S S. GUSAU | 74 | 27 | 36.47 |
| 07. GOVT. SCIENCE S S. B/KEBBI | 59 | 19 | 32.20 |

| 08. A. B. ACADEMY SOKOTO | 58 | 19 | 31.03 |
|---|---|---|---|
| 09. GOVT. COLLEGE SOKOTO | 56 | 16 | 29.09 |
| 10. GOVT. SCIENCE S S. ZURU | 77 | 19 | 24.68 |
| 11. GOVT.TECH COLL FARFARU | 164 | 23 | 14.47 |
| 12. GOVT. SCIENCE S S. FARFARU | 58 | 8 | 14.29 |
| 13. GOVT.TECH COLLEGE SURU | 164 | 6 | 3.66 |
| 14. GOVT.GIRL S.S. TAMBAWAL | 170 | 3 | 1.77 |
| 15. GOVT.TECH COL K/ NAMODA | 64 | -- | -- |

Lagos as principal staff officer. His departure undoubtedly slowed down the momentum of the implementation process. When asked

### Table 7.8
### 1988 "O" Level Examination Results of the Magnet Schools

| Schools | Number of Candidates | Number of Passes in 5 Subjects | % Passes |
|---|---|---|---|
| 01. SULTAN BELLO S.S. SOKOTO | 60 | 52 | 86 |
| 02. KANTA COLLEGE ARGUNGU | 52 | 31 | 59.62 |
| 03. GOVT. S.S. GWANDU | 60 | 21 | 35 |
| 04. GOVT. S.S. ANKA | 158 | 29 | 18.4 |
| 05. GOVT. S.S. KAMBA | 57 | 4 | 7 |
| 06. GOVT. GIRLS SS MAHUTA | 98 | 13 | 13.2 |
| 07. GOVT. S.S. G\BAWA | 121 | 15 | 12.3 |
| 08. GOVT. S.S. KAURA | 100 | 26 | 26 |
| 09. GOVT. S.S. KOKO | 121 | 4 | 3.3 |
| 10. GOVT. COLLEGE SOKOTO | 56 | 16 | 29.09 |

| 11. GOVT. GIRLS COLL SOKOTO | 55 | 27 | 49.09 |
|---|---|---|---|
| 12. GOVT. SCIENCE S.S.GUSAU | 74 | 27 | 36.47 |

about the current position of Operation Move Ahead, an official of the Ministry of Education stated: "Operation Move Ahead has gone with its initiator, Col. Garba Mohammed."

## Table 7.9
## 1988 Teachers Grade-II Examination Results

| Schools | Number of Candidates | Number of Passes in 5 Subjects | % Passes |
|---|---|---|---|
| 01. GSTC BAKURA | 84 | 3 | 3.57 |
| 02. WATC GUSAU | 64 | 5 | 7.80 |
| 03. STC SOKOTO | 112 | 2 | 1.78 |
| 04. GTC ZURMI | 160 | 20 | 12.50 |
| 05. SAC SOKOTO | 18 | 0 | 0 |
| 06. WSTC BODINGA | 58 | 3 | 5.17 |
| 07. WTC YELWA | 61 | 1 | 1.63 |
| 08. WTC B\ KEBBI | 162 | 17 | 10.49 |
| 09. GTC WASAGU | 139 | 16 | 11.50 |
| 10. GTC ARGUNGU | 276 | 10 | 3.6 |
| 11. CAAS SOKOTO | 54 | 4 | 7.40 |
| TOTAL | 1,188 | 81 | 6.8 |

Key: GSTC.= Government Science Teachers College; WATC = Women Arabic Teachers College; STC = Sokoto Teachers College; GTC = Government Teachers College; SAC = Sultan Abubakar College; WSTC = Women Science Teachers College; WTC = Women Teachers College; CAAS = College of Arts and Arabic Studies.
Source: Ministry of Education 1989.

Although his successor, Colonel Ahmad Muhammad Daku, like other governors before him, was interested in the educational development of the state, as manifested in the continuation of remodeling of ninety-one primary schools in 1987, he did not pay special attention to the overall program. He clearly had other priorities and policies to pursue.

Not very long after the departure of Colonel Mohammed, Dr. M. Bunza, the commissioner of education, resigned and took up appointment with the University of Sokoto as its registrar. Dr. Bunza's background and interest in educational matters had contributed significantly to the formulation and implementation of Operation Move Ahead. He was a teacher, educational administrator, and former provost of College of Education, Sokoto, before becoming commissioner of education. His exit from the ministry was also a blow to the implementation of OMA.

On January 31, 1987, the secretary to the military government and head of service, Alhaji M. B. Alkali, who had been very close to the former military governor, Colonel Mohammed, and who had played an important role in the formulation and implementation of OMA, retired from service.

With the departure of these key figures in the formulation and implementation of OMA, the collapse of the policy was imminent. Although the new SMG/HS, Alhaji Yahaya Maigari, who moved from the Department of Primary and Secondary Education, was interested in, and conversant with, the objectives and strategies of OMA (for it was he who began the reorganization of the Department of Primary and Secondary Education as part of the implementation process of OMA), his new responsibilities for seeing to the implementation of the overall government policies could not allow him to continue to pay particular attention to OMA, as he used to do. Besides, there were both a new commissioner and a new permanent secretary to take charge of the Ministry of Education.

Apart from the effect of the governmental changes on the implementation of OMA, the staff of the Ministry of Education, like the staff of other ministries, were mostly overloaded with work. It was common to see bundle of files on the trays of many senior officers. From the observations made in the interview conducted with some senior civil servants from salary grade level 08 to the highest grade level 16 and to the commissioners (cabinet members) on the volume of work they had to contend with, their responses were that they were overloaded with work. Some officers usually returned to the office after it had closed in order to complete their assignments, although they were not paid any extra allowances. When the Mobile Classroom was to be established at Bado Ukku-Ukku officials of the Ministries of Education and Local Government could not sleep the night before, all in an effort to make the launching a success. This is not unusual in the implementation of other policies.

This overload is accentuated by the socioeconomic problems of the implementers, which make it hard for them to stay in office for the consecutive hours required. By midday many officers could not be found in their offices. They were out either to attend to an official assignment or to fulfil a private engagement. The author had to visit both the Ministries of Education and Local Government several times to be able to find certain officers for interviews. This undoubtedly affected the level of their performance to the extent that work that was supposed to be completed in a day took several days.

Nonetheless, in August 1988 the federal government formulated a policy establishing the National Primary Education Commission. The commission was to be responsible for, among other things, prescribing the minimum standards of primary education throughout Nigeria and contributing 65 percent to the calculated cost of primary school teachers and non-teachers salaries (Federal Republic of Nigeria Official Gazette 1988, 75, 53). With the establishment of this commission, all states of the federation established their primary school management boards to conform with the federal government policy. Thus, responsibility for primary education shifted from ministries of local governments, as in some states, to the new boards.

In Sokoto State, the responsibilities of the Division of Primary Education in the Ministry of Education were transferred, along with its staff, to the new school board. Similarly, the responsibilities of the Ministry of Local Government, as regards primary education, was transferred, along with its staff, to the new board.

This new policy undoubtedly affected the organization and direction of Operation Move Ahead. The new board had its own policy goals and strategy that might be different from those of Operation Move Ahead. However, this was neither a policy shift (since the federal government was not the formulator of Operation Move Ahead), a state policy, nor was it a policy reformulation since the federal government policy was not based on the philosophy of Operation Move Ahead. It is rather a new federal policy to be implemented by all the state governments irrespective of existing state policies. All the same, this new federal government policy, relevant as it is, disrupted the organization and strategy of Operation Move Ahead.

On the whole, as evidenced by the above account, Operation Move Ahead had registered some successes but its overall goals could not be achieved. This failure could neither be attributed to the Ministry of Education or the bureaucrats in it, nor to the policy or its context.

In the first place, the Ministry of Education, the main organization responsible for the implementation of the policy, was reorganized essentially to see to the effective implementation of the program. The reorganization itself was the first level of the implementation process, which was effectively carried out.

Regarding the bureaucrats, some officers were compulsorily retired from the Ministry of Education in order to give room for more competent and dedicated officers who, it was assumed, could ensure the success of the policy. This was in line with the argument of Sabatier and Mazmanian (1980, 544–8) that policy makers are capable of controlling the implementation process by appointing officers who could successfully implement their policies.

As for the policy itself, it was by no means ambiguous at least to the policy makers and the implementers who are familiar with their bureaucratic and policy terminologies. The language of the policy was drafted by the bureaucrats in the Ministry of Education, Ministry of Local Government, and the governor's office, having received the general guidelines from the policy makers and contributed their own ideas, based on their values and experiences, to the policy. The policy had no conflicting goals. Its general goals are to increase enrollment in primary schools and to ensure the production of qualified students in post-primary institutions who would fill the state quota in high institutions of learning and in the federal government establishments. Besides, the policy was very popular and, in response to people's aspiration, it generated enormous support. The policy, furthermore, was based on adequate causal theory. Many studies in Nigeria and elsewhere have shown the relevance and positive relationships between the causal variables contained in the policy and the policy goals. That is, there are positive relationships between provision of qualified and responsible head teachers for schools and the schools' performance; adequate school facilities and pupils' better performance; involvement of parents in the education of their children and the children's better performance; and making the school environment conducive for learning and students' better performance (Agu 1986, 36).

In the context of policy, contrary to the bottom-uppers' argument, there were no conflicts and no bargaining between the policy makers and implementers during the implementation process that might have hampered the realization of the policy goals. Rather, the implementation process was characterized by cooperation and coordination within and between the organizations involved.

In spite of the presence of all these important conditions for policy success, the program could not achieve its overall goals because it was not given enough time and chances to succeed, as a result of governmental instability, governmental overload, implementers' socioeconomic problems, and infrastructural inadequacies. These four variables constitute the main problems of implementing Operation Move Ahead in particular and other policies in general in the Sokoto State bureaucracy. Examination of these variables is important because "implementation is not necessarily being measured in terms of action which successfully meets policy objectives. Rather, only those factors are being examined which tend either to facilitate or to hinder the process of implementation" (Nixon 1980, 128).

# Explaining Policy Success and Failure

## Governmental Instability

It has been indicated in Chapter Three that the Nigerian political system (of which Sokoto State is a part) is characterized by instability. Governments are frequently changed through military coups d'état. Governments are hardly allowed to settle before they are toppled. Even during the life of the same regime, leadership changes are noticeable. On July 21, 1988, the Babangida administration, which came into office in August 1985, made its third reshuffle of the state governors. Nine new governors were appointed, eight sent back to the barracks, seven retained their assignments, and five posted to other states (West Africa 1 August 1988, 1410).

Reacting to comments on this change, *West Africa Magazine* (8 August 1988, 1433) reported:

> Nigerians are asking whether the latest reshuffle is not one change too many. How can there be continuity when some states of the federation had an average of one governor each year? Even some governors felt that they had not had "enough time to complete programmes initiated in the state." Colonel Anthony Ukpo, appointed governor in 1986, and now redeployed to the barracks said, on being asked what his greatest achievement was: "Two years is not enough to say this is my greatest achievement. I ordered ferries, it took one whole year to build a ferry."

During the twelve years of its existence (1976–1988), Sokoto State had seven different governors: late Colonel Umaru Alhaji Muhammed (1976–1978), Colonel Muhammadu Gado Nasko (1978–1979), Alhaji Shehu Muhammed Kangiwa (1979–1981), Dr. Garba Nadama (1981–1983), Brigadier Garba Duba (1984–1985), Colonel Garba Muhammed (1985–1986), and Colonel Ahmad Muhammad Daku (1986–1990).

Each of the governors tended to pay special attention to the implementation of the policies formulated during their tenure, and they gave little or no serious attention to the implementation of policies initiated by their predecessors. *West Africa Magazine* (8 August 1988, 1433) notes: "Usually when new governors are sworn-in, on-going projects are jettisoned, and new ones initiated."

In its report, the Task Force Committee on the Evaluation of Effectiveness and Efficiency of the Sokoto State Civil Service (1986, 15) observes:

> Over the years, many Ministries and Parastatals complain, the changing government policies have had a lot to do with reducing efficiency in their services. Ministries and Departments have had to do one thing only to have it completely reversed by a succeeding administration in the state.... Boarding of students in post primary institutions ... was completely reversed, ... the policy abolishing Haraji ... was also reversed. In an atmosphere of unstable government policies, Ministries and Parastatals are at times forced to go at opposite directions all at once.

All this, it should be noted, is not deliberate, but due largely to the different perceptions of the governors regarding the problems they considered pressing. Another possible explanation is work overload as well as the socioeconomic pressures on the actors. The late Colonel Muhammed inherited in 1976 from his predecessor an education policy designated Primary Education Improvement Programme (PEIP), which had been formulated in 1972 (by the then North-Western State government). Its implementation continued until 1978 when its momentum lagged during the time of his successor, Colonel Nasko, and it was eventually abandoned in 1979 during Alhaji Kangiwa's administration.

The 1976 transport policy, which established the Rima Transport Service and SUDA Bus Service, formulated during the late Colonel Muhammed's time, was given less attention during the time of both Alhaji Kangiwa and Dr. Nadama, and it was eventually scrapped by Brigadier Duba in 1984. The 1982 Marriage Law, formulated under Dr. Nadama, was welcomed by everybody but, by 1984, its implementation had run into problems and nothing was done by

Nadama's successor, Brigadier Duba. The implementation of the 1984 Housing Policy, initiated by Brigadier Garba Duba to save costs in the government renting of private accommodation was reversed by his successor, Colonel Muhammed. The implementation of the 1985 Environmental Sanitation Edict, formulated during Brigadier Duba's term, upon the directive of the federal military government, under Major General Muhammadu Buhari, was slowed down after General Buhari was overthrown in a military coup d'état and Brigadier Duba was reassigned to a new job from Sokoto. As pointed out in Chapter One, the policy was not all that popular. Nevertheless, it was being implemented while its initiators were still in charge.

These changes are not, of course, limited to the level of governors; they very much affect the top echelon of the bureaucracy. With every change of government, the Secretary to the Government (SSG) and Head of the Civil Service (HS) or Secretary to the Military Government and Head of Service (SMG/HS) are in most cases changed. There has been, from 1976 to date, seven different SMG/ HS, as shown in Table 7.10:

### Table 7.10 Governors and Secretaries to State Governments/Heads of Service

| Date | Governors | Secretaries |
|------|-----------|-------------|
|  |  |  |
| 1976–8 | Colonel Umaru Muhammed (Mili) | Alh. M. Carpenter (SMG/HS) |
| 1978–9 | Colonel Gado Nasko (Mili) | Alh. M. Carpenter (SMG/HS) |
| 1979–81 | Alh. Shehu Kangiwa (Civi) | Alh. Yarima A. Sani (SSG) |
|  |  | Alh. Idrisu Koko (HS) |
| 1981–3 | Dr. Garba Nadama (Civi) | Alh. Yarima A. Sani (SSG) |
|  |  | Alh.Idrisu Koko (HS) |
|  |  | Alh Ahmed Dogon Daji (SSG) |
|  |  | Alh. Muhammadu Jega (HS) |

| Date | Governors | Secretaries |
|------|-----------|-------------|
| 1984–5 | Brigadier Garba Duba (Mili) | Alh. Muhammadu Jega (SMG/HS) |
| | | Alh. M. B. Alkali (SMG/HS) |
| 1985–6 | Colonel Garba Muhammed (Mili) | Alh. M. B. Alkali (SMG/HS) |
| 1986–9 | Colonel Ahmad M. Daku (Mili) | Alh. M. B. Alkali (SMG/HS) |
| | | Alh. Yahaya Maigari (SMG/HS) |

Muhammadu Carpenter (SMG/HS), 1976–9; Abubakar Yarima Sani (Secretary to the State Government SSG), 1979–83; Alhaji Idrisu Koko (Head of Service), 1979–83; Alhaji Ahmed Dogon Daji (SSG), October to December 1983; Alhaji Muhammadu Jega (Head of Service), October to December 1983; Alhaji Muhammadu Jega (SMG/HS), 1984–5; Alhaji Muhammadu Bello Alkali (SMG/HS), 1985–6; Yahaya Maigari (SMG/HS), 1987 to date. Their appointments were made by the governors as follows: late Colonel Muhammed appointed Alhaji Carpenter; late Alhaji Kangiwa appointed Yarima Sani and Alhaji Koko, respectively; Dr. Nadama appointed Alhaji D/Daji and Alhaji Jega, respectively; Brigadier Duba appointed Alhaji Jega, and later Alhaji Alkali; Colonel Daku appointed Maigari.

On their part too, with every change, the secretaries to the government and heads of service reassigned the permanent secretaries, although with the governor's approval. Almost every year, from 1979 to 1989, permanent secretaries were posted from one ministry to another, as presented in Table 7.11. Yet, the problem was not their reassignment, for that was the nature of their work. The problem, however, was the frequency that characterized the postings and that invariably affected the continuity of the implementation process, particularly when even the political officials (commissioners) were not only changed, but also reassigned from time to time. Table 7.11 shows the number of times posting of permanent secretaries was carried out every year from 1979 to 1989, and the number affected in each posting. For example, in 1984, there were three postings. In the first posting, twenty-five officers were affected; in the second, two were affected; and in the third, four were affected. It is not unusual that those who were affected in the first posting also could have been affected in the second or third posting. For example, two permanent secretaries (Alhaji Sulaiman Bawa and Alhaji Hanafi Sa'ad) were featured in five consecutive postings as follows: on May 18, 1987, March 29, 1988, June 28, 1988, May 29, 1989, and September 18, 1989. With every posting, a lot of time was wasted on handing over and taking over notes and on introducing the officer taking over. After he had taken over, the new officer would need time to study his new organization. All this affects the pace of implementation process. A permanent secretary may initiate a policy in a given ministry and start its implementation, but before its full implementation he is posted to another organization. Another permanent secretary may be posted to the ministry, but may have different views about the policy of his predecessor. He may not have any inclination to the policy. Thus his commitment toward the successful implementation of the policy will not be total.

Apart from the direct implementation problem it causes, the redeployment posting of permanent secretaries adversely affects the relationship between the secretaries to the government and heads of service who initiated the posting, and some

**Table 7.11**
**Posting of Permanent Secretaries in the Sokoto Bureaucracy,**
**1979–1989**

| Year | Number of Times | Number Affected |
|------|-----------------|-----------------|
| 1979 | 1 | 17 |
| 1980 | 1 + 1 | 2 + 11 |
| 1981 | 1 | 4 |
| 1982 | 1 | 3 |
| 1983 | 1 + 1 | 2 + 27 |
| 1984 | 1 + 1 + 1 | 25 + 2 + 4 |

| 1985 | 1 + 1 | 3 + 13 |
|------|-------|--------|
| 1986 | | |
| 1987 | 1 + 1 + 1 | 16 + 3 + 4 |
| 1988 | 1 + 1 | 9 + 23 |
| 1989 | 1 + 1 | 10 + 5 |
| Source: Military Governor's Office, Sokoto, 1989. | | |

permanent secretaries moved from preferred to less attractive posts. Generally, the bureaucrats have categorized government posts into two: those that are regarded as lucrative and those that are not. The lucrative ministries are involved in the award of large- and small-scale contracts, unlike the nonlucrative ones. Among the lucrative ministries are Education, Health, Works and Transport, and Finance. Among the nonlucrative ones are the Governor's Office, Social Development, Information, Commerce, and Industry. Thus, some permanent secretaries, when posted to nonlucrative ministries, tend to blame the head of service, although without saying so openly, for posting them there. This attitude tends to affect the morale and invariably the performance of the officers concerned. It might also undermine the effective implementation of policies and programs, particularly when socioeconomic problems and overload have to be faced.

# Work Overload

Associated with the governmental instability is the problem of governmental overload. Some studies have indicated that about 60 percent of the civil servants were overloaded with work, while 30 percent had insufficient work to do. In this regard, Asiodu (1970, 133) observes:

The Civil Services in Nigeria are increasingly required to prepare development plans, to appraise and select industrial and agricultural projects, to decide when new roads, railways, harbours, bridges or telecommunications facilities should be constructed and the optimum size of investments in these projects at any given time in the light of carefully analyzed projections of demand, and on the basis of cost/ benefits analysis. These things are now the every day tasks of government.

Overload has characterized the activities of many governments. In attempting to answer the question "why Britain is becoming harder to govern," King (1976, 12) observes that:

the range of matters for which British Governments hold themselves responsible—and for which they believe that the electorate may hold them responsible—has increased greatly over the past ten or twenty years, as well as over the past fifty, and is still increasing at a rapid rate.

In Sokoto State, there has been, during the last twelve years, an enormous expansion of government activities: education, health services, water, power supply, roads, and housing. However, it should be pointed out that the expansion of government activities in Sokoto State is not attributable to its venturing into new areas outside its traditional jurisdiction, as in Britain. The state government, as well as the Nigerian government as a whole, has been the main initiator of socioeconomic development, the main provider of social services, and the largest employer of labor. The expansion is, rather, largely due to more demands on the existing services, following rapid increases in the population, on the one hand, and the improved financial position of the government, as a result of the oil revenue, on the other. The Sokoto State population increased from 4.5 million in 1976 to over 8 million in 1988. Similarly, its budget rose in the same period from N208.8 million to N910.8 million.

Between 1984 and 1987 the bureaucracy was so overworked that a permanent secretary commented that the bureaucracy had lost its sense of direction and had no chance to even initiate policy or to even implement policy effectively. The federal government might send a circular to the state requesting a detailed report of the state activities in the last quarter or requesting a detailed report on one kind of a program or another to be submitted within a very short time. For example, *West Africa Magazine* (1989, 983) reported:

> All Ministries were ... directed by President Ibrahim Babangida on May 17 to submit reports by May 31 detailing their achievements since the inception of his administration in 1985.... The Government intended to compare original target levels with actual performance, as a basis for an objective assessment of each Minister's achievement.

These reports, in most cases, were not readily available. Fresh efforts had to be made to gather relevant information for the report. In doing so, circulars would be sent from the military governor's office to all ministries and departments concerned to prepare their reports accordingly. In the absence of computer facilities everything had to be started from scratch and, invariably, all other works such as implementation of other policies would virtually come to a standstill until the report was prepared. Before the report was completed, or no sooner was it completed, other similar circulars would be issued either by the federal or the state government.

While this was going on, committees were likely to be appointed to investigate or solve one problem or another. For example, seventy-eight committees of inquiries were established between January 1984 and November 1989, thirteen in 1984, twelve in 1985, four in 1986, five in 1987, fifteen in 1988, and twenty-nine in 1989 (Military Governor's Office 1989). The minimum number of members of these committees was five, and their membership, except for eight committees, consisted completely of civil servants. They had to combine their ministerial or organizational responsibilities with their role as members of the committees. There was an instance during which a permanent secretary was to be appointed to head a committee, he vehemently rejected the idea, arguing that he was presently serving on nine different committees, which was making it impossible for him to do his routine administrative work in his ministry. It was a situation where the bureaucrats were busy implementing different policies at

## Table 7.12
## Number of Policy Documents Submitted by Ministries to the Sokoto State Executive Council, 1979–1988

| Ministries | '79 | '80 | '81 | '82 | '83 | '84 | '85 | '86 | '87 | '88 |
|---|---|---|---|---|---|---|---|---|---|---|
| Agriculture | 13 | 30 | 10 | 8 | - | 14 | 13 | 9 | 15 | 5 |
| Commerce | 16 | 7 | - | 4 | - | 9 | 4 | 2 | 6 | 10 |
| Education | 13 | 11 | 7 | 8 | 3 | 9 | 9 | 13 | 14 | 14 |
| Finance/Economic | 42 | 37 | 19 | 20 | 5 | 14 | 18 | 24 | 18 | 11 |
| Governor's Office | 32 | 16 | 3 | 6 | 4 | 4 | 24 | 11 | 16 | 19 |
| Health | 20 | 19 | 4 | 6 | 1 | 6 | 13 | 20 | 14 | 10 |
| Information/Sports | 24 | 10 | 9 | 1 | 4 | 9 | 6 | 5 | 2 | 4 |
| Justice | 1 | 3 | 2 | 1 | - | 4 | - | 1 | 3 | 1 |
| Local Government | 17 | 3 | 1 | 2 | - | 2 | 4 | 12 | 7 | 2 |
| Works/Housing | 20 | 18 | 5 | 6 | 3 | 7 | 11 | 7 | 9 | 19 |
| Total | 198 | 154 | 60 | 59 | 22 | 78 | 82 | 117 | 99 | 92 |

Source: Military Governor's Office, Sokoto, 1989.

the same time but achieving very little. As Ingram and Mann (1980, 18) conclude, "the more densely packed the policy space, the less likelihood that policies can be successful."

Along with this is the speed with which those policies were expected to be implemented. It should be noted that with the exception of the 1979–1983 civilian governments that came through democratic elections, all the other governments came through military coups d'état. Usually the military regimes criticize their predecessors for achieving nothing while in office, taking into account the continuing underdevelopment of the state. It is not by accident, therefore, that successive governments in the state from 1976 to 1987 have always been in a hurry to formulate and implement one kind of policy or another so as to improve the situation of the state and, in doing so, legitimize their stay in power. Since the priority of each administration is to implement its own policies, the implementation of inherited policies is bound to be neglected or abandoned, particularly when the actors are faced with enormous socioeconomic pressures from the social environment.

The empirical evidence on overload is suggestive, but hardly conclusive. To prove it convincingly will involve a prohibitive statistical calculation; the number of memos bureaucrats write each day will be counted and the amount of time devoted to such memos, the number of visitors they receive, the number of meetings and conferences they attend, and the number of telephone calls they make and receive. In short, it is an impressionistic view that bureaucrats are overloaded with work that unduly slows down implementation process.

## Implementers' Socioeconomic Problems

The implementation of public policies is greatly constrained by implementers' socioeconomic problems. Relatives, fellow townsmen, and friends of the bureaucrats, particularly from the rural areas, visit them in their offices in the urban centers mostly during official hours and request them for assistance to solve one problem or another. In most cases the bureaucrats would have to leave their offices—some may ask for permission while others may not—in order to solve those problems. The problem might be to purchase prescribed drugs for a hospitalized relative who could not afford to buy them; it might be to show empathy to a relative who had a court case and had suffered untold hardship as a result of continuous adjournment; it might be to get some money for urgent domestic needs; or it might be to get a job for a relative or friend. In doing this their official performance is seriously constrained. Observing this phenomenon, Kingsley (1963, 306) said, "[C]ivil servants ... are under extreme and constant pressures to support or give assistance to a circle of relatives which seems geometrically as one's status and income go up." Yet providing such assistance is necessary, if one has the means, taking into account that the people are generally Muslims and the religion has made it mandatory for them to help those in need. Secondly, the extended family system in the state requires mutual assistance among the family. It may appear that the extended family system is a constraint on the performance of the bureaucrats. On the contrary, it seems that it is the state of underdevelopment that makes life hard for people so that they must solicit assistance from their relations, friends, and townsmen who are employed in the bureaucracy. As pointed out in Chapter Four, 80 percent of the Sokoto State population was engaged in agricultural activities, particularly farming (which lasts, in most cases, for four months in a year). Thus, with limited rainfall, desert encroachment, and the use of inappropriate farming technology, it is difficult to improve production and its consequence on poor income. Besides, in the face of increasing population and urbanization on the one hand, and the grossly inadequate job opportunities on the otehr, as there are very few industries and factories to complement government efforts in that direction, it is hard for the people to make ends meet. In all this, the inability of the successive administrations to cope with these enormous problems make it impossible for people not to seek the assistance of their relations or friends in the bureaucracy who are seemingly regarded as better off. Thus, the extended family in itself is not the problem. If anything, it enhances social integration in the society and limits crime waves.

This view on the implementers' problems may be subject to different interpretations. Some may see the bureaucrats as inefficient, for as Allison argues, "what we see and judge to be important ...

depends not only on the evidence but also on the conceptual lenses through which we look at the evidence" (Elmore 1978, 189). Some may even dispute whether Sokoto State, or Nigerian bureaucracy, conforms with Weber's type. There is no doubt that structurally, Sokoto State bureaucracy is based on legal-rational authority, but behaviorally it has some limitations. The point, however, is to highlight that implementers are confronted with socioeconomic problems, which invariably affect the pace of implementation process.

# Infrastructural Inadequacies

Apart from the socioeconomic pressures of families and friends on the individual bureaucrats, the inadequacy of infrastructure (notably health, water, power, transport, and communications) constrains their performance. Bureaucrats may leave their offices at any time to travel to their original home villages (most of them are from rural areas) to see sick relatives and arrange for their transport to general hospitals, as there are only ten in the state, or to rural health centers (only sixteen) or to health clinics (only thirty-eight in a population of 8 million). The inadequacy of the health facilities is not only in terms of numbers, but also in terms of the internal facilities, such as drugs, medical instruments, and equipment. Thus, even when the sick relatives are admitted into hospitals, the problem of constant visits continues.

Similarly, whenever there is a water shortage from the main supply (a dominant feature of water supply in the urban centers), officers leave their offices to fetch water from wherever they can get it for their domestic needs. Official work is also disrupted whenever there is a power failure, a rampant problem in the state.

Furthermore, a large number of officers leave their offices to take their children home from school, as there is only inadequate transport. To this extent, government vehicles are uneconomically used by officers for taking their children to and from school. There are two types of government vehicles: those that are specifically attached to some officers (with drivers) and those that are in the common pool for general official use. In the first category are commissioners, permanent secretaries, secretaries, general managers, and other officers on grade level 16 and above. In the second category are all other officers who are assigned official duties that require the use of vehicles. Although in both cases the use of the vehicles is supposed to be for only official purposes, they are mostly used for private purposes: to take children, families, relatives, and friends to the hospital, to attend some ceremonies, and to go to the market for purchasing foodstuffs and other goods. It is not surprising, therefore, a number of circulars were issued in order to control the misuse of government vehicles. One of such circulars reads:

> It has been observed that there is daily increase in the continuous misuse of Government vehicles. In order to arrest the current wave of misuse of Government Vehicles in the State, a surprise check would soon be conducted by the army in the State Capital (Governor's Office Sokoto 1985).

Thus, the frequency with which officers go out for their private engagements (conditioned by the nature of the socioeconomic problems) during official hours is high and definitely affects the level of their performance and invariably the extent of implementation, particularly when there is much work to be done.

On the other hand, the terrible condition of some rural roads or the absence of motorable roads in some rural areas makse it difficult for the bureaucrats to ensure effective implementation of government programs in those areas. In his study of health policy in Benue State, Mato (1986, 71) noted that the problem of inadequate transport in the state Ministry of Health inhibited efficient health delivery services.

That apart, a work that involves coordination of efforts of different organizations at both the state capital and local government headquarters and that is supposed to take just a day will take between three and five days to finish in view of the inadequacy of telephone services in the state. As indicated in Chapter Four, only eight out of the nineteen local government areas of the state have telephone services. Apart from Sokoto, Gusau, and Birnin Kebbi, whose telephone services were provided in the 1950s, the other five towns have had their telephones only since the early 1980s.

On the whole, it seems to me, as evidenced by the above analysis, that implementation of public policy could hardly succeed in an atmosphere characterized by constant change of governments and officials, by too many policies being undertaken by government, and by all of it taking place in an environment of severe socioeconomic inadequacies.

> Failure to recognize that these … ordinary circumstances present serious obstacles to implementation inhibits learning. If one is always looking for unusual circumstances and dramatic events, he cannot appreciate how difficult it is to make the ordinary happen (Pressman and Wildavsky 1973, xii).

Having examined the constraining variables of implementation in Sokoto State, it is appropriate to go further, for implementation analysis is not just about understanding implementation problems, but also about finding solutions to the problems. Toward this end most of the implementation studies have provided some recommendations for improving the chances of implementation success. However, some of the recommendations are either unclear or unpersuasive, or even unsupported by the empirical research base (O'Toole 1986, 191). This notwithstanding, some implementation scholars, particularly the top-downers, having identified dominant factors that contribute to implementation failures, through their own studies and the studies of pioneering implementation scholars (Pressman and Wildavsky 1973; Van Meter and Van Horn 1975; Hood 1976; Bardach 1977), have provided a list of variables (checklists) that, they suggested, are sufficient for effective implementation. In particular, Gunn (1978) provides ten conditions necessary for achieving perfect implementation:

## Conditions for Effective Implementation

For implementation of policy to succeed, it is essential that a number of conditions be fulfilled. First, the circumstances external to the implementing agency must not impose crippling constraints. Second, adequate time and sufficient resources should be set aside for the program. Third, the implementers must see to it that not only are there no constraints in terms of overall resources but also that, at each stage in the implementation process, the required combination of resources is actually available. Fourth, the policy to be implemented should be based upon a valid theory of cause and effect. Fifth, the relationship between cause and effect should be direct and that there are few, if any, intervening links. Sixth, a single implementing agency should be identified, which does not necessarily depend upon other agencies for success. Seventh, there must be complete understanding of, and agreement upon, the objectives to be achieved. Eighth, in moving toward agreed objectives it should be possible to specify, in complete detail and perfect sequence, the tasks to be performed by each participant. Ninth, there is perfect communication among, and coordination of, the various elements or agencies involved in the program. Tenth, those in authority can demand and expect their directives to be faithfully carried out (1978, 169-176).

Although these conditions of "perfect implementation" are unattainable, they nonetheless provide a guide to policy makers and implementers, and they sensitize them to the complex issues involved in policy implementation. As Gunn points out,

> [the] purpose is to help us think more systematically about the reasons for implementation failures and about approaches to improving the implementation process.... [I]t should be said that we are here concerned with exploring the idea of perfect implementation and not necessarily offer it as an ideal (1978, 169–70).

In the same fashion, Sabatier and Mazmanian (1979, 484–500) have provided another checklist as necessary conditions for effective implementation. Though there are some overlaps with Gunn's, they have limited their conditions to only five and specified some variables that have not been explicitly considered by Gunn. They are:

1.  The program is based on a sound theory relating changes in target group behavior to the achievement of desired end-state (objectives).

2. The statute (or other basic policy decision) contains unambiguous policy directives and structures the implementation process so as to maximize the likelihood that target groups will perform as desired.
3. The leaders of the implementing agencies possess substantial managerial and political skill and are committed to statutory goals.
4. The program is supported by organized constituency groups and a few key legislators or the chief executive throughout the implementation process, with the courts being neutral or supportive.
5. The relative priority of statutory objectives is not significantly undermined over time by the emergence of conflicting public policies or by changes in relevant socioeconomic conditions that undermine the statute's "technical" theory or political support.

Yet, another checklist is the one provided by Cleaves. Having reviewed the pioneering implementation studies in the Third World (the broader area of the present study) covering seven countries, namely Zambia, Kenya, India, Peru, Colombia, Mexico, and Brazil, contained in Grindle (1980), Cleaves arrived at similar conclusions as those of the pioneering implementation scholars mentioned above. He noted that the following six factors are crucial for successful implementation: (1) simple technical organizational features, (2) marginal change from the status quo, (3) one-actor target, (4) one-goal objective, (5) clearly stated goals, and (6) short duration.

As can be observed in this chapter, some of the above mentioned conditions may be necessary, others are certainly necessary, and still others are already internalized into the day-to-day bureaucratic procedures and practices. Taken together, and as evidenced by the examination of Operation Move Ahead, the conditions may be necessary but not sufficient to ensure successful implementation.

The checklists reproduced are meant to demonstrate the extent to which implementation scholars have gone in providing solutions to implementation problems. However, it is not clear whether the recommendations have influenced the choices made by practitioners.

Except for the original work by O'Toole (1986), there have not been efforts to examine the extent of application of the results of implementation research. As noted by O'Toole (1986, 189–90),

> No such questions seem to have been asked, let alone conclusively answered, in the literature of implementation research. The field lacks any information whatsoever concerning the degree to which social scientific knowledge about ... implementation ... has been tapped, and to what end.

As mentioned in Chapter Five, the critical variables involved in the implementation process are the policy, the organization or organizations in which implementation takes place, the actors, and the political and socioeconomic environment in which implementation is conducted. In short, this chapter, apart from anything else, has demonstrated the strengths and weaknesses of the top-down approach to the problems of implementation.

# Chapter Eight
# Conclusion

In this book I have attempted to indicate what constitutes the main problems of implementation in the Sokoto State civil service. The conclusions on the state are largely applicable to other states of the Nigerian federation. In looking for explanations why policies succeed or fail, the book began with a literature survey. It then proceeded to provide a bird's-eye view of Nigerian public administration, paying particular attention to its origin, development, and key challenges.

Since the book's primary focus is on how policies get implemented or fall short at the critical stages of implementation, it was necessary to examine the two dominant approaches in the implementation literature: the top-down and the bottom-up perspectives. Whereas the top-downers emphasize the distinction between policy and implementation and the importance of policy goal in influencing the action of implementers, the bottom-uppers make no distinction between policy and implementation and instead emphasize the relevance of implementers' strategy in the implementation process. The pioneers in the field are top-downers, but they have been challenged by the bottom-uppers, who provide another methodological approach to understanding categories of the actors involved in the implementation. A critical review of both perspectives reveals more similarities than differences. This, in any case, is not the point of this book. While challenging the distinction between the two approaches and demonstrating that the substantive analytic concepts of the implementation process advanced by the bottom-uppers are neither new nor adequate to challenge the position of the top-downers, the book has highlighted the choices open to the federal and state governments in coping with the challenges facing them in one important sector: education.

In addition to demonstrating the relevance of the top-down perspective in conceptualizing and analyzing implementation problems in general, the book cites Operation Move Ahead in Sokoto State as a case study in policy implementation. One clear lesson is that the formal implementation process may be one thing, but the actual implementation problem is another. In other words, implementation problems may not necessarily be directly related to the subject of implementation.

Implementation analysis is about understanding implementation problems, which are the preoccupation of contemporary implementation scholars. In the Third World so far, implementation problems have been attributed to either bureaucracy and bureaucrats or to the policy and the policy context. One view is that the bureaucracy is too hierarchical, and the bureaucrats are incompetent, uncommitted, and corrupt. These factors are enough to undermine successful implementation. A contrary view, however, is to attribute policy failures to ambiguity and to the neglect of the stakeholders' needs or preferences at the formulation stage. The context under which such a policy is conducted is likely to be characterized by tension and conflict. However, having reviewed both arguments, I find them inadequate in explaining the problems of implementation in the Sokoto State bureaucracy.

The bureaucracy, with its hierarchy and the long chain of command, is not necessarily the problem. Rather it is the sheer workload that the implementers have to contend with. In the absence of overload, communication tends to be clearer and faster. It is the overload that tends to hamper speedy action. It is not by accident that most of the policies initiated in Sokoto State between 1967 and 1975 (in the days of the North-Western government) were implemented by Faruk's regime in spite of the enormous corruption of the day. This was attributable to the limited number of programs. The administration, both at the state and federal levels, was for the most part of its tenure not under any serious pressure to provide expanded social services.

Regarding the bureaucrats, when they fail to achieve policy objectives, the problems in most cases are due not to internal bureaucratic constraints, incompetence, or mismanagement, but rather to external factors (Milward and Brinton 1983, 163). Thus, attributing the poor implementation of Nigeria's national economic development plans to corruption and lack of committed bureaucrats, as asserted by Anigboh, is wrong. The First Plan (1962–1968), launched by the civilian regime of the First Republic, was interrupted in 1966 following a military coup d'état of January 1966, the counter-military coup d'état of July in the same year, and the subsequent civil war that started in 1967 and ended in January 1970. It would be a miracle if the plan was well implemented under those trying circumstances. The Second Plan (1970–1974), on the other hand, was not affected by any significant crisis. It is not surprising, therefore, that most of the policies formulated during the period were implemented. The buoyancy of the economy might have been an enabling factor, but the government's determination to achieve plan objectives could not be dismissed as irrelevant. The Third Plan (1975–1980), launched in March 1975, was interrupted in July of the same year by another military coup d'état. In February 1976, another unsuccessful coup d'état led to the death of the then-head of state, General Murtala Muhammed. In 1979, the military transferred power to the elected civilians. The civilians came in with their new programs and obviously paid little attention to the plan formulated by the military. The Fourth Plan (1981–1985), launched by the civilian government, was interrupted at the end of 1983 by the military, which reversed the civilian programs. The proposal for the Fifth Plan to take off in 1986 was interrupted by yet another military coup d'état in August 1985. Under this circumstance, to blame the bureaucrats is to make them the scapegoat. Besides, "they are asked to do things which are immensely difficult or sometimes impossible, and are often overloaded with responsibilities relative to the resources they have for carrying out those responsibilities" (Milward and Brinton 1983, 163–4). And yet, they are blamed for such shortcomings. Milward and Brinton (1983, 150) contend that "[u]sing the public bureaucracy as a scapegoat for a variety of social and economic ills can effectively 'prevent' the proper analysis of those problems."

Concerning the problems of policy and its context, it has been argued that since bureaucrats who implement policy participate effectively in its formulation, the problem of ambiguity and conflicts are likely to be minimized and implementation expedited. In explaining why the Japanese government seems to be much more successful than the American government in implementing public policy, Cothran (1987, 421) said that "better implementation would result from allowing civil servants to participate more fully in policy formulation."

In the light of this, alternative explanations for policy successes and failures are needed. The position advanced in this book is that implementation is undermined by governmental instability, governmental overload, implementers' socioeconomic problems, and infrastructural inadequacies. Focusing on these variables, particularly governmental instability, the book demonstrates how the factors undermined the implementation of Sokoto State's education policy, Operation Move Ahead. Although some scholars have discussed the problem of governmental overload in constraining implementation, consideration has not yet been given to the problems of governmental instability, implementers' socioeconomic problems, and infrastructural inadequacies in the implementation literature. By conceptualizing the problems of governmental instability, implementers' socioeconomic problems, and infrastructural inadequacies, and by showing the linkages between them and other variables (overload), one has at least further advanced the literature on implementation.

As indicated earlier, few implementation scholars have discussed the problems of overload and still other scholars have generally mentioned socioeconomic problems of implementers; thus, what needs to be highlighted is the featuring of governmental instability in the failures of many policies, whether in the industrialized world or the Third World. In Britain, for example, Burch and Wood (1983, 182) commented that "three post-war Labour governments legislated to reduce profits made from land ownership, but Conservative successors reversed the policy before it was fully carried out." Even in Pressman and Wildavsky's famous study of implementation of the Oakland Project there were problems of governmental instability, involving the change of the first head of the Oakland Project, his representative at Oakland, and other key staff who had helped run the program in its first year. They were changed to new jobs before the program they started could achieve its aim. Their departure, Pressman and Wildavsky confirmed, had "marked a drastic shift in the emphasis of the Oakland programme" (1973, 48). New implementers were appointed, but they had to study and understand the program before they could move forward. All these caused further delays in the implementation process. Instead of creating three thousand jobs four years after the program had taken off, only a few jobs had been created and major public works had not been built (Pressman and Wildavsky 1973, 2–3).

In Nigeria, Babangida's mass mobilization program for Economic Reconstruction, Social Justice, and Self-Reliance (MAMSER), is not the first of its kind to aim at mobilizing Nigerians. There have been similar policies in the past that aimed at achieving the same set of objectives: Shagari's Ethical Revolution and Buhari's War Against Indiscipline (WAI), which was directed against disorderliness and all kinds of corruption in the public life (Keesings Contemporary Record 1984, 33261). Other policies include Obasanjo's Operation Feed the Nation (OFN) and Shagari's Green Revolution. All these previous programs were never fully implemented due to governmental instability.

Following their experience of the time it takes to implement a policy, the drafters of the 1989 Nigerian constitution provide for a six-year term for the president, believing that a six-year period is adequate to implement all projects embarked upon (*West Africa Magazine* 1989, 470).

As argued in this book, one of the outstanding contributions of the implementation study is to identify the variables that could be manipulated in order to ensure successful implementation. In other words, implementation study is about understanding and solving implementation problems. Toward that end, some implementation scholars, having reviewed the works of the pioneering implementation scholars and their own research, have provided complementary checklists as conditions for effective implementation. Specifically, Gunn provides ten conditions, Mazmanian and Sabatier six, and Cleaves six, as presented in Chapter Seven. The conditions, on the whole, are necessary but not sufficient to ensure successful implementation. Hence, the relevance of governmental instability and socioeconomic inadequacies as crucial variables to be incorporated on the agenda of the checklist tradition — governmental overload is already incorporated.

In the same vein, it has been illustrated that, in any implementation processes, four variables are essential: the policy, the organization or organizations in which implementation is pursued, the actors in the process, and the overall environment of implementation.

The implication of all this for both theoretical and empirical purposes is to show that there are implementation problems that arise from the policy, there are those that arise from the actors, those within and across bureaucracies, and those that arise outside bureaucracies. In this context, while governmental instability and governmental overload arise both within and outside bureaucracy, socioeconomic problems of bureaucrats and infrastructural inadequacies arise outside the bureaucracy. Those problems that arise outside the policy arena (i.e., those that are beyond the reach or control of policy makers and the career bureaucracy) are precisely those that are critical to implementation success. By understanding the implementation process and the variables that constrain it, policy formulators and implementers will be better placed to avoid the problems or to cope with them when they arise.

# Bibliography

Abba, A. et al. 1985. *The Nigerian Economic Crises: Causes and Solutions.* Zaria: Academic Staff Union of Universities of Nigeria.

Abdu, S. P. et al. 1982. *Sokoto State in Map: An Atlas of Physical and Human Resources.* Ibadan: University Press.

Abdullahi, Musa. 1977. *Traditional Elites and Political Modernization: Local Government Reforms in the North-Western State of Nigeria.* University of Chicago.

Adamolekun, Ladipo. 1983. *Public Administration: A Nigerian and Comparative Perspective.* London: Longman.

Adamolekun, Ladipo. 1985. "A Critical Time for the Civil Service," *West Africa Magazine* Jan 28–Feb 4. 143–4.

Adamolekun, Ladipo. 1985. *The Fall of the Second Republic.* Ibadan: Spectrum Books Ltd.

Adebayo, Augustus. 1981. *White Man in Black Skin.* Ibadan: Spectrum Books Ltd.

Adedeji, Adebayo. (ed).1969. *Nigerian Administration and its Political Setting.* London: Hutchinson.

Agu, Augustine O. 1986. *The Implementation of Universal Primary Education in Nigeria: Nation, States, and Schools.* Harvard University.

Ake, Claude. 1974. "Modernization and Political Instability: A Theoretical Exploration," *World Politics* 26:576–91.

Ake, Claude. 1975. Definition of Political Instability, *Comparative Politics.* 271–83.

Anigboh, Uzobeyi A. 1985. *The Extent to Which Corruption Has Hindered the Effective Implementation of Economic Development in Africa: A Case Study of Nigeria from 1970 to 1983* (Howard Unpublished PhD).

Asiodu, Phillip. 1970. "The Structure of the Federal and State Civil Services in the Context of the Twelve states structure,"

*Administrative and Political Development: Prospect for Nigeria.* Kaduna: Baraka Press.

Awa, E. O. 1964. *Federal Government of Nigeria.* Berkeley: University of California Press.

Babangida, Ibrahim. January 21, 1986. *Presidential address to federal ministers and permanent secretaries.* 1–3.

Balogun, M. J. 1983. *Public Administration in Nigeria: A Developmental Approach.* London: Macmillan Press.

Balogun, M. J. 2009. *The Route to Power in Nigeria: A Dynamic Engagement Option for Current and Aspiring Leaders.* New York: Palgrave Macmillan.

Bardach, Engene. 1977. *The Implementation Game: What Happens After a Bill Becomes a Law.* Massachusetts: MIT.

Barret, Lindsay. 1984. "The Return of the Nigerian Military: The Pattern of Military Rule," *West Africa Magazine.* July 9–August 6.

Barrett, Susan and Fudge, Colin (eds). 1981. *Policy and Action: Essays on the Implementation of Public Policy.* London: Methuen.

Barrett, S. and Hill, M. 1984. "Policy, Bargaining and Structure in Implementation Theory: Towards an Integrated Perspective," *Policy and Politics* 12, 3:219–240.

Baumer, Donald C. 1978. "Implementing Public Service Employment," *The Policy Cycle*, Sage Yearbooks in Politics and Public Policy, vol. 5. London: Sage.

Berman, Paul. 1978. "The Study of Macro- and Micro-Implementation," *Public Policy* 26, 2:157–184.

Berman, Paul. 1980. "Thinking about Programmed and Adaptive Implementation," *Why Policies Succeed or Fail*, Sage Yearbooks in Politics and Public Policy, vol. 8. London: Sage.

Bienen, H. and Fitton, M. 1978. "Soldiers, Politicians and Civil Servants," *Soldiers and Oil: The Political Transformation of Nigeria.* London: Frank Cass.

Blanche, Robin. 1984. "Education: How Humberside went comprehensive," *Policies into Practice.* London: Heinemann.

Blitz, L. F. (ed). 1965. *The Politics and Administration of Nigerian Government.* London: Sweet and Maxwell.

Boorer, David R. 1985. *Secondary Teacher Education in Sokoto State: An Examination of the Quality of the Training Given by a College of Education in Northern Nigeria.* University of Wales.

Bowen, Elinor R. 1982. "The Pressman-Wildavsky Paradox: Four Addenda or Why Models Based on Probability Theory Can Predict Implementation Success and Suggest Useful Tactical Advice for Implementers," *Journal of Public Policy* 2, 1:1–22.

Bretton, Henry L. 1962. *Power and Stability in Nigeria: The Politics of Decolonization.* New York: Frederick A. Preager.

Brownsberger, W. N. 1983. "Development and Governmental Corruption—Materialism and Political Fragmentation in Nigeria," *The Journal of Modern African Studies* 21, 2:215–233.

Bunker, Douglas R. 1972. "Policy Sciences Perspectives on Implementation Process," *Policy Sciences* 3:71–80.

Bunza, Mustapha M. 1984. *Growth and Development of Higher Education in Sokoto and Niger States of Nigeria.* University of Wales.

Burch, M. and Wood, B. 1983. *Public Policy in Britain.* Oxford: Martin Robertson.

Burns, Sir Alan. 1949. *Colonial Civil Servant.* London: George Allan & Unwin Ltd.

Campbell, M. J. 1965. "The Structure of Local Government," *The Politics and Administration of Nigerian Government.* London: Sweet & Maxwell.

Carland, John M. 1985. *The Colonial Office and Nigeria, 1898–1914.* London: Macmillan.

Chapman, L. 1979. *Your Disobedient Servant.* London: Penguin.

Chase, Gordon. 1979. "Implementing A Human Services Program: How Hard Will It Be," *Public Policy* 27, 4:385–435.

Chick, John D. 1965. "The Structure of Government at the Regional Level," *The Politics and Administration of Nigerian Government.* London: Sweet & Maxwell.

Ciroma, A. L. 1980. "Public Service and Nation Building," *Public Service Lecture.* Lagos: Federal Civil Service.

Clark, Robert P. 1978. *Power and Policy in the Third World.* New York: John Wiley & Sons.

Coleman, James S. 1958. *Nigeria: Background to Nationalism.* Berkeley: University of California Press.

Coleman, James S. 1965. *Education and Political Development.* Princeton: Princeton University Press.

Collins, P. (ed). 1980. *Administration for Development in Nigeria.* Lagos: African Education Press.

Cothran, Don A. 1987. "Japanese Bureaucrats and Policy Implementation: Lessons for America?" *Policy Studies Review* 6, 3:439–458.

Davies, T. and Mason, C. 1982. "Gazing Up at the Bottoms: Problems of Minimal Response in the Implementation of Manpower Policy," *European Journal of Political Research* 10:145–157.

Dlakwa, H. Dantaro. 1984. *Implementing Federal Development Project at the State Level in Nigeria: The Case of Federal Low Cost Housing Scheme 1980–83.* University of Pittsburgh.

Dudley, B. J. 1973. *Instability and Political Order: Politics and Crisis in Nigeria.* Ibadan: Ibadan University Press.

Dunsire, Andrew. 1978. *Implementation in a Bureaucracy.* Oxford: Martin Robertson.

Edward III, G. C. and Sharkansky, Ira. 1978. *The Policy Predicament: Making and Implementation of Public Policy.* San Francisco: W. H. Freeman & Company.

Egerton, H. Edward. 1922. *British Colonial Policy in the XXth Century.* London: Methuen.

Egonmwan, J. A. 1982. *The Effect of Structure on Policy Implementation: An Organizational Analysis of Bendel State of Nigeria Ministry of Local Government in Relation to the Implementation of the 1976 Reform* (MDS, Institute of Social Studies, The Hague). 3.

Elmore, Richard F. 1978. "Organizational Models of Social Program Implementation," *Public Policy* 26, 2:185–228.

Elmore, Richard F. 1979. "Backward Mapping: Implementation Research and Policy Decisions," *Political Science Quarterly* 94, 4:601–616

Elmore, Richard F. 1985. "Forward and Backward Mapping: Reversible Logic in the Analysis of Public Policy," *Policy*

*Implementation in Federal and Unitary Systems.* Dordrecht: Martinus Nijhoff Publishers.

Elmore, Richard F. 1987. "Instrument and Strategy in Public Policy," *Policy Studies Review* 7, 1:174–186.

Fafunwa, A. Babs. 1974. *History of Education in Nigeria.* London: George Allan & Unwin.

Flint, John. 1983. "Planned Decolonization and Its Failure in British Africa," *African Affairs: The Journal of the Royal African Society* 82, 328:389–411.

Goggin, Malcom. 1986. "The 'Too Few Cases/Too Many Variables' Problem in Implementation Research," *Western Political Quarterly.* 328–347.

Goodin, Robert and Waldner, Ilmar. 1979. "Thinking Big, Thinking Small, and Not Thinking At All," *Public Policy* 27, 1:1–24.

Graham, Sonia F. 1966. *Government and Mission Education in Northern Nigeria 1900–1919.* Ibadan: University of Ibadan Press.

Grindle, M. S. (ed). 1980. *Politics and Policy Implementation in the Third World.* Princeton: Princeton University Press.

Grindle, M. S. 1981. "Anticipating Failure: The Implementation of Rural Development Programs," *Public Policy* 29, 1:51–74.

Gulma, A. Abubakar. 1983. *The Growth and Development of Grade II Teachers' Colleges in the Sokoto State of Nigeria, 1970–1980.* University of Wales.

Gunn, L. A. 1978. "Why is Implementation So Difficult?" *Management Services in Government,* November. 169–176.

Haily, Lord. 1951. *Native Administration in British African Territories.* London: HMSO.

Ham, C. and Hill, M. 1984. *The Policy Process in the Modern Capitalist State.* London:

Hanf, Kenneth and Scharpf, F.(eds). 1978. *Interorganizational Policy Making: Limits to Coordination and Central Control,* London: Sage.

Hanf, Kenneth. 1982. "Regulatory Structure: Enforcement as Implementation," *European Journal of Political Research* 10:159–172.

Hanf, Kenneth and Toonen, T. A. (eds). 1985. *Policy Implementation in Federal and Unitary Systems.* Dordrecht: Martinus Nijhoff Publishers.

Hanusch, Horst, (ed). 1983. *Anatomy of Government Deficiencies.* Berlin: Springer-Verlag.

Hargrove, E. C. 1975. *The Missing Link.* Washington DC: The Urban Institute.

Hargrove, E. C. 1983. "The Search for Implementation Theory," in Zechhausev, R and Leebart, D. (eds). *What Role for Government? Lessons from Policy Research.* Duke Press, Policy Studies.

Harris, Richard L. 1965. "The Role of the Civil Servant in West Africa," *Public administration Review* 25:308.

Heussler, Robert. 1963. *Yesterdays Rulers: The Making of the British Colonial Service.* Syracuse: Syracuse University Press.

Higgins, Thomas J. 1984/85. "Implementation Revisited: The Case of Federal Demonstration," *Journal of Policy Analysis and Management* 4, 3:436–440.

Hill, Michael. 1979. "Appendix II: Implementation and the Central-Local Relationship," *Central-Local Government Relationship: A Panel Report to the Research Initiatives.* London: Social Science Research Council.

Hjern, B. and Porter, D. 1981. "Implementation Structure: A New Unit of Administrative Analysis," *Organization Studies* 2:211–27.

Hjern, B. and Hull, C. 1982. "Implementation Research as Empirical Constitutionalism," *European Journal of Political Research* 10:105–115.

Hjern, B. and Hull, C. 1985. "Small Firm Employment Creation: An Assistance Structure Explanation," *Policy Implementation in Federal and Unitary Systems.* Dordrecht: Martinus Nijhoff Publishers.

Hogwood, B. and Gunn, L. 1984. *Policy Analysis for the Real World.* Oxford: OUP.

Hood, C. C. 1976. *The Limit of Administration.* London: John Wiley

Huntington, Samuel. 1968. *Political Order in Changing Societies.* New Haven: Yale University Press.

Hyder, Masood. 1984. "Implementation: The Evolutionary Model," *Policies into Practice: National and International Case Studies in Implementation.* London: Heinemann.

Ingram, Helen. 1977. "Policy Implementation through Bargaining: Federal Grants in Aid," *Public Policy* 25.

Ingram, Helen M. and Mann, Dean (eds). 1980. *Why Policies Succeed Or Fail.* Sage Yearbooks in Politics and Public Policy, vol. 8. London: SAGE.

Jalingo, Ahmed Usman. 1980. *The Radical Tradition in Northern Nigeria.* University of Edinburgh.

Johnson, Ronald D. and O'Connor, R. E. 1979. "Intra-agency Limitations on Policy Implementation: You Can't Always Get What You Want, but Sometimes You Get What You Need," *Administration and Society* 11, 2:193–215.

Junaidu, Muhammad. 1987. *Education and Cultural Integrity: An Ethnographic Study of the Problems of Formal Education and Pastoral Fulani in Sokoto State, Nigeria.* University of York.

Kelman, Steven. 1984–85. "Using Implementation Research to Solve Implementation Problems: The Case of Energy Emergency Assistance," *Journal of Policy Analysis and Management* 4, 1.

King, Anthony. 1975. "Overload: Problems of Governing in the 1970s," *Political Studies* 23:284–296.

King, Anthony. 1985. "Governmental Responses to Budget Scarcity: Great Britain," *Policy Studies Journal* 13, 3:476–493.

Kingsley, J. Donald. 1963. "Bureaucracy and Political Development, with Particular Reference to Nigeria," *Bureaucracy and Political Development. Princeton:* Princeton University Press.

Kirk-Greene, A. H. M. 1965. "The Higher Civil Service," *The Politics and Administration of Nigeria.* London: Maxwell.

Kirk-Greene, A. H. M. and Rimmer, Douglas. 1981. *Nigeria since 1970: A Political and Economic Outline.* London: Hodder & Stoughton.

Kumo, S. and Aliyu, A. (ed). 1977. *Research and Public Policy in Nigeria.* Zaria: Department of Research and Consultancy, Institute of Administration, ABU.

La-Palombara, J. 1963. *Bureaucracy and Political Development.* Princeton: Princeton University Press.

Lane, Jan-Erik. 1987. "Implementation, Accountability and Trust," *European Journal of Political Research* 15:527–546.

Lane, Jan-Erik (ed). 1987. *Bureaucracy and Public Choice.* Sage Modern Politics Series vol.15 Sponsored by the European Consortium for Political Research/ECPR London: Sage Publication.

Larson, James S. 1980. *Why Government Program Fail: Improving Policy Implementation.* New York: Praeger.

Lester, J. et al. 1987. "Public Policy Implementation: Evolution of the Field and Agenda for Future Research," *Policy Studies Review* 7, 1:200–216.

Linder, S. and Peters, G. 1987. "A Design Perspective on Policy Implementation: The Fallacies of Misplaced Prescription," *Policy Studies Review* 6, 3:459–75.

Linder, S. and Peters, G. 1987. "Relativism, Contingency, and Definition of Success in Implementation Research," *Policy Studies Review* 7, 1:116–127.

Lewis, David and Wallace, H. (eds). 1984. *Policies into Practice: National and International Case Studies in Implementation.* London: Heinemann Educational Books.

Lewis, J., and Flynn, R. 1979. "The Implementation of Urban and Regional Planning Policies," *Policy and Politics* 7, 2:123–142.

Longe, G. A. E. 1984. "The Civil Servant and the Nation," (unpublished) August 24. 1–14.

Longe, G. A. E. 1984. *Civil Service Reform: Myth or Necessity.* Lagos: Federal Government Printing Press.

Love, Janice and Sederberg, Peter C. 1987 "Euphony and Cacophony in Policy Implementation: Scf and The Somali Refugee Problem," *Review of Policy Research,* vol. 7, issue 1:155–173

Lugard, Lord. 1970. *Political Memoranda: Instruction to Political Officers 1913–18, 3rd ed.* London: Frank Cass & Company Ltd.

Maipose, G. C. S. 1984. *Constraints on Administration of Rural Development in Zambia.* University of Manchester.

Mason, C. and Davies, T. 1982. "Gazing Up at the Bottoms: Problems of Minimal Response in the Implementation of Manpower Policy," *European Journal of Political Research.* 10:145–57.

Majone, G. and Wildavsky, Aaron. 1978. "Implementation As Evolution," *Public Studies Review Annual* 2:103–117.

Mato, Akume Clement. 1986. *Public Policy Formulation: The Case of Benue state, Nigeria.* Indiana University.

Maududi, S. Abul A'la. 1955. *The Islamic Constitution.* Lahore: Islamic Publication.

May, Judith V. and Wildavsky, A. (eds). 1978. *The Policy Cycle.* Sage Yearbooks in Politics and Public Policy, vol. 5. London: SAGE Publications.

Mazmanian, D. A. and Sabatier, P. (eds). 1981. *Effective Policy Implementation.* Lexington: D. C. Heath & Company.

Migdal, Joel S. 1978. "Policy and Power: A Framework for the Study of Comparative Policy Contexts in Third World Countries," *Policy Studies Review Annual* 2, 12:167–186.

Milward, H. B. and Rainey, Hal G. 1983. "Don't Blame the Bureaucracy," *Journal of Public Policy* 3, 2:149–168.

Mohammed, Col. G. 1985. "Maiden Speech of the Military Governor of Sokoto State, Col. Garba Mohammed to the People of Sokoto State on Tuesday, September 10, 1985, outlining the priority of his administration," (unpublished).

Mohammed, Col. G. 1986. "Speech of the Military Governor of Sokoto State, Col. Garba Mohammed on the Occasion of Graduation Ceremony of the State College of Arts and Science, Sokoto, 25 January" (unpublished).

Mohammed, Col. G. 1986. An Address of the Military Governor of Sokoto State, Col. Garba Mohammed, on 7 August 1986 on the occasion of the 19th Meeting of the Principals/Directors of Schools and colleges of Basic and Preliminary Studies, reiterated his commitment to the goals and implementation of Operation Move Ahead.

Mohammed, Yakubu. 1988. "Enter Super Ministers," *Newswatch* February 1, 4.

Montjoy, R. S.et al. 1979. "Toward a Theory of Policy Implementation: An Organizational Perspective," *Public Administration Review* September/October, 465–476.

Mueller, Keith J. 1984. "Local Implementation of National Policy," *Policy Studies Review* 4, 1:86–98.

Nafziger, E. Wayne. 1983. *The Economics of Political Instability: The Nigerian-Biafra War.* Colorado: Westview Press.

Nakamura, R. T. 1987. "The Textbook Policy Process and Implementation Research," *Policies Studies Review* 7, 1:142–154.

Ngu, Sylvester M. 1985. *Administrative Probity and Public Accountability: An Analytical Study of Administrative Corruption, Maladministration and Institutional Arrangement for Administrative Control in Kaduna State, Nigeria up to 1983.* The University of Liverpool.

Nicolson, I. F. 1965. "The Structure of Government at the Federal Level," *The Politics and Administration of Nigerian Government.* London: Sweet & Maxwell.

Nicolson, I. F. 1969. *The Administration of Nigeria 1900–1960: Men, Methods, and Myth.* Oxford: Clarendon Press.

Nixon, Jaqi. 1980. "The Importance of Communication in the Implementation of Government Policy at Local Level," *Policy and Politics* 8, 2:127–144.

Nwosu, Humphrey N. 1977. *Political Authority and the Nigerian Civil Service.* Enugu: Fourth Dimension Publishing Company.

Nwosu, H. N. (ed). 1980. *Problems of Nigerian Administration: A Book of Reading.* Enugu: Fourth Dimension.

Odekunle, Femi (ed). 1982. *Nigeria: Corruption in Development.* Ibadan: Ibadan University Press.

Odumosu, L. Idowu. 1965. "Constitutional Development," *The Politics and Administration of Nigeria.* London: Sweet & Maxwell.

Odunlami, Thomas A. 1986. *The Effectiveness of Land Use Policies: A Case Study of Nigeria.* Cambridge University PhD Thesis.

Ogunsheye, Ayo. 1965. "Nigeria," *Education and Political Development.* Princeton: Princeton University Press.

Okonjo, Isaac M. 1974. *British Administration in Nigeria 1900–1950: A Nigerian View.* New York: NOK Publishers.

Onabamiro, Sanya. 1983. *Glimpses into Nigerian History.* Nigeria: Macmillan.

Orr, Captain C. W. J. 1911. *The Making of Northern Nigeria.* London: Macmillan.

Ostheimer, John O. 1973. *Nigerian Politics*. New York: Harper & Row.

O'Toole, L. J. Jr. and Montjoy, Robert S. 1984. "Inter-organizational Policy Implementation: A Theoretical Perspective," *Public Administration Review* November/December, 491–503.

O'Toole, L. J. Jr. 1986. "Policy Recommendations for Multi-Actor Implementation: An Assessment of the Field," *Public Policy* 6, 2:181–210.

Ozigi, A. and Ocho, L. 1981. *Education in Northern Nigeria*. London: George Allen & Unwin.

Paden, John N. 1986. *Ahmadu Bello Sardauna of Sokoto: Values and Leadership in Nigeria*. Zaria: Hudahuda Publishing Company.

Palumbo, Dennis J. and Harder, M. (eds). 1981. *Implementing Public Policy*. Lexington: Lexington Books.

Palumbo, Dennis J. 1987. "Introduction: Symposium: Implementation: What Have We Learned and Still Need To Know," *Policy Studied Review*. 7, 1:91–102.

Panter-Brick, K. (ed). 1978. *Soldiers and Oil: The Political Transformation of Nigeria*. London: Frank Cass.

Pearce, Robert. 1984. "The Colonial Office and Planned Decolonization in Africa," *African Affairs: The Journal of the Royal African Society* 83, 330:77–93.

Peil, Magaret. 1976. *Nigerian Politics: The Peoples View*. London: Cassel.

Pressman, Jeffery and Wildavsky, Aaron. 1973. *Implementation*. Berkeley: University of California Press.

Qutb, Sayyed. 1977. *Islam and Universal Peace*. American Trust Publication.

Rhodes, R. A. W. 1985. *Power-Dependence, Policy Communities and Intergovernmental Networks*. Essex Papers in Politics and Government.

Riggs, Fred W. 1964. *Administration in Developing Countries: The Theory of Prismatic Society*. Boston: Houghton Mifflin Company.

Riggs, Fred W. 1975. "Organizational Structure and Context," *Administration and Society* 7, 2:150–190.

Sabatier, Paul and Mazmanian, Daniel. 1979. "The Condition of Effective Implementation: A Guide to Accomplishing Policy Objectives," *Policy Analysis* 5, 4:481–504.

Sabatier, Paul and Mazmanian, Daniel. 1980. "The Implementation of Public Policy: A Framework of Analysis," *Policy Studies Journal* Symposium on Successful Policy Implementation 8:538–560.

Sabatier, P., and Hanf, K. 1985. "Strategic Interaction, Learning and Policy Evolution: A Synthetic Model," *Policy Implementation in Federal and Unitary Systems.* Dordrecht: Martinus Nijhoff Publishers.

Sabatier, P. A. 1986. "Top-Down and Bottom-Up Approaches to Implementation Research: A Critical Analysis and Suggested Synthesis," *Public Policy* 6, 1:21–48.

Sanderson, Lilian. 1975. "Education and Administrative Control in Colonial Sudan and Northern Nigeria," *African Affairs: The Journal of the Royal African Society* 74, 297:427–441.

Schwarz, A. O. Jr. 1965. *Nigeria: The Tribes, the Nations, or the Race—The Politics of Independence.* Massachusetts: MIT.

Schwarz, Walter. 1968. *Nigeria.* London: Pall Mall.

Sharkansky, Ira. 1980. "Policy Making and Service Delivery on the Margins of Government: The Case of Contractors," *Public Administration Review* March/April, 116–123.

Smith, Brain. 1983. "Federal-State Relation in Nigeria," *African Affairs: The Journal of the Royal African Society* 80, 320:355–378.

Smith, Thomas B. 1973a. "The Policy Implementation Process," *Policy Sciences* 4:197–209.

Smith, Thomas B. 1973b. "The Study of Policymaking in Developing Nations," *Policy Studies Journal* 1, 4:244–9.

Symonds, Richard. 1966. *The British and Their Successors: A Study in the Development of the Government Services in the New States.* London: Faber & Faber.

Thrasher, Michael, and Dunkerley, David. 1982. "A Social Exchange Approach to Implementation Analysis," *Social Science Information.* 349–382.

Thrasher, Michael. 1983. "Exchange Networks and Implementation," *Policy and Politics* 11, 4:375–391.

Tukur, Mahmud (ed). 1970. *Administrative and Political Development: Prospect for Nigeria*. Kaduna: Baraka Press.

Tukur, Mahmud (ed). 1971. *Reform of the Nigerian Public Service*. Zaria: Ahmadu Bello University Press.

Tukur, Mahmud. 1977. *Values and Public Affairs: The Relevance of the Sokoto Caliphate Experience to the Transformation of the Nigerian Polity*. Ahmadu Bello University Zaria.

Turabian, Kate L. 1982. *A Manual for Writers of Research Papers, Thesis and Dissertations*. London: Heinemann, 1st British ed.

Van Meter, D. S. and Van Horn, Carl E. 1975. "The Policy Implementation Process: A Conceptual Framework," *Administration and Society* 6, 4:445–488.

Wali, Mohammad A. 1984. *The Medicalization of Health in Sokoto State*. University of Liverpool M.A. Thesis.

Wali, M. A. and Ong, B. N. 1985. "Curative and Preventive Health Care in Sokoto State, Nigeria," *Ambio: Journal of the Human Environment*. XIV, 2:121.

Weber, Max. 1947. *The Theory of Social and Economic Organization* (Translated by A.M. Henderson and Talcott Parsons, and edited with an Introduction by Talcott Parsons.) London: Macmillan.

Welton, J., and Evans, J. 1986. "The Implementation of Special Education Policy: Where Did the 1981 Act Fit In?" *Public Administration* 64:209–227.

Wildavsky, Aaron. 1989. "Ubiquitous Anomie: Reflections and Rejoinder," *Public Administration Review* 49, 1:77.

Williams, Walter. 1975. "Implementation Analysis and Assessment," *Policy Analysis* Special Issue on Implementation, 1, 3:531–566.

Wilton, J. and Evans, J. 1986. "The Development and Implementation of Special Education Policy: Where Did the 1981 Act Fit In?" *Public Administration* 64:209–27.

Wittrock, B. et al. 1982. "Implementation Beyond Hierarchy: Swedish Energy Research Policy," *European Journal of Political Research* 10:131–143.

Wittrock, Bjorn. 1985. "Beyond Organizational Design: Contextuality and the Political Theory of Public Policy," *Policy Implementation in Federal and Unitary Systems*. Dordrecht: Martinus Nijhoff Publishers.

## Magazines, Newspapers, and Other Documents

*Africa Report* 1985.
*African Concord*. 1987. 5 November No. 165.
African Concord Magazine. 1988, Vol. 2: 3.
Annual Abstract of Statistics 1970, 149–50. Lagos: Federal Office of Statistics.
Annual Abstract of Statistics 1970, 1972. Lagos: Federal Office of Statistics.
*Annual Abstract of Statistics*. 1972. Lagos: Federal Office of Statistics.
Annual Abstract of Statistics 1972, 148. Lagos: Federal Office of Statistics.
Annual Abstract of Statistics 1974, 151–2. Lagos: Federal Office of Statistics.
*Annual Report on Nigeria for the Year 1947*. 1949. London: His Majesty's Stationary Office.
"Babangida Demands Progress Reports," 1989. *West Africa*. 8–12 June, 983. *Newswatch Magazine* 1988. 11 January, 34.
Constitution of the Federal Republic of Nigeria 1979, 14.
Constitution of the Federal Republic of Nigeria 1999 .
"Democracy on Trial," 1989. *West Africa*. 23 March to 2 April, 470.
Directorate of Budget Sokoto. 1976; 1977; 1978; 1979; 1980; 1981; 1982; 1983; 1984; 1985; 1986; 1987; 1988; 1989. *Recurrent and Capital Estimates of the Government of Sokoto State of Nigeria*. Sokoto: Directorate of Budget.
Directorate of Information Services. 1955. *Social and Economic Progress in the Northern Region of Nigeria*. Kaduna: Directorate of Information.
Executive Office of the President. *The Challenge of Change: Collected Speeches of President Shehu Shagari*. Lagos: Federal Government Press.
Federal Ministry of Education. 1985. *Statistics of Education in Nigeria 1980–1984*. Lagos: Federal Ministry of Education.

Federal Republic of Nigeria. 1988. *Official Gazette*. Lagos: Federal Government Press, Vol 75, no. 53.

"Focus on Sokoto State," 1989. *West Africa*. 12–11 June, 970–80.

Governor's Office Sokoto 1985.

Governor's Office Sokoto 1986.

Military Governor's Office, Sokoto 1989.

Ministry of Education, Sokoto. 1978. *Educational Statistics 1976–77*. Sokoto: Ministry of Education.

Ministry of Education, Sokoto 1988. *Post Primary Statistics 1988*. Sokoto: Ministry of Education.

Ministry of Education, Sokoto 1988. *Primary School Statistics II 1988*. Sokoto: Ministry of Education.

Ministry of Education, Sokoto 1989.

*National Policy on Education [Revised], Federal Republic o     f Nigeria*. 1981. Lagos: Federal Government Press.

National Population Bureau Estimate of 1978.

"Nigeria: Penal Decrees," 1984. *Keesings Contemporary Archives: Records of World Events*. London: Longman. 33261. 17.

"Nigeria: Successful Coup by Senior Members of the Supreme Military Council," 1985. *Keesings Contemporary Archives: Records of World Events*. London: Longman, 33956.

"Nigeria: Trials by Special Tribunals," 1984. *Keesings Contemporary Archives: Records of World Events*. London: Longman. 33261–2.

*Nigeria Year Book*. 1959. Lagos: Nigerian Printing and Publishing Company LtD.

Nigerian Observer 1988, May 17, 5.

Office of the Head of the Civil Service of the Federation 1988.

Scholarship Board Sokoto. 1986; 1987; 1988. *Annual Comprehensive List of sponsored students*.

Scholarship Board Sokoto. 1986; 1987; 1988. File records.

"Sending Nigerians to School," 1974. *West Africa*. 25 March, 325–6.

Social & Economic Progress in the Northern Region of Nigeria 1955, 38.

"Sokoto Government to release report on multi-million Naira contracts," 1984. *The New Nigeria*. 20 August.

Sokoto State. 1984. *Report of the Administrative Panel of Inquiry on Projects Financed by External Loans [5 Star Giginya Hotel 240 D.U Housing and Motels at Sokoto, Gusau, Argungu and Illela].*

Sokoto State. 1986. *Committee Report on Infrastructure in Sokoto State* 1986, 8.

Sokoto State Economic Planning Department, 1985:39.

Sokoto State Government. 1987. Introducing Sokoto State.

Sokoto State Government Circular. 1985. Misuse of Government Vehicles [SMG/545/VOL.II/198].

Sokoto State Government Circular. 1986. Special Arrangement for Appointment of Headmasters [SMG/94/vol.vii/1440] Office of the Secretary to State government & Head of Service

Sokoto State Government Circular. 1986. Control of Government Vehicles [SMG/545/III/357].

Sokoto State Government Circular on Operation Move Ahead, 1986. Ministry of Education Sokoto

"State Governors Reshuffled," 1988. *West Africa.* 1 August, 1410.

Statistics of Education in Nigeria, 1985

Task Force Committee on the Evaluation of Effectiveness and Efficiency of the Sokoto State Civil Service 1986

"The final shuffle?" 1988. *West Africa.* 8 August, 1433.

The New Nigeria 20 August 1984.

The New Nigeria Tuesday 25 February 1986, 9.

The New Nigeria Sunday 23 February 1986, 16.

The Nigeria Handbook 1933, 180. Lagos: Government Printer.

The Nigeria Handbook 1954, 108, 115. Lagos: Government Printer.

The Nigeria Year Book 1959, 127 Lagos: Government Printer.

USA Department of Bureau of Public Affairs 1982, 6, 19.

West Africa 1 August 1988.

West Africa. 1989. 17–23 July pp. 1188.

West Africa Magazine 1974, No. 2962, 326.

West Africa Magazine (8 August 1988:1433).

West Africa Magazine (1989, 27 March–2 April).

West Africa Magazine (1989, 12–11 June, 970).

West Africa Magazine (1989, 12–18 June, 983).

www.ingramcontent.com/pod-product-compliance
Lightning Source LLC
Chambersburg PA
CBHW030302290526
45785CB00001B/188